Modern Algorithms for Image Processing

Computer Imagery by Example Using C#

Vladimir Kovalevsky

Apress®

Modern Algorithms for Image Processing: Computer Imagery by Example Using C#

Vladimir Kovalevsky
Berlin, Germany

ISBN-13 (pbk): 978-1-4842-4236-0
https://doi.org/10.1007/978-1-4842-4237-7

ISBN-13 (electronic): 978-1-4842-4237-7

Library of Congress Control Number: 2018965475

Managing Director, Apress Media LLC: Welmoed Spahr
Acquisitions Editor: Joan Murray
Development Editor: Laura Berendson
Coordinating Editor: Jill Balzano

Cover image designed by Freepik (www.freepik.com)

Distributed to the book trade worldwide by Springer Science+Business Media New York, 233 Spring Street, 6th Floor, New York, NY 10013. Phone 1-800-SPRINGER, fax (201) 348-4505, e-mail orders-ny@springer-sbm.com, or visit www.springeronline.com. Apress Media, LLC is a California LLC and the sole member (owner) is Springer Science + Business Media Finance Inc (SSBM Finance Inc). SSBM Finance Inc is a **Delaware** corporation.

For information on translations, please e-mail rights@apress.com, or visit http://www.apress.com/rights-permissions.

Apress titles may be purchased in bulk for academic, corporate, or promotional use. eBook versions and licenses are also available for most titles. For more information, reference our Print and eBook Bulk Sales web page at http://www.apress.com/bulk-sales.

Any source code or other supplementary material referenced by the author in this book is available to readers on GitHub via the book's product page, located at www.apress.com/9781484242360. For more detailed information, please visit http://www.apress.com/source-code.

Printed on acid-free paper

Dedicated to my wife, Dr. Baerbel Kovalevsky

Table of Contents

About the Author

Vladimir Kovalevsky received his diploma in physics from the Kharkov University (Ukraine), his first doctoral degree in technical sciences from the Central Institute of Metrology (Leningrad), and his second doctoral degree in computer science from the Institute of Cybernetics of the Academy of Sciences of the Ukraine (Kiev) where he headed the Department of Pattern Recognition for more than a decade.

Vladimir has been living in Germany since 1983. He was a researcher at the Central Institute of Cybernetics of the Academy of Sciences of the GDR, Berlin, a professor of computer science at the University of Applied Sciences Berlin, and a scientific collaborator at the University of Rostock.

He has been a visiting researcher at the University of Pennsylvania, a professor at the Manukau Institute of Technology in New Zealand, and a professor at the Chonbuk National University in South Korea. He has reviewed for the journals *Applied General Topology, Computer Vision and Image Understanding, IEEE Transactions on Pattern Analysis and Machine Intelligence*, and others.

Vladimir has been a plenary speaker at conferences in Europe, the United States, and New Zealand. His research interests include digital geometry, digital topology, computer vision, image processing, and pattern recognition. He has published four monographs and more than 180 journal and conference papers on image analysis, digital geometry, and digital topology.

Acknowledgments

I wish to acknowledge valuable and fruitful discussions with Boris Flach, Reinhard Klette, Ulrich Koethe, Alexander Kovalevsky, Volkmar Miszalok, and Peer Stelldinger. These discussions have significantly contributed to this work.

I would like to express my special appreciation to Alexander V. Kovalevsky, who helped significantly as an experienced programmer in the development of my projects.

Introduction

This book presents a collection of algorithms and projects for processing two-dimensional images. I developed and investigated the algorithms. Special emphasis is placed on computer solutions of problems related to the improvement of the quality of images, with image analysis and recognition of some geometrically definable objects. New data structures useful for image analysis are presented. The description of all algorithms contains examples of source code in the C# programming language. Descriptions of projects contain source code that can be used by readers.

With this book I intend to help you develop efficient software for processing two-dimensional images. There are a lot of books on image processing, but important algorithms are missing from these books. I have developed many efficient algorithms as a new and important contribution to this area.

I have paid great attention to solutions of problems in image analysis. On the other hand, problems of improving the quality of images are important for the arts. My wife is a recognized specialist in the history of the arts, and her publications often use copies of famous pictures and drawings. The photographs of these artworks are often of low quality. Often photographs of historical drawings illustrating the work of a painter are of such low quality that it is almost impossible to clearly see the contents of the image. Improving these images is therefore very important. In such cases, the programs I have developed for improving the quality of pictures are very useful.

I have developed efficient algorithms for recognizing circles and ellipses in noisy images. These algorithms can be used for recognizing objects with a shape approximating a circle; for example, apples, mushrooms, and so on. They can also be used for recognizing bicycles in images of traffic because the wheels of bicycles are ideal circles, but if the bicycle is positioned in such a way that the plane of its frame is not orthogonal to the viewing ray, then its wheels look like ellipses rather than circles. I was therefore forced to develop efficient algorithms for recognizing ellipses in noisy images as well. My efforts were successful and the book contains a chapter devoted to the recognition of bicycles in noisy images.

The book contains descriptions of numerous algorithms for image analysis, including these:

- Manually controlled thresholding of shading corrected images.

- A fast algorithm for simultaneously labeling all connected components in a segmented image.

- A new efficient method of edge detection.

- A fast algorithm for approximating digital curves by polygons and for estimating the curvature of circular arcs approximating the curve.

- Algorithms for recognition and measurement of circular or elliptical objects in color images.

Among the algorithms for image improvement, the most important are the following:

- The algorithm for rectifying photographs of paintings taken at an oblique angle.

- An algorithm correcting images of nonuniformly illuminated scenes.

- The algorithm for improving the contrast of images of nonuniformly illuminated scenes.

- The best algorithm for reducing Gaussian noise (the so-called Sigma-Filter).

- The algorithm for reducing impulse noise.

All descriptions are followed by a pseudo-code similar to the C# programming language. Most of the descriptions contain source code that can be copied from the text and used directly in a Windows Forms program written in the C# .NET language.

All source code and figures are included in a download file (which you can access via the **Download Source Code** button located at www.apress.com/9781484242360) so you can see the colors.

PART I

Image Processing

CHAPTER 1

Introduction

This book contains descriptions of algorithms for image processing such as noise reduction, including reduction of impulse noise, contrast enhancement, shading correction, edge detection, and many others. The source codes of the projects in the C# programming language implementing the algorithms are included on the book's companion web site. The source codes are Windows Forms projects rather than Microsoft Foundation Classes Library (MFC) projects. The controls and the graphics in these projects are implemented by means of simple and easily understandable methods. I have chosen this way of implementing controls and graphics services rather than those based on MFC because the integrated development environment (IDE) using MFC is expensive. Besides that, the software using MFC is rather complicated. It includes many different files in a project and the user is largely unable to understand the sense and usefulness of these files. On the contrary, Windows Forms and its utility tools are free and are easier to understand. They supply controls and graphics similar to that of MFC.

To provide fast processing of images we transform objects of the class `Bitmap`, which is standard in Windows Forms, to objects of our class `CImage`, the methods of which are fast because they use direct access to the set of pixels, whereas the standard way of using `Bitmap` consists of implementing the relatively slow methods of `GetPixel` and `SetPixel` or methods using `LockBits`, which are fast, but not usable for indexed images.

The class `CImage` is rather simple: It contains the properties `width`, `height`, and `nBits` of the image and methods used in the actual project. My methods are described in the chapters devoted to projects. Here is the definition of our class `CImage`.

```
class CImage
{ public Byte[] Grid;
   public int width, height, nBits;

   public CImage() { } // default constructor
```

© Vladimir Kovalevsky 2019
V. Kovalevsky, *Modern Algorithms for Image Processing*, https://doi.org/10.1007/978-1-4842-4237-7_1

```
    public CImage(int nx, int ny, int nbits) // constructor
    {
       width = nx;
       height = ny;
       nBits = nbits;
       Grid = new byte[width * height * (nBits / 8)];
    }

    public CImage(int nx, int ny, int nbits, byte[] img) // constructor
    {
       width = nx;
       height = ny;
       nBits = nbits;
       Grid = new byte[width * height * (nBits / 8)];
       for (int i = 0; i < width * height * nBits / 8; i++) Grid[i] = img[i];
    }
} //********************** end of class CImage ****************
```

Methods of the class CImage are described in the descriptions of projects.

CHAPTER 2

Noise Reduction

Digital images are often distorted by random errors usually referred to as *noise*. There are two primary kinds of noise: Gaussian noise and impulse noise (see Figure 2-1). Gaussian noise is statistical noise having a probability distribution similar to a Gaussian distribution. It arises mainly during acquisition (e.g., in a sensor). It could be caused by poor illumination or by high temperature of the sensor. It comes from many natural sources, such as the thermal vibrations of atoms in conductors, referred to as thermal noise. It influences all pixels of the image.

Impulse noise, also called salt-and-pepper noise, presents itself as sparsely occurring light and dark pixels. It comes from pulse distortions like those coming from electrical welding near the electronic device taking up the image or due to improper storage of old photographs. It influences a small part of the set of pixels.

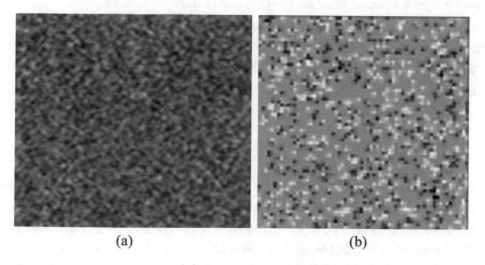

(a)   (b)

Figure 2-1. *Examples of noise: (a) Gaussian noise; (b) impulse noise*

V. Kovalevsky, *Modern Algorithms for Image Processing*, https://doi.org/10.1007/978-1-4842-4237-7_2

The Simplest Filter

We consider first the ways of reducing the intensity of Gaussian noise. The algorithm for reducing the intensity of impulse noise is considered later in this chapter.

The most efficient method of reducing the intensity of Gaussian noise is replacing the lightness of a pixel P by the average value of the lightness of a small subset of pixels in the neighborhood of P. This method is based on the fact from the theory of random values: The standard deviation of the average of N equally distributed random values is by the factor $\sqrt{N}$ less than the standard deviation of a single value. This method performs a two-dimensional convolution of the image with a mask, which is an array of weights arranged in a square of $W \times W$ pixels, and the actual pixel P lies in the middle of the square. Source code for this filter is presented later in this chapter. This method has two drawbacks: It is rather slow because it uses $W \times W$ additions for each pixel of the image, and it blurs the image. It transforms fine edges at boundaries of approximately homogeneous regions to ramps where the lightness changes linearly in a stripe whose width is equal to W pixels. The first drawback is overcome with the fast averaging filter. However, the second drawback is so important that it prevents use of the averaging filter for the purpose of noise removal. Averaging filters are, however, important for improving images with shading (i.e., those representing nonuniformly illuminated objects), as we see later. I propose another filter for the purpose of noise removal as well.

First, let us describe the simplest averaging filter. I present the source code of this simple method, which the reader can use in his or her program. In this code, as well as in many other code examples, we use certain classes, which are defined in the next section.

The Simplest Averaging Filter

The nonweighted averaging filter calculates the mean gray value in a gliding square window of $W \times W$ pixels where W is the width and height of a square gliding window. The greater the window size W, the stronger the suppression of Gaussian noise: The filter decreases the noise by the factor W. The value W is usually an odd integer $W = 2 \times h + 1$ for the sake of symmetry. The coordinates $(x + xx, y + yy)$ of pixels inside the window vary symmetrically around the current center pixel (x, y) in the intervals: $-h \leq xx \leq +h$ and $-h \leq yy \leq +h$ with $h = 1, 2, 3, 4$, and so on.

Near the border of the image the window lies partially outside of the image. In this case, the computation loses its natural symmetry because only pixels inside the image can be averaged. A reasonable way to solve the border problem is to take control of the coordinates $(x + xx, y + yy)$ if they point out of the image. If these coordinates are out of the image the summation of the gray values must be suspended and the divisor nS should not be incremented.

An example of the algorithm for averaging the colors is presented here. We often use in our code comments denoted by lines of certain symbols: lines marked with = label the start and the end of a loop, lines with minus signs label if instructions, and so on. This makes the structure of the code more visible.

The simplest slow version of the algorithm has four nested for loops.

```
public void CImage::Averaging(CImage input, int HalfWidth)
{ int nS, sum;
  for (int y=0; y<height; y++) //===================================
  { for (int x=0; x<width; x++) //===============================
    { nS=sum=0;
      for (int yy=-HalfWidth; yy<=HalfWidth; yy++) //========
      { if (y+yy>=0 && y+yy<input.height )
          for (int xx=-HalfWidth; xx<=HalfWidth; xx++) //===
          { if (x+xx>=0 && x+xx<input.width)
            { sum+=input.Grid[x+xx+width*(y+yy)];
              nS++;
            }
          } //====== end for (xx... ===================
      } //======== end for (yy... ========================
      Grid[x+width*y]=(sum+nS/2)/nS; //+nS/2 is for rounding
    } //============ end for (x... ========================
  } //============== end for (y... ========================
} //**************** end Averaging **************************
```

This is source code: The reader can copy it and put into its C# source, and it will work.

The parameter HalfWidth is half the width of the gliding window. The width and height of the window are both equal to 2*HalfWidth+1. The variables x and y in the preceding code are the indexes of pixels in Grid, and xx and yy are the indexes of the pixels inside the gliding averaging window.

The computation of sum in the innermost for loop needs $W \times W$ additions and $W \times W$ accesses to the image for each pixel of the input image, which is quite time consuming.

Let us remark once again that averaging filters, although they are very efficient at reducing the intensity of Gaussian noise, strongly blur the image. Therefore they should not be used for noise reduction. I suggest using the sigma filter described later in this chapter for this purpose. Averaging is used for the purpose of shading correction (see Chapter 4). Therefore it will be mostly used with a rather large gliding window, as large as half the width of the image. Then the simplest averaging routine becomes so time consuming that it is practically impossible to use it. For example, in the case of a grayscale image of 1000×1000 pixels and a gliding window of 400×400 pixels, which is typical for shading correction, the runtime of the function Averaging on a standard PC can take about 20 minutes.

The Fast Averaging Filter

The simplest averaging filter makes W^2 additions and one division for each pixel of the image. For example, it makes $5 \cdot 5 + 1 = 26$ operations for each pixel in the case of a gliding window of $5 \times 5 = 25$ pixels. There are applications (e.g., the shading correction) that are using much greater gliding windows; for example, one of $400 \times 400 = 160{,}000$ pixels. If an application uses the simplest averaging filter with such a great gliding window, it can run for several minutes.

It is possible to accelerate the averaging filter using the following basic idea: It is possible to calculate first the sums of gray values in small one-dimensional windows of $1 \times W$ pixels. We call the arrays of these sums the *columns*. In the following description of the basic idea we use a Cartesian coordinate system, the index of a column of the image being the abscissa x and the index of a row being the ordinate y. We consider the ordinate axis as directed downward, from top to bottom, which is usual in image processing and different from the direction of the ordinate axis in mathematics.

The fast averaging filter solves the same problem as the simplest filter, but it is much faster. The fast filter blurs the image in the same way as the simplest filter does. Therefore its main application is shading correction rather than noise suppression.

When using the basic idea just mentioned, it is possible to reduce the number of operations per pixel from $W \times W$ to ≈ 4: The fast filter calculates and saves the sum of the gray values in each column of W pixels, and the middle pixel of each column lies in the actual row of the image (Figure 2-2). The filter then directly calculates the sum over the window having its central pixel at the beginning of a row; that is, by adding up the sums saved in the columns. Then the window moves one pixel along the row, and the filter calculates the sum for the next location by adding the value of the column sum at the right border of the window and by subtracting the value of the column sum at the left border. It is necessary to check whether the column to be added or subtracted is inside the image. If it is not, the corresponding addition or subtraction must be skipped.

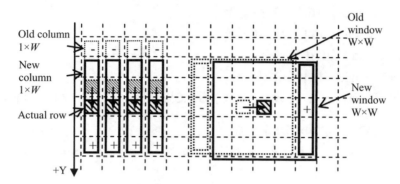

Figure 2-2. *Explanation of the functioning of the fast average filter*

Due to applying a similar procedure for the calculation of the column sums, the average number of additions or subtractions per pixel is reduced to $\approx 2 + 2 = 4$. The sum inside the window must be calculated directly (i.e., by the addition of HalfWidth + 1 sums of columns) only for a pixel at the beginning of each row. The sums of columns must be calculated directly only for the pixels of the first row of the image.

The filter updates the values of the columns when proceeding to the next row of the image by adding the gray value below the lower end and subtracting the gray value at the upper end of each column (Figure 2-2). In this case it is also necessary to check whether the gray value to be added or subtracted is in the image. The filter divides (with rounding) the sum by the number of pixels in the intersection of the window with the image as soon as the sum of the gray values in a window is calculated and saves the result in the corresponding pixel of the output image.

Here is the source code of the simplest version of the fast averaging filter designed for filtering grayscale images.

```
public int FastAverageM(CImage Inp, int hWind, Form1 fm1)
// Filters the grayscale image "Inp" and returns the result in 'Grid' of the
// calling image.
{
   width  = Inp.width ; height = Inp.height; // elements of class CImage
   Grid = new byte[width  * height];
   int[] SumColmn; int[] nPixColmn;
   SumColmn = new int[width];
   nPixColmn = new int[width];
   for (int i = 0; i < width ; i++) SumColmn[i] = nPixColmn[i] = 0;

   int nPixWind = 0, SumWind = 0;
   for (int y = 0; y < height + hWind; y++) //===============================
   {
     int yout = y - hWind, ysub = y - 2 * hWind - 1;
     SumWind = 0; nPixWind = 0;
     int y1 = 1 + (height + hWind) / 100;
     for (int x = 0; x < width + hWind; x++) //===========================
     {
       int xout = x - hWind, xsub = x - 2 * hWind - 1;    // 1. and 2.
                                                          addition
       if (y < height && x < width )
       {
         SumColmn[x] += Inp.Grid[x + width  * y];
         nPixColmn[x]++;        // 3. and 4. addition
       }
       if (ysub >= 0 && x < width )
       {
         SumColmn[x] -= Inp.Grid[x + width * ysub];
         nPixColmn[x]--;
       }
       if (yout >= 0 && x < width )
       {
```

```
      SumWind += SumColmn[x];
      nPixWind += nPixColmn[x];
    }
    if (yout >= 0 && xsub >= 0)
    {
      SumWind -= SumColmn[xsub];
      nPixWind -= nPixColmn[xsub];
    }
    if (xout >= 0 && yout >= 0)
      Grid[xout + width  * yout] = (byte)((SumWind + nPixWind / 2) /
      nPixWind);
  } //===================== end for (int x = 0; =====================
} //===================== end for (int y = 0; =====================
return 1;
} //*********************** end FastAverageM ***********************
```

I present next the universal source code of the fast average filter designed both for color and grayscale images. It uses the variable int nbyte, which is set to 3 for color and to 1 for grayscale images. We define for the sum of color intensities in the gliding window of $(2*hWind + 1)^2$ pixels an array SumWind[3] of three elements for sums of red, green, and blue intensities. In the case of a grayscale image, only the element SumWind[0] is being used. We use the following variables as described next.

The location with the coordinates (c+nbyte*x, nbyte*y) is the location of a color channel, one of red, green, or blue channels whose intensity is added to the corresponding element of the array SumColmn. The location (c+nbyte*x, nbyte*ysub) is that of a color channel whose intensity is to be subtracted from SumColmn. The variable c+nbyte*x is the abscissa of the short column whose contents are to be added to SumWind[c]. The variable c+nbyte*xsub is the abscissa of the short column whose contents are to be subtracted from SumWind[c].

```
public int FastAverageUni(CImage Inp, int hWind, Form1 fm1)
// Filters the color or grayscale image "Inp" and returns the result in
// 'Grid' of calling image.
{ int c = 0, nByte = 0;
   if (Inp.N_Bits == 8) nByte = 1;
   else nByte = 3;
```

```
width   = Inp.width ; height = Inp.height; // elements of the class "Cimage"
Grid = new byte[nByte * width  * height];
int[] nPixColmn;
nPixColmn = new int[width];
for (int i = 0; i < width ; i++) nPixColmn[i] = 0;
int[,] SumColmn;
SumColmn = new int[width, 3];
int nPixWind = 0, xout = 0, xsub = 0;
int[] SumWind = new int[3];
for (int y = 0; y < height + hWind; y++) //===============================
{ int yout = y - hWind, ysub = y - 2 * hWind - 1;
   nPixWind = 0;
   for (c = 0; c < nByte; c++) SumWind[c] = 0;
   int y1 = 1 + (height + hWind) / 100;
   for (int x = 0; x < width  + hWind; x++) //============================
   { xout = x - hWind;
     xsub = x - 2 * hWind - 1;     // 1. and 2. addition
     if (y < height && x < width) // 3. and 4. addition
    { for (c=0; c< nByte; c++)
        SumColmn[x, c] += Inp.Grid[c + nByte*(x + width*y)];
      nPixColmn[x]++;
   }
   if (ysub >= 0 && x < width )
   { for (c=0; c<nByte; c++)
        SumColmn[x, c] -=Inp.Grid[c+nByte*(x+ width*ysub)];
     nPixColmn[x]--;
   }
   if (yout >= 0 && x < width )
   { for (c = 0; c < nByte; c++) SumWind[c] += SumColmn[x, c];
     nPixWind += nPixColmn[x];
   }
   if (yout >= 0 && xsub >= 0)
   { for (c = 0; c < nByte; c++) SumWind[c] -= SumColmn[xsub, c];
     nPixWind -= nPixColmn[xsub];
   }
```

```
   if (xout >= 0 && yout >= 0)
      for (c = 0; c < nByte; c++)
         Grid[c+nByte*(xout+width*yout)]=(byte)( SumWind[c] / nPixWind);
   } //============= end for (int x = 0;   ==============================
 } //============= end for (int y = 0;   ==============================
 return 1;
} //**************** end FastAverageUni ********************************
```

This source code can be used in a corresponding Windows Forms project. It is not the fastest version; it can be made 50 percent faster by removing the multiplications from the interior loop. Some multiplications can be performed before starting the loop; some others can be replaced by additions. A still faster version can be made containing the following nine loops instead of the two loops with the indexes y and x in FastAverageM or in FastAverageUni:

```
for (int yOut=0; yOut<=hWind; yOut++)
{ for(int xOut=0; xOut<=hWind; xOut++){...} //Loop 1
   for(xOut=hWind+1; xOut<=width-hWind-1; xOut++) {...} //Loop 2
   for(xOut=width-hWind; xOut<width; xOut++) {...} //Loop 3
}
for(yOut=hWind+1; yOut<=height-hWind-1; yOut++)
{ for(xOut=0; xOut<=hWind; xOut++) {...} //Loop 4
   for(xOut=hWind+1; xOut<=width-hWind-1; xOut++) {...} //Loop 5
   for(xOut=width-hWind; xOut<width; xOut++) {...} //Loop 6
}
for(yOut=height-hWind; yOut<height; yOut++)
{ for(xOut=0; xOut<=hWind; xOut++) {...} /Loop 7
   for(xOut=hWind+1; xOut<=width-hWind-1; xOut++) {...} //Loop 8
   for(xOut=width-hWind; xOut<width; xOut++) {...} //Loop 9
}
```

Each of the nine loops processes a part of the image (see Figure 2-3) that is either hWind + 1 pixels wide or hWind + 1 pixels high.

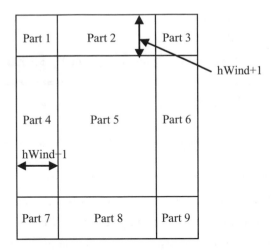

Figure 2-3. *The nine parts of the image corresponding to the nine loops*

This version of the fast averaging filter can be used only if the condition hWind $\leq$ min (width, height)/2 - 1 is fulfilled. In such a version of the routine the interior loops with the variable xOut contain no multiplications and no if instructions. The routine is about 60 percent faster than the previously described FastAverageM. However, it is much longer and much more difficult to debug. The gain in speed is not essential: This code uses 0.7 seconds to process a big color image of 2448 × 3264 pixels with the gliding window of 1200 × 1200 pixels, whereas FastAverageM takes 1.16 seconds. These calculation times are almost independent from the size of the gliding window: They are 0.68 and 1.12 seconds correspondingly for the case of a gliding window of 5 × 5 pixels.

The Fast Gaussian Filter

The averaging filter produces a smoothed image in which some rectangular shapes not present in the original image can be seen. These shapes appear because the averaging filter transforms each light pixel to a homogeneously light rectangle of the size of the gliding window. As soon as a pixel has an outstanding lightness strongly differing from the values of adjacent pixels, the rectangle becomes visible. This is an unwanted distortion. It can be avoided when using the Gaussian filter that multiplies the gray values to be added by values that decay with the distance from the center of the window according to the two-dimensional Gauss law. In addition, the Gaussian filter provides a better suppression of noise. An example of the weights is shown in Figure 2-4.

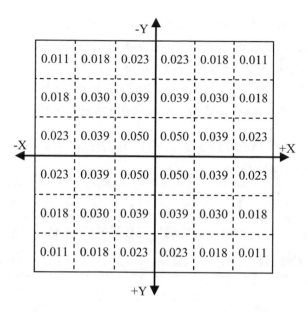

Figure 2-4. *Example of weights in the gliding window of the classical Gauss filter*

These values are called the weights of the filter. The weights corresponding to the two-dimensional Gauss law are floats less than one:

$$w(x, y) = (2\pi\sigma_x\sigma_y)^{-1}\exp(-x^2/2\sigma^2_x - y^2/2\sigma^2_y).$$

They can be calculated in advance and saved in a two-dimensional array whose size corresponds to the size of the gliding window (Figure 2-4). Then the gray values or color channels of the filtered image are multiplied with the weights and the sum of the products is calculated. This procedure needs W^2 floating point multiplications and W^2 additions per pixel of the grayscale image to be filtered where W is the width of the gliding window. In the case of a color image, this number is $3W^2$.

There is a possibility of obtaining approximately the same results using the knowledge of the statistics that says that the convolution of many equivalent probability distributions tends to the Gaussian distribution. The convergence of this process is so fast that it is sufficient to calculate the convolution of only three rectangular distributions to obtain a good approximation. A rectangular distribution has a constant density in an interval and a zero density outside the interval. If an image is processed with a filter three times, the result is equivalent to the filtering with weights being convolutions of three rectangular weights. Thus to perform approximately a Gaussian filtering of an image it is sufficient to filter the image three times with a fast averaging filter. This procedure requires $4 \times 3 = 12$ integer additions per color channel of a pixel independent from the size of the window. We have calculated that the standard of the equivalent Gaussian distribution is proportional to the half-width of the gliding window of the averaging filter. In Table 2-1 hWind is the half-width of the averaging window, and Sigma is the standard of a random variable whose distribution corresponds to the weights calculated by the triple filtering with the fast filter.

Table 2-1. *Relation Sigma/hWind tending to 1 with increasing hWind*

hWind	1	2	3	4	5
Sigma	1.414	2.456	3.459	4.456	5.49
Sigma/hWind	1.414	1.218	1.153	1.114	1.098

You can see that the relation Sigma/hWind tends to 1 when the width of the window increases.

Figure 2-5 shows how the weights of the approximate Gauss filter differ from true Gauss weights.

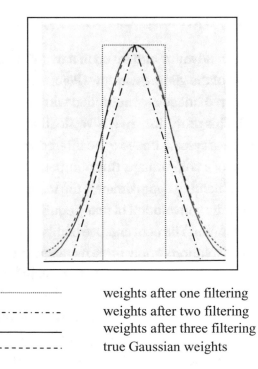

....	weights after one filtering
- . - . - . - . - . -	weights after two filtering
———————	weights after three filtering
- - - - - - - - - -	true Gaussian weights

Figure 2-5. *Weights of the approximate and true Gauss filters*

The Median Filter

The averaging and the Gaussian filters provide the most efficient suppression of Gaussian noise. The averaging filter with a gliding window that has the width of $W = 2h + 1$ pixels transforms steep edges of homogeneous regions to ramps of the width W. In the case of a Gaussian filter, the ramp is steeper. However, both these filters blur the image, so they should not be used for noise suppression.

Most textbooks on image processing recommend using median filters for noise suppression. A median filter sorts the intensities of colors in the gliding window and replaces the intensity in the middle of the gliding window by the intensity staying in the middle of the sorted sequence. Median filters can also be used for suppressing impulse noise or salt-and-pepper noise.

Almost no textbook, though, draws the attention of the reader to very important drawbacks of the median filter. First, it heavily distorts the image. A median filter with a gliding window of $(2 * h + 1)^2$ pixels deletes each stripe of the width of less than h pixels. It also deletes a triangular part of approximately $2h$ pixels at each corner of a rectangular shape. Even more, it inverts a part of the image containing some parallel stripes of the width h if the width of the spaces between the stripes is also equal to h (compare Figure 2-6 with Figure 2-7). This is easily understandable if the reader notices that median makes decisions according to the majority: The central pixel becomes dark if the majority of pixels in the gliding window are dark.

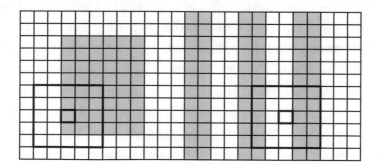

Figure 2-6. *Original image and the gliding window of 5 × 5 pixels*

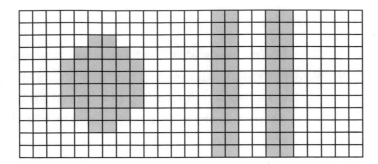

Figure 2-7. *The same image after filtering with median of 5 × 5 pixels*

Using the median for the suppression of impulse noise is also not recommended because it will delete objects having the shape of thin lines that have nothing to do with noise. I suggest an efficient method in a later chapter.

Sigma Filter: The Most Efficient One

The sigma filter reduces noise in the same way as the averaging filter: by averaging many gray values or colors. The idea of the sigma filter is averaging only those intensities (i.e., gray values or intensities of color channels) in a gliding window that differ from the intensity of the central pixel by no more than a fixed parameter called *tolerance*. According to this idea, the sigma filter reduces the Gaussian noise and retains the edges in the image not blurred.

The sigma filter was suggested by John-Sen Lee (1983). However, it remained almost unknown until recently: It has been mentioned in no textbook for image processing that I am aware of. It was mentioned in a professional paper only once Chochia (1984).

A filter similar to the sigma filter was suggested by Tomasi and Manduchi (1998), which they called the *bilateral filter.* They suggested assigning two kinds of weights to the colors being averaged: a domain weight becoming smaller with the increasing distance of the averaged pixel from the central pixel of the gliding window and a range weight becoming smaller with increasing difference between the intensities of colors of the pixel being averaged and that of the central pixel. Both weights can be defined as densities of the Gauss distribution. The filter works well: It reduces the Gaussian noise and preserves the sharpness of the edges. However, it is essentially slower than the sigma filter; for example, to process a color image of 2500 × 3500 pixels the bilateral filter needs 30 seconds, whereas the simplest sigma filter needs only 7 seconds. Thus the bilateral filter is approximately four times slower than the sigma filter. The authors of the bilateral filter did not mention the sigma filter among the references.

To explain why the sigma filter works so well, it can be regarded as the first iteration of the well-known expectation-maximization (EM) algorithm. The subdivision of the colors in the gliding window into two subsets, those being close to the color of the central pixel and those being far away from it, can be considered the expectation step, whereas the averaging of the close colors is the maximization step. It is well known that the EM algorithm converges rather quickly. Therefore the single first iteration brings a result that is close to the mean value of the subset of pixels in the gliding window whose colors are close to the color of the middle pixel with a high probability.

When comparing the sigma filter with the bilateral filter, it is possible to remark that the sigma filter uses an algorithm similar to that of the bilateral filter where Gaussian distributions are replaced by simpler rectangular distributions that can be calculated much faster.

Let us first present the pseudo-code for filtering grayscale images with the sigma filter. We denote with Input the input image and with Output the output image. Let a pixel with coordinates (X, Y) glide through the input image. Let M be the gray value at (X, Y). For each position (X, Y) do:

```
sum=0; number=0; M=Input(X,Y);
Let another pixel (x, y) run through the gliding window with the center of
window at (X, Y).
for each pixel Input(x,y) do:
if (abs(Input(x,y) - M) < tolerance)
{ sum+=Input(x,y);
   number++;
}
Output(X,Y)=Round(sum / number);
```

Now let us present the source code of this simple solution. We have replaced often repeated multiplications by additions to make the method faster (13 percent).

```
public int SigmaSimpleColor (CImage Inp, int hWind, int Toleranz)
// The sigma filter for 3 byte color images.
{
   int[] gvMin = new int[3], gvMax = new int[3], nPixel = new int[3];
   int [] Sum = new int[3];
   int c, hWind3 = hWind * 3, NX3 = width * 3, x3, xyOut;
   N_Bits = Inp.N_Bits; // "N_Bits is an element of the class CImage
```

```
for (int y = xyOut = 0; y < height; y++) // ================================
{
   int y1, yStart = Math.Max(y - hWind, 0) * NX3,
            yEnd = Math.Min(y + hWind, height - 1) * NX3;
   for (int x = x3 = 0; x < width; x++, x3+=3, xyOut+=3) //==================
   {
      int x1, xStart = Math.Max(x3 - hWind3, 0),
              xEnd = Math.Min(x3 + hWind3, NX3 - 3);
     for (c=0; c<3; c++)
     {
        Sum[c] = 0;
        nPixel[c] = 0;
       gvMin[c] = Math.Max(0, Inp.Grid[c + xyOut] - Toleranz);
       gvMax[c] = Math.Min(255, Inp.Grid[c + xyOut]+Toleranz);
     }
     for (y1 = yStart; y1 <= yEnd; y1 += NX3)
       for (x1 = xStart; x1 <= xEnd; x1 += 3)
         for (c = 0; c < 3; c++)
         {
            if (Inp.Grid[c+x1+y1]>=gvMin[c] && Inp.Grid[c+x1+y1]<=
            gvMax[c])
            { Sum[c]+=Inp.Grid[c+x1+y1];
              nPixel[c]++;
            }
         }
     for (c = 0; c < 3; c++) //=======================================
     { if (nPixel[c] > 0) Grid[c+xyOut] = (byte)((Sum[c] + nPixel[c]/2)/
     nPixel[c]);
       else Grid[c+xyOut]=0;
     } //================ end for (c... ==========================
   } //================ end for (int x... ==========================
} //================ end for (int y... ==========================
return 1;
} //******************** end SigmaSimpleColor ************************
```

This solution works well, but it is rather slow if the size of the gliding window is greater than 5 × 5 pixels: It needs approximately OPP = 4*W^2 operations per pixel for gray images or 9*W^2 for color images. In the most practical cases it suffices to use the sigma filter with the window size of 3 × 3 or 5 × 5 pixels. Thus `SigmaSimpleColor` can be used almost everywhere.

Later we will see a faster version of the sigma filter. Unfortunately, it is impossible to apply in this case the method used in the fast averaging filter because the procedure is nonlinear. The procedure can be made faster due to the use of a local histogram. The histogram is an array in which each element contains the number of occurrences of the corresponding gray value or color intensity in the window. The sigma filter calculates the histogram for each location of the window by means of the updating procedure: Gray values or color intensities in the vertical column at the right border of the window are used to increase the corresponding values of the histogram, whereas the values at the left border are used to decrease them.

Let OPP be the number of operations per pixel. 2*3*W is the number of operations necessary to actualize the histogram and 2*3*(2*tol+1) is the number of operations necessary to calculate the sum of 3*(2*tol+1) values of the histogram and the corresponding number of pixels. Thus the overall OPP = 2*3*W+2*3*(2* tol +1).

Here is the source code for the sigma filter with a local histogram for color images.

```
public int SigmaColor(CImage Inp, int hWind, int Toleranz, Form1 fm1)
// The sigma filter for color images with 3 bytes per pixel.
{
  int gv, y1, yEnd, yStart;
  int[] gvMin = new int[3], gvMax = new int[3], nPixel = new int[3];
  int Sum = new int[3];
  int[,] hist = new int[256, 3];
  int c;
  for (y1 = 0; y1 < 256; y1++) for (c = 0; c < 3; c++) hist[y1, c] = 0;
  N_Bits = Inp.N_Bits;
  fm1.progressBar1.Value = 0;
  int yy = 5 + nLoop * height / denomProg;
  for (int y = 0; y < height; y++) //=====================================
  {
    if ((y % yy) == 0) fm1.progressBar1.PerformStep();
    yStart = Math.Max(y - hWind, 0);
```

```
yEnd = Math.Min(y + hWind, height - 1);
for (int x = 0; x < width; x++) //=====================================
{
  for (c = 0; c < 3; c++)  //=====================================
  {
    if (x == 0) //---------------------------------------------
    {
      for (gv = 0; gv < 256; gv++) hist[gv,c] = 0;
      for (y1 = yStart; y1 <= yEnd; y1++)
        for (int xx = 0; xx <= hWind; xx++)
          hist[Inp.Grid[c + 3 * (xx + y1 * width)], c]++;
    }
    else
    {
      int x1 = x + hWind, x2 = x - hWind - 1;
      if (x1 < width - 1)
        for (y1 = yStart; y1 <= yEnd; y1++)
          hist[Inp.Grid[c + 3 * (x1 + y1 * width)], c]++;
      if (x2 >= 0)
        for (y1 = yStart; y1 <= yEnd; y1++)
        {
          hist[Inp.Grid[c + 3 * (x2 + y1 * width)], c]--;
          if (hist[Inp.Grid[c + 3 * (x2 + y1 * width)], c] < 0) return -1;
        }
    } //---------------- end if (x==0) ------------------------

    Sum[c] = 0; nPixel[c] = 0;
    gvMin[c] = Math.Max(0, Inp.Grid[c + 3 * x + 3 * width * y] -
    Toleranz);
    gvMax[c] = Math.Min(255, Inp.Grid[c + 3 * x + 3 * width * y] +
    Toleranz);
    for (gv = gvMin[c]; gv <= gvMax[c]; gv++)
    {
      Sum[c] += gv * hist[gv, c]; nPixel[c] += hist[gv, c];
    }
    if (nPixel[c] > 0)
```

```
      Grid[c + 3 * x + 3 * width * y] = (byte)((Sum[c] + nPixel[c] / 2)
      / nPixel[c]);
    else Grid[c + 3 * x + 3 * width * y] = Inp.Grid[c + 3 * x + 3 *
    width * y];
  } //=============== end for (c... =============================
 } //=============== end for (int x... ===========================
} //=============== end for (int y... ===========================
  return 1;
} //********************* end SigmaColor *****************************
```

The method SigmaSimpleColor is faster than SigmaColor if the width of the gliding window is less than seven (hWind less than three). At greater values of the width SigmaColor is faster. The working time of SigmaColor changes rather slowly with the width of the gliding window. Refer to Table 2-2.

Table 2-2. *Working Times for a Color Image of 1200 × 1600 Pixels in Seconds*

	hWind			
Method	1	2	3	6
SigmaSimpleColor	0.71	1.68	3.11	10.26
SigmaColor	2.43	2.55	2.63	3.02

The method SigmaSimpleColor and similar methods for grayscale images are used in almost all projects described in this book.

Suppression of Impulse Noise

As already specified, the impulse noise affects singular, occasionally chosen pixels or small groups of adjacent pixels rather than all pixels of the image. The latter is characteristic for Gaussian noise. We distinguish between dark and light impulse noise. The dark noise contains pixels or groups of pixels whose lightness is lower than that of their neighborhood, whereas in the case of the light noise the pixels have a higher lightness than their neighborhood.

The problem of suppressing impulse noise in grayscale or color images is rather complicated: It is necessary to automatically detect all subsets S of pixels that satisfy, in the case of dark noise, the following conditions:

1. All pixels of a subset S must have a lightness that is lower than or equal to a threshold T.

2. The subset S is connected.

3. The number of pixels (i.e., the area of S) is lower than a predefined value M.

4. All pixels that do not belong to S but are adjacent to pixels of S must have a lightness that is higher than T.

5. The threshold T can be different for different subsets S.

The problem is difficult because the threshold T is unknown. Theoretically it is possible to solve the problem while testing all possible values of T one after another. However, such an algorithm would be very slow.

M. I. Schlesinger (1997) suggested the following idea of a fast solution:

"We propose such a procedure that the "noise removing" with subsequent thresholding gives the same results as thresholding with subsequent commonly used noise removing in the binary picture. This equivalency holds for every threshold's value.

The algorithm of the project PulseNoise *consists of four steps: (1) sorting of pixels in increasing order of their brightness, (2) white noise removal, (3) sorting of pixels in decreasing order of their brightness, and (4) black noise removal.*

Ordering of pixels is fulfilled during twofold scanning of the pixels using an additional array with the length equal to the number of different brightness.

White noise removal is carried out during onefold scanning of ordered pixels. Let t_i be a pixel having brightness $v(t_i)$. Processing of the pixel consists of checking whether there exists white noise region G that contains this pixel. Initially the region contains only t_i. Then the region grows so that some pixel t' is included into it if (1) t' is a neighbor of the region G; and (2) $v(t')\geq v(t_i)$. The region grows until one of the following conditions is satisfied:

1. The size of the obtained region G exceeds the predefined size. In this case the region G is not considered as noise and the next pixel $t_{(i+1)}$ is processed.

2. No pixel can be included in G. In this case G is a noise and the brightness of all its pixels is equal to maximum brightness of the neighboring pixels.

Removal of black noise is similar to white noise removal."

A detailed description and the source code of our implementation of this algorithm in the Windows Forms project `PulseNoiseWF` follows. We have made some inessential changes: Instead of sorting the pixels according to their lightness, which would be too slow, we use a histogram `histo[256]` of the lightness and define a two-dimensional array `Index[256][*]`. This array contains for each value `light` of the lightness a different number `Index[light][histo[light]]` of indexes `(x + Width*y)` of pixels. The value `(x + Width*y)` is the index of the pixel with coordinates (x, y), by which the pixel can be found in the image. Thus, for example, the value `Index[light][10]` is the index of the tenth pixel in the set of all pixels with the lightness equal to `light`. When reading the array `Index` while starting with small lightness, we obtain the indexes of pixels sorted in the order of increasing lightness, but when reading it in the opposite direction, we obtain the indexes of pixels sorted in the order of decreasing lightness.

The project contains a file `CImage.cs` with the definition of the class `CImage` containing methods used for preprocessing the images. These methods work with objects of the class `CImage`, which is easier and faster than working with Bitmaps in Windows Forms.

The project contains also the file `CPnoise.cs` with the class `CPnoise` containing methods realizing the suppression of the impulse noise. There is also a small file `Queue.cs` containing the class Queue, which defines simple methods realizing the well-known structure Queue. A queue is a first-in-first-out (FIFO) data structure. In a FIFO data structure, the first element added to the queue will be the first one to be removed. This is equivalent to the requirement that once a new element is added, all elements that were added before it have to be removed before the new element can be removed. I describe the methods of the project in what follows.

We consider the cases of grayscale and color images together because the only difference between these cases is that in the case of color images the common lightness of the three channels—red, green, and blue—of a pixel is considered in the same way as the gray value of the grayscale image. We use for the calculation of the lightness of color pixels our method `MaxC(byte R, byte G, byte B)` described in Chapter 3. We use in this project the color information directly only in instructions assigning a color to the pixels of the found set *S*.

The project PulseNoiseWF displays a form shown in Figure 2-8. When the user clicks Open image, the openFileDialog1 dialog box opens and the user can choose an image. The image opens and is transformed into the object CImage.Orig by means of the methods BitmapToGrid or BitmapToGridOld, depending on the pixel format of the opened image. BitmapToGrid uses the method LockBits of the class BitmapData, which permits direct assessment to the pixels of the bitmap; this is much faster than the standard assessment with GetPixel. The code of BitmapToGrid is shown here.

Figure 2-8. *The form of the project* PulseNoiseWF

```
private void BitmapToGrid(Bitmap bmp, byte[] Grid)
{
  Rectangle rect = new Rectangle(0, 0, bmp.Width, bmp.Height);
  BitmapData bmpData = bmp.LockBits(rect, ImageLockMode.ReadWrite,
                                               bmp.PixelFormat);
  int nbyte;
  switch (bmp.PixelFormat)
  {
    case PixelFormat.Format24bppRgb:        nbyte = 3; break;
    case PixelFormat.Format8bppIndexed:    nbyte = 1; break;
```

```csharp
    default: MessageBox.Show("Not suitable pixel format=" + bmp.PixelFormat);
                return;
  }
  IntPtr ptr = bmpData.Scan0;
  int length = Math.Abs(bmpData.Stride) * bmp.Height;
  byte[] rgbValues = new byte[length];
  System.Runtime.InteropServices.Marshal.Copy(ptr, rgbValues, 0, length);

  progressBar1.Visible = true;
  for (int y = 0; y < bmp.Height; y++)
  {
    int y1 = 1 + bmp.Height / 100;
    if (y % y1 == 1) progressBar1.PerformStep();

    for (int x = 0; x < bmp.Width; x++)
    {
      if (nbyte == 1)  // nbyte is global according to the PixelFormat of "bmp"
      {
        Color color = bmp.Palette.Entries[rgbValues[x+Math.Abs(bmpData.
        Stride)*y]];
        Grid[3 * (x + bmp.Width * y) + 0] = color.B;
        Grid[3 * (x + bmp.Width * y) + 1] = color.G;
        Grid[3 * (x + bmp.Width * y) + 2] = color.R;
      }
      else
        for (int c = 0; c < nbyte; c++)
          Grid[c + nbyte * (x + bmp.Width * y)] =
                        rgbValues[c + nbyte * x + Math.Abs
                        (bmpData.Stride) * y];
    }
  }
  bmp.UnlockBits(bmpData);
  progressBar1.Visible = false;
} //********************* end BitmapToGrid *********************
```

The method `BitmapToGridOld` uses `GetPixel`. In the case of an 8-bit image, the color table `Palette` must be used to define the color of each pixel. This goes faster with `GetPixel` than with `Palette.Entries`, as this was the case in `BitmapToGrid`. Therefore we use `BitmapToGridOld` in the case of 8-bit original images.

The form `Form1` contains the following definitions:

```
private Bitmap origBmp;
private Bitmap Result; // result of processing
CImage Orig;  // copy of original image
CImage Work;  // work image
public Point[] v = new Point[20];
// "v" are corners of excluded rectangles
int Number, // number of defined elements "v"
   maxNumber = 8;
bool Drawn = false;
```

The image is shown in `pictureBox1` on the left side of the form. The user can now change the values of the maximum sizes (number of pixels) of the dark and light spots to be eliminated. This can be done with the tool `numericUpDown` with labels `Delete dark` and `Delete light`.

When the user clicks Impulse noise, the corresponding program stump will be started. Here is the code of the stump.

```
private void button3_Click(object sender, EventArgs e)      // Impulse noise
{
  Work.Copy(Orig);  // "Work" is the work image defined outside
  int nbyte = 3;
  Drawn = true;
  Work.DeleteBit0(nbyte);
  int maxLight, minLight;
  int[] histo = new int[256];
  for (int i = 0; i < 256; i++) histo[i] = 0;
  int light, index;
  int y1 = Work.height / 100;
  for (int y = 0; y < Work.height; y++) //============================
  {
    if (y % y1 == y1 - 1) progressBar1.PerformStep();
```

```
  for (int x = 0; x < Work.width; x++) //=======================
  {
    index = x + y * Work.width; // Index of the pixel (x, y)
    light = MaxC(Work.Grid[3 * index+2] & 254,
                 Work.Grid[3 * index + 1] & 254,
                 Work.Grid[3 * index + 0] & 254);
    if (light < 0) light = 0;
    if (light > 255) light = 255;
    histo[light]++;
  } //=============== end for (int x=1; .. ====================
} //=============== end for (int y=1; .. ====================
progressBar1.Visible = false;
for (maxLight = 255; maxLight > 0; maxLight--) if (histo[maxLight] != 0)
break;
for (minLight = 0; minLight < 256; minLight++) if (histo[minLight] != 0)
break;
CPnoise PN = new CPnoise(histo, 1000, 4000);
PN.Sort(Work, histo, Number, pictureBox1.Width, pictureBox1.Height,
this);
progressBar1.Visible = false;
int maxSizeD = 0;
if (textBox1.Text != "") maxSizeD = int.Parse(textBox1.Text);
int maxSizeL = 0;
if (textBox2.Text != "") maxSizeL = int.Parse(textBox2.Text);
PN.DarkNoise(ref Work, minLight, maxLight, maxSizeD, this);
progressBar1.Visible = false;
Work.DeleteBit0(nbyte);
PN.LightNoise(ref Work, minLight, maxLight, maxSizeL, this);
progressBar1.Visible = false;
Result = new Bitmap(origBmp.Width, origBmp.Height,
                                        PixelFormat.Format24bppRgb);
progressBar1.Visible = true;
int i1 = 1 + nbyte * origBmp.Width * origBmp.Height / 100;
for (int i = 0; i < nbyte * origBmp.Width * origBmp.Height; i++)
{
```

```
    if (i % i1 == 1) progressBar1.PerformStep();
    if (Work.Grid[i] == 252 || Work.Grid[i] == 254) Work.Grid[i] = 255;
  }
  progressBar1.Visible = false;
  GridToBitmap(Result, Work.Grid);
  pictureBox2.Image = Result;
  Graphics g = pictureBox1.CreateGraphics();
  Pen myPen = new Pen(Color.Blue);

  // Drawing the excluded rectangles
  for (int n = 0; n < Number; n += 2)
  {
    g.DrawLine(myPen, v[n + 1].X, v[n + 0].Y, v[n + 1].X, v[n + 1].Y);
    g.DrawLine(myPen, v[n + 0].X, v[n + 0].Y, v[n + 1].X, v[n + 0].Y);
    g.DrawLine(myPen, v[n + 0].X, v[n + 0].Y, v[n + 0].X, v[n + 1].Y);
    g.DrawLine(myPen, v[n + 0].X, v[n + 1].Y, v[n + 1].X, v[n + 1].Y);
  }
  progressBar1.Visible = false;
} //*************************** end Impulse noise ***************
```

The stump calls the method DeleteBit0, deleting the bit 0 of all pixels of the image to make possible the labeling of pixels that have already been used. Then the histogram of the lightness of the image is computed, and the minimum lightness MinLight and maximum lightness MaxLight are defined.

Then the method Sort for sorting the pixels by their lightness is called. It is not necessary to sort the pixels by means of a known sorting algorithm, as this would take too much time. Instead our method Sort obtains the histogram histo[256] of the lightness of the image and fills the two-dimensional array Index[256][ ] of indexes. The argument light of Index[light] is the lightness of a pixel. The subarray Index[light][ ] is an array of indexes where nPixel[light] is the number of pixels having the lightness light. The value nPixel[light] is equal to histo[light]. Each element of the subarray Index[light][ ] is an index equal to x+width*y of a pixel with coordinates (x, y) whose lightness is equal to light. Here x is the number of a column, y is the number of a row, and width is the number of columns in the image. The method Sort saves the index ind=x+ width*y of the ith pixel with the lightness light and with coordinates (x, y) in Index[light][i]. Thus all pixels of the image are sorted in increasing order of their lightness. If a decreasing order is needed, the array Index can be read in the opposite direction. Here are the source codes of the definition of the class CPnoise and its methods. We describe the methods and show their codes outside of the definition of the class CPnoise although according to the prescription of C# .NET they should be inside. This method is more convenient because we can locate the description of a method near the code of the method.

```
class CPnoise
{ unsafe
  public int[][] Index; // saving indexes of all pixels ordered by lightness
  int[] Comp; // contains indexes of pixels of the connected subset
  int[] nPixel; // number of pixels with certain lightness
  int MaxSize;// admissible size of the connected subset
  Queue Q1;
  unsafe
  public CPnoise(int[] Histo, int Qlength, int Size)  // Constructor
  {
    this.maxSize = Size;
    this.Q1 = new Queue(Qlength);//necessary to find connected subsets
    this.Comp = new int[MaxSize];
    this.nPixel=new int[256];//256 is the number of lightness values
    for (int light = 0; light < 256; light++) nPixel[light] = 0;
    Index = new int[256][];
    for (int light = 0; light < 256; light++)
      Index[light] = new int[Histo[light] + 1];
  } //*********************** end of Constructor *****************
```

As we see in the preceding code of button3_Click, the method Sort is called after the computation of the histogram. It inserts indexes of all pixels of the image to the two-dimensional array Index[256][ ] of indexes. The image in which the impulse noise should be eliminated sometimes contains small spots that are not noise and should not be eliminated. For example, the eyes of a person in an image are sometimes small, dark spots of a size similar to the size of the spots of the dark noise. To prevent their elimination we have developed a simple procedure: The user should draw with the mouse in the input image some rectangles including the locations that should not be eliminated. The method Sort obtains the parameters v[ ] of these rectangles and skips the insertion of the pixels inside these rectangles into the array Index[256][ ]. For this purpose the simple method getCond is employed, which uses the array v[ ] of Points defined in Form1. The code is not presented here. The following is the source code of the method Sort.

```
public int Sort(CImage Image, int[] histo, int Number, int picBox1Width,
                                        int picBox1Height, Form1 fm1)
{
int light, i;
double ScaleX = (double)picBox1Width / (double)Image.width;
double ScaleY = (double)picBox1Height / (double)Image.height;
double Scale; // Scale of the presentation of the image in "pictureBox1"
if (ScaleX < ScaleY) Scale = ScaleX;
else Scale = ScaleY;
bool COLOR;
if (Image.nBits == 24) COLOR = true;
else COLOR = false;
double marginX = (double)(picBox1Width - Scale *Image.width)*0.5; // left of
                                                                        image
double marginY=(double)(picBox1Height - Scale*Image.height)*0.5; // above
                                                                        image
bool Condition = false; // Skipping pixel (x, y) if it lies in a global
rectangles "fm1.v"
fm1.progressBar1.Value = 0;
fm1.progressBar1.Step = 1;
fm1.progressBar1.Visible = true;
fm1.progressBar1.Maximum = 100;
for (light = 0; light < 256; light++) nPixel[light] = 0;
for (light = 0; light < 256; light++)
  for (int light1 = 0; light1 < histo[light]; light1++) Index[light]
  [light1] = 0;

int y1 =  Image.height / 100;
for (int y = 1; y < Image.height; y++) //===================================
{
  if (y % y1 == y1 - 1) fm1.progressBar1.PerformStep();
```

```
for (int x = 1; x < Image.width; x++) //====================================
{
  Condition = false;
  for (int k = 0; k < Number; k += 2)
    Condition = Condition || getCond(k, x, y, marginX, marginY, Scale, fm1);
  if (Condition)  continue;
  i = x + y * Image.width; // Index of the pixel (x, y)
  if (COLOR)
    light = MaxC(Image.Grid[3 * i+2] & 254, Image.Grid[3 * i + 1] & 254,
                                        Image.Grid[3 * i + 0] & 254);
  else light = Image.Grid[i] & 252;
  if (light < 0) light = 0;
  if (light > 255) light = 255;
  Index[light][nPixel[light]] = i; // record of index "i" of a pixel with
  lightness "light"
  if (nPixel[light] < histo[light]) nPixel[light]++;
} //============== end for (int x=1; .. ==============================
} //============== end for (int y=1; .. ==============================
fm1.progressBar1.Visible = false;
return 1;
} //**************** end Sort ****************************************
```

The method Sort reads all pixels of the image and fills the two-dimensional array Index[256][ ] with indexes of the pixels. This array is used by the methods DarkNoise and LightNoise.

We consider first the case of dark noise. The method DarkNoise contains a for loop with the variable light, which scans the values of light starting with the maximum lightness minus 2 until the minimum lightness minLight. This loop contains the other loop with the variable i, which scans the values of the second index of the two-dimensional array Index[light][i] from 0 to nPixel[light]. It reads the index of a pixel from the array Index[light][i] and tests whether the pixel with this index has the lightness equal to light and whether its label is equal to zero. If both conditions are fulfilled, then the method BreadthFirst_D is called for the pixel with the index Index[light][i]. This method constructs a connected subset of pixels with lightness less than or equal to light containing the starting pixel with the index Index[light][i].

Here is the source code of DarkNoise:

```
public int DarkNoise(ref CImage Image, int minLight, int maxLight, int
maxSize, Form1 fm1)
{
  bool COLOR = (Image.nBits == 24);
  int ind3 = 0, // index multiplied with 3
    Label2, Lum, rv = 0;
  if (maxSize == 0) return 0;
  fm1.progressBar1.Maximum = 100;
  fm1.progressBar1.Step = 1;
  fm1.progressBar1.Value = 0;
  fm1.progressBar1.Visible = false;
  int bri1 = 2;
  fm1.progressBar1.Visible = true;
  for (int light = maxLight - 2; light >= minLight; light--) //==============
  {
    if ((light % bri1) == 1) fm1.progressBar1.PerformStep();
    for (int i = 0; i < nPixel[light]; i++) //===============================
    {
      ind3 = 3 * Index[light][i];
      if (COLOR)
      {
        Label2 = Image.Grid[2 + ind3] & 1;
        Lum = MaxC(Image.Grid[2 + ind3] & 254, Image.Grid[1 + ind3] & 254,
                                          Image.Grid[0 + ind3] & 254);
      }
      else
      {
        Label2 = Image.Grid[Index[light][i]] & 2;
        Lum = Image.Grid[Index[light][i]] & 252;
      }
      if (Lum == light && Label2 == 0)
      {
        rv = BreadthFirst_D(ref Image, i, light, maxSize);
      }
```

```
  } //================= end for (int i.. ===========================
  } //================= end for (int light.. =========================
  fm1.progressBar1.Visible = false;
  return rv;
} //********************** end DarkNoise *****************************
```

The method DarkNoise calls the method BreadthFirst_D( ) with the values Image, i, light, and maxSize as its arguments. The value of maxSize is the maximum allowed number of pixels in the sought for connected set of pixels having lightness less than or equal to light. This method implements the known algorithm breadth-first search, designed to label all vertices of a tree structure. The connected set of all pixels having lightness less than or equal to light is a tree. Here is the code for BreadthFirst_D( ):

```
private int BreadthFirst_D(ref CImage Image, int i, int light, int maxSize)
{
  int lightNeib,    lightness of the neighbor
      index, Label1, Label2,
      maxNeib, // maxNeib is the maximum number of neighbors of a pixel
      Neib, // the index of a neighbor
      nextIndex, // index of the next pixel in the queue
      numbPix; // number of pixel indexes in "Comp"
  bool small; // equals "true" if the subset is less than "maxSize"
  bool COLOR = (Image.nBits == 24);
  index = Index[light][i];
  int[] MinBound = new int[3]; // color of pixel with min. lightness near
  the subset
  for (int c = 0; c < 3; c++) MinBound[c] = 300; // a value out of [0, 255]
  for (int p = 0; p < MaxSize; p++) Comp[p] = -1; // MaxSize is element of
  the class
  numbPix = 0;
  maxNeib = 8; // maximum number of neighbors
  small = true;
  Comp[numbPix] = index;
  numbPix++;
  if (COLOR)
    Image.Grid[1 + 3 * index] |= 1; // Labeling as in Comp (Label1)
```

```
else
  Image.Grid[index] |= 1; // Labeling as in Comp
Q1.input = Q1.output = 0;
Q1.Put(index); // putting index into the queue
while (Q1.Empty() == 0) //=  loop running while queue not empty ============
{
  nextIndex = Q1.Get();
  for (int n = 0; n <= maxNeib; n++) // == all neighbors of "nextIndex"
  {
    Neib = Neighb(Image, nextIndex, n); // the index of the nth neighbor
    of nextIndex
    if (Neib < 0) continue; // Neib < 0 means outside the image
    if (COLOR)
    {
      Label1 = Image.Grid[1 + 3 * Neib] & 1;
      Label2 = Image.Grid[2 + 3 * Neib] & 1;
      lightNeib = MaxC(Image.Grid[2 + 3 * Comp[m]],
                       Image.Grid[1 + 3 * Comp[m]], Image.Grid[0 + 3 *
                       Comp[m]]) & 254;
    }
    else
    {
      Label1 = Image.Grid[Neib] & 1;
      Label2 = Image.Grid[Neib] & 2;
      lightNeib = Image.Grid[Neib] & 252; // MaskGV;
    }
    if (lightNeib == light && Label2 > 0) small = false;
    if (lightNeib <= light) //-------------------------------------------
    {
      if (Label1 > 0) continue;
      Comp[numbPix] = Neib; // putting the element with index Neib into Comp
      numbPix++;
      if (COLOR)
        Image.Grid[1 + 3 * Neib] |= 1; // Labeling with "1" as in Comp
```

```
        else
          Image.Grid[Neib] |= 1; // Labeling with "1" as in Comp
        if (numbPix > maxSize)  // Very important condition
        {
          small = false;
          break;
        }
        Q1.Put(Neib);
      }
      else // lightNeib<light
      {
        if (Neib != index) //-----------------------------------------------
        {
          if (COLOR)
          {
            if (lightNeib < (MinBound[0] + MinBound[1] + MinBound[2]) / 3)
              for (int c = 0; c < 3; c++) MinBound[c] = Image.Grid[c + 3 *
              Neib];
          }
          else
            if (lightNeib < MinBound[0]) MinBound[0] = lightNeib;
        } //--------------- end if (Neib!=index) ------------------------
      } //--------------- end if (lightNeib<=light) and else -----------
    } // ==================== end for (n=0; .. ========================
    if (small == false) break;
} // ==================== end while ===========================
int lightComp; // lightness of a pixel whose index is contained in "Comp"
for (int m = 0; m < numbPix; m++) //==================================
{
  if (small != false && MinBound[0] < 300) //"300" means MinBound not
  calculated ---
  {
    if (COLOR)
```

```
      for (int c = 0; c < 3; c++) Image.Grid[c + 3 * Comp[m]] = (byte)
      MinBound[c];
    else
      Image.Grid[Comp[m]] = (byte)MinBound[0];
  }
  else
  {
    if (COLOR)
      lightComp = MaxC(Image.Grid[3 * Comp[m]],
                     Image.Grid[1 + 3 * Comp[m]], Image.Grid[2 + 3 *
                     Comp[m]]) & 254;
    else
      lightComp = Image.Grid[Comp[m]] & 252; // MaskGV;
    if (lightComp == light) //---------------------------------------------
    {
      if (COLOR) Image.Grid[2 + 3 * Comp[m]] |= 1;
      else Image.Grid[Comp[m]] |= 2;
    }
    else // lightComp!=light
    {
      if (COLOR)
      {
        Image.Grid[1 + 3 * Comp[m]] &= (byte)254; // deleting label 1
        Image.Grid[2 + 3 * Comp[m]] &= (byte)254; // deleting label 2
      }
      else
        Image.Grid[Comp[m]] &= 252; // deleting the labels
    } //-------------- end if (lightComp == light) and else--------------
  } //-----------------end if (small != false) and else ----------------
} //==================== end for (int m=0 .. ========================
return numbPix;
} //********************* end BreadthFirst_D *************************
```

The method BreadthFirst_D obtains as parameters the lightness light and the number i of a pixel P in the array Index[light][i]. The task of this method is to find a connected set S of pixels having the lightness less than or equal to light and containing the pixel P. If this set contains a number numbPix of pixels that is less or equal to the parameter maxSize then the pixels of S obtain a lighter color and become invisible as dark pixels. Otherwise all pixels of S obtain a label indicating that these pixels have the lightness light and belong to a connected subset of more than maxSize pixels.

The method takes the index from Index[light][i], puts it into the queue Q and starts a while loop running as long as Q is not empty. In the loop the value nextIndex is taken from the queue Q and each of its eight neighbors with the index Neib is tested whether its lightness is less than or equal to light. Besides that the label of Neib is tested.

We use the least significant bits of a pixel in Image.Grid to label a pixel. In the case of a grayscale image we use two least significant bits: Bit 0 is LabelQ1 and Bit 1 is LabelBig2. In the case of a color image we use one bit of the green channel as LabelQ1 and one bit of the red channel as LabelBig2.

LabelQ1 is set if the index was already put into the queue. LabelBig2 is set if a pixel belongs to a connected big set S of pixels that is greater than maxSize and the lightness of the pixel is equal to light.

If LabelQ1 of the pixel with the index Neib is not set and its lightness is less than or equal to light, then the index Neib is saved in the array Comp containing the indexes of all pixels whose lightness is less than or equal to light. Then the index Neib is put into the queue and the pixel obtains the label LabelQ1. If, however, the lightness of Neib is greater than light, this lightness will be used for calculating the color MinBound used for filling all pixels of a small set S to be made lighter.

Both labels are important to make the method BreadthFirst_D faster: A pixel with a set LabelQ1 must not be input into the queue again and one with a set LabelBig2 indicates that the set S containing this pixel is not small. The method DarkNoise does not call the method BrightFirst_D for a pixel labeled with LabelBig2.

In the while loop of BrightFirst_D, the index nextIndex is taken from the queue as its next element. The indexes Neib of all eight neighbors of nextIndex are delivered by a method Neighb(Image, nextIndex, n) (n runs from 0 to 7) one after another. If a neighbor Neib lies outside the image (nextIndex was at the border of the image), the method Neighb returns a negative value and Neib will be ignored. Otherwise the lightness lightNeb of Neib is taken from Image. If lightNeb is greater than light, then

Neib does not belong to the sought for set *S* of pixels composing the connected set (component) of pixels darker than or equally dark as light. The value lightNeb is then used to calculate the color MinBound which is the color with minimum lightness of pixels adjacent to *S*.

If lightNeb is equal to light and the pixel Neib has LabelBig2 set, then the logical variable small is set to false. Otherwise, if lightNeb is greater than or equal to light, there are two cases: In the case that Neib has LabelQ1 set, the pixel Neib is ignored; otherwise the number numbPix of pixels already included into the sought for set *S* is compared with maxSize. If it is greater than maxSize, then the variable small is set to false and the while loop is broken. If, however, numbPix is less than or equal to maxSize, then Neib is included into the set *S* (Neib is saved in the array Comp), the pixel Neib gets LabelQ1 set, and Neib is put into the queue.

After the end of the while loop the value of small is being checked. If it is true, then all pixels of *S* whose indexes are saved in the array Comp get the color MinBound. Otherwise the pixels of Comp having the lightness equal to light get the label LabelBig2. All other pixels of *S* get no label. The method returns the value numbPix.

The method BreadthFirst_L is similar to BreadthFirst_D. The difference consists mainly in interchanging some > and < operators (but not that of the instruction if (numbPix > maxSise) {...}). The method BreadthFirst_L is called by the method LightNoise, which is similar to DarkNoise. The method LightNoise reads the array Index starting with the lowest lightness and calls the method BreadthFirst_L.

All methods work with both grayscale and color images. This is reached due to the employment of the method MaxC(Red, Green, Blue) (see the explanation in Chapter 3), which calculates the lightness of a pixel with the color (Red, Green, Blue) according to this simple formula:

$$\text{lightness} = \max(0.713*R,\ G,\ 0.527*B).$$

The reader can see in Figure 2-9 an example of applying this project to an old photograph of a drawing made by a famous German female painter, Louise Seidler.

Figure 2-9. *Example of applying the project* `PulseNoiseWF` *to an old photograph of a drawing by Louise Seidler (left). Dark spots of less than 380 pixels are removed (right).*

The results obtained for grayscale images representing old photos of drawings are much better when we use suppressing of impulse noise after a correction of shading as described in Chapters 4 and 5. The images in Figure 2-9 will also look much better after applying methods of shading correction.

Figure 2-10 is another example of an image with light noise. It is a fragment of a photograph of the painting "Jesus and the Children" by Louise Seidler.

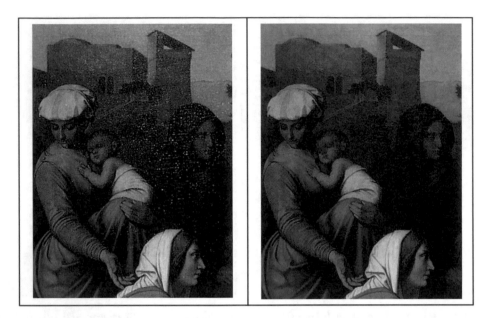

Figure 2-10. *Example of applying the project* PulseNoiseWF *to a fragment of a photograph of the painting of Louise Seidler (left). Light spots of less than 30 pixels are removed (right).*

CHAPTER 3

Contrast Enhancement

We define the contrast of a digital image as follows:

$$C_{ip} = (Li_{max} - Li_{min})/Domain$$

where Li_{max} is the maximum and Li_{min} is the minimum lightness in the image and *Domain* is the domain of the lightness or maximum possible value of the difference $Li_{max} - Li_{min}$.

The contrast measure just defined obviously depends on the lightness of a single pixel. To get a more robust measure it is necessary to know the frequencies of the lightness values: A value occurring in a small number of pixels is not important. The frequencies are contained in the histogram of the image. It is possible to find such values `MinInp` and `MaxInp` of the lightness, that the number of pixels with lightness below `MinInp` and that with lightness above `MaxInp` are less than a predefined value, which we call the *discard area* (because the number of pixels is the measure of the area). Then the robust contrast measure is

$$C_r = (MaxInp - MinInp)/Domain.$$

Automatic Linear Contrast Enhancement

Most programs for contrast enhancement, such as IrfanView, use a mapping of the set of the lightness values in the image to another such set by means of a function whose derivative in the middle part is greater than 1 (see Figure 3-1).

© Vladimir Kovalevsky 2019
V. Kovalevsky, *Modern Algorithms for Image Processing*, https://doi.org/10.1007/978-1-4842-4237-7_3

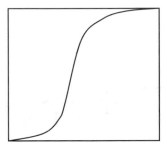

Figure 3-1. *Example of the graph of a function used for increasing the contrast in other programs*

Another approach is suggested here based on investigating the histogram of the image. The idea of our algorithm consists in mapping the interval between the lowest and the highest lightness in the image onto the whole interval; for example, onto [0, 255]. It is important to notice that a small number of pixels having extremely low or extremely high values can essentially influence the results of the mapping.

Therefore it is necessary to exclude a predefined portion (e.g., 1 percent) of the pixels having extreme values from the mapping. It is necessary to find for this purpose the values MinInp and MaxInp such that the number of pixels having lightness less than MinInp and having lightness greater than MaxInp is less than 1 percent of the whole number of pixels in the image.

To increase the contrast of the image we must increase the difference between the maximum and minimum lightness. This can be done by reducing the small values of the lightness in the image and increasing the greater ones. To get the maximum possible contrast of 1 it is necessary to transform the values of the lightness in such a way that MinInp is replaced by 0 and MaxInp by 255, and the intermediate values change monotonically; that is, their order remains unchanged.

It is possible to increase the contrast by an automatic procedure. The user must only define the value of the discard areas in percentage of the image size. It is advisable to use a look-up table (LUT) to make the calculation of the output lightness faster. LUT is an array containing as many elements as the number of possible input values; for example, 256, or from 0 to 255. Each element of the LUT contains the precalculated output value. Therefore, it becomes sufficient to calculate the output values only 256 times instead of width × height times, although the number width × height could be as large as many thousands or even millions. Getting a value from an array takes much less time than the calculation of this value.

It is also easy to reduce the contrast. When calculating the LUT, it is sufficient to set the following values: `MinInp=0`, `MaxInp=255`, `MinOut>0`, and `MaxOut<255`. It is a fun experiment to drastically reduce the contrast and then automatically increase it!

The simplest way to increase the contrast (see Figure 3-2) is by means of the following piecewise linear transformation:

```
if (Linp <= MinInp) Lout = 0;
else if (Linp >= MaxInp) Lout = 255;
        else Lout = 255*(Linp - MinInp)/(MaxInp - MinInp);
```

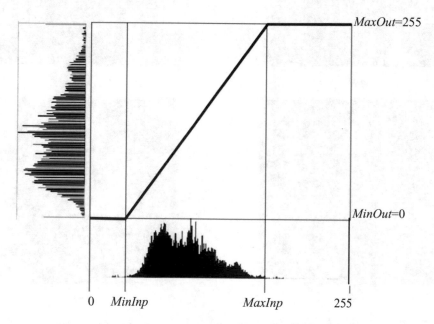

Figure 3-2. *Simplest piecewise linear contrast enhancement*

This very simple method yields very good results, but not for images containing large dark or large light areas. It is possible to obtain much better results in such cases when employing the method of histogram equalization, explained in the next section.

Histogram Equalization

Some images contain large dark areas with low contrast (see Figure 3-3a). The previously described simplest piecewise linear method stretches the lightness values homogeneously, whereas for such an image the low values in the dark region must be moved apart more strongly than the values in other regions. Such transformation cannot be performed by the simplest piecewise linear method.

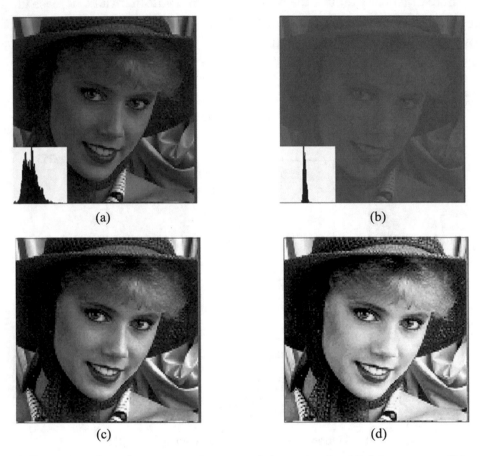

Figure 3-3. *Examples of contrast changes: (a) original with histogram; (b) reduced contrast with histogram; (c) linear contrast enhancement; (d) histogram equalization*

A well-known idea for increasing the contrast of such images is that of *histogram equalization:* It is necessary to transform the lightness values in such a way that all values get almost the same frequencies. To accomplish this, a pixel with a gray value inp_1 having a relatively high frequency (Figure 3-4a) must be replaced by many pixels with different gray values having lower frequencies. These gray values out_1, out_2, and so on must compose a sequence of adjacent values (Figure 3-4b). There is no known method to decide which of these pixels must get a certain value. Fortunately this is not necessary: It is sufficient to replace the original gray values with other values with greater differences between the values in such a way that the average frequency becomes constant (Figure 3-4c). This can be achieved by histogram equalization.

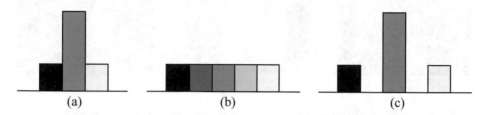

Figure 3-4. *Transforming a histogram to make the frequencies or average frequencies constant: (a) part of the histogram with a great frequency; (b) the gray value with a high frequency replaced by many values with lower frequencies; (c) values with greater differences of the values making the average frequency constant*

To implement histogram equalization it is necessary to calculate the *cumulative histogram*. This is an integer array with 256 elements. The element corresponding to a lightness value L contains the number of pixels with lightness values less than or equal to L. To calculate the value of the cumulative histogram for L it is sufficient to sum up the values of the usual histogram for all values less than or equal to L:

$$Cum[L] = \sum_{i \le L} Hist[i];$$

The LUT for histogram equalization can be calculated by means of the cumulative histogram. Most of the textbooks on image processing suggest the following formula for the elements of the LUT:

$$EquLUT[L] = 255 \cdot Cum[L] / MaxCum; \qquad (3.1)$$

where *MaxCum* is the maximum value of the cumulative histogram, which is obviously equal to the size width*height of the image.

However, when using this formula, difficulties occur if the original image contains a large number of pixels with a gray value equal to *gMin,* which is the minimum gray value for which the histogram is greater than 0. In this case the image transformed by means of the LUT calculated according to Equation 3.1 can be very poor because many pixels have a large gray value proportional to *Cum[gMin]*, which is much greater than 0. An example of such a transformation is shown in Figure 3-5b.

(a)   (b)   (c)

Figure 3-5. *Examples of histogram equalization: (a) original image; (b) transformed with LUT according to Equation 3.1; (c) transformed with LUT according to Equation 3.2*

To solve the problem it is sufficient to set the value of the *L*th element of the LUT *EquLUT* proportional to the difference *Cum*[*L*] – *MinHist* rather than to *Cum*[*L*] where *MinHist* = *Cum*[*gMin*] = *Hist*[*gMin*]. The elements of the LUT must be calculated according to the following formula:

$$\text{If } L \text{ is less or equal to } gMin \text{ then } EquLUT[L] = 0; \text{ else}$$

$$EquLUT[L] = 255 \cdot (Cum[L] - MinHist)/(MaxCum - MinHist) \qquad (3.2)$$

where *MaxCum*=width*height is the maximum value of *Cum*[*L*].

An example of the transformation with the LUT calculated according to Equation 3.2 is shown in Figure 3-5c.

The results of histogram equalization are not always satisfactory. Therefore it is rational to use a combination of the piecewise linear method with that of equalization called mixed method (see Figure 3-6):

$$CombiLUT[L] = W_1 \cdot LUT[L] + W_2 \cdot EquLUT[L]; \qquad (3.3)$$

where *LUT*[*L*] is the piecewise linear LUT and the weights W_1 and W_2 can be chosen as nonnegative brakes whose sum is equal to 1. Figure 3-6c shows the results of using *CombiLUT* with $W_1 = 0.2$ *and* $W_2 = 0.8$.

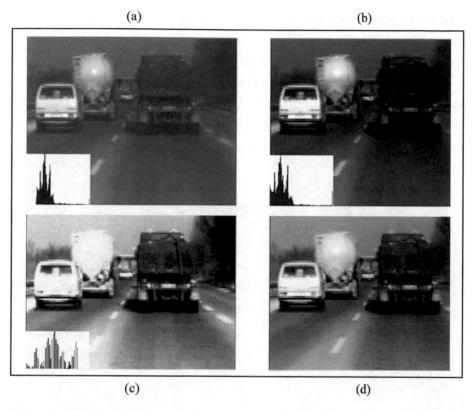

Figure 3-6. *Combined contrast enhancement: (a) original image; (b) piecewise linear; (c) histogram equalizing; (d) mixed method (20 percent)*

Measuring the Lightness of Color Images

To define the contrast of a color image it is necessary to calculate its brightness or lightness in each pixel. There are many different definitions of the lightness of a color pixel in the literature. Wikipedia suggests in the paper "HSL and HSV" different definitions of the "lightness"; for example:

$$I = (R+G+B)/3 \text{ or}$$

$$V = \max(R, G, B) \text{ or}$$

$$L = (\max(R, G, B)+\min(R, G, B))/2 \text{ or}$$

$$Y = 0.30R + 0.59G + 0.11B$$

where *R, G,* and *B* are the intensities of the color channels red, green, and blue, respectively. The author has developed a project WFluminance to experimentally test different definitions of the lightness.

The project shows in the left part of the form eight rectangles with different colors (Figure 3-7) and provides the possibility to change the lightness of each rectangle without changing its hue by means of the corresponding tool numericUpDown. The lightness of each color rectangle has been changed until all rectangles look like they have the same visually acceptable lightness equal to the lightness of the gray rectangle on the left. It is well known that a gray color has the intensities of all three color channels equal to each other: R = G = B. Thus the lightness of a gray color can be assumed to be equal to this constant intensity.

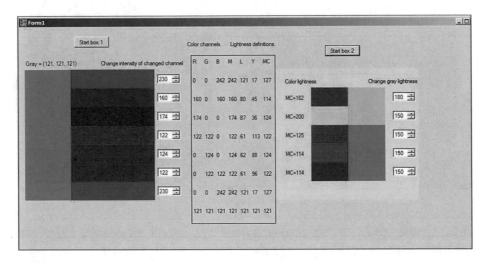

Figure 3-7. *Rectangles with constant visual lightness*

The project calculates the values of the lightness for each rectangle according to different definitions. The results are shown in Table 3-1. As one can see from Table 3-1, the value of MC is almost constant for all eight rectangles of Figure 3-7, which look like they have a constant lightness. The value of MC was also successfully tested for other colors as shown on the right side of Figure 3-7, representing pairs of rectangles with visually equal lightness.

Table 3-1. *Values of the Lightness According to Different Definitions*

Rectangle	Color	R	G	B	M	L	Y	MC
1	Blue	0	0	242	242	121	17	127
2	Magenta	160	0	160	160	80	45	114
3	Red	174	0	0	174	87	36	124
4	Yellow	122	122	0	122	61	113	122
5	Green	0	124	0	124	62	88	124
6	Cyan	0	122	122	122	61	96	122
7	Blue	0	0	242	242	121	17	127
8	Gray	121	121	121	121	121	121	121

Note: $M = max(R, G, B)$; $L = (M + min((R, G, B)$; $Y = 0.2126*R + 0.7152*G + 0.0722*R$; $MC = max(0.713*R, G, 0.527*B)$.

The text left of the color rectangle in the right half shows the MC value of the color in the rectangle. The user of the project can change the gray value of the adjacent gray rectangle by changing the value of the corresponding `numericUpDown` tool until the visual lightness of the gray rectangle is equal to the visual lightness of the color rectangle. If the value of `numericUpDown` is approximately equal to the MC value then this is proof that the MC method gives a good estimation of the luminance of that color. As you can see, the values for all rectangles are approximately equal.

There is a question whether an exact definition of the lightness of color pixels is important. This definition is used in converting a color image into a grayscale image and in the shading correction. We have tried to use different methods for calculating the lightness of color pixels while converting different color images into grayscale images. In most cases, the results do not depend on the choice of the method. However, in the example shown in Figure 3-8 a rather big part of the color image disappears when using method Y (Table 3-1).

We have also tested how the results of shading correction depend on the choice of the method of measuring the lightness. Similarly as in the case of converting a color image into a grayscale image, the results of shading correction mostly do not depend on that choice. However, there are images for which the shading correction strongly depends on that choice. See, for example, the image in Figure 3-9.

Original   Method MC   Method Y

Figure 3-8. *Example of an image where a part disappears under Method Y*

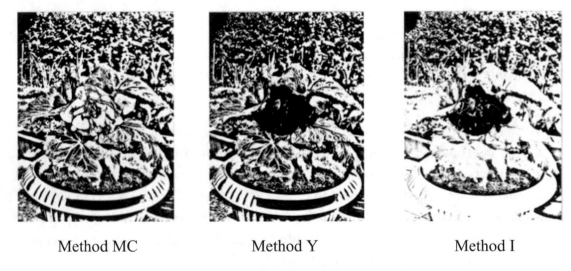

Method MC   Method Y   Method I

Figure 3-9. *Example of an image where shading correction strongly depends on the method of measuring the lightness; Method Y and Method I*

Taking into account the results just described, we have decided to use the method MC everywhere (as method MaxC).

Contrast of Color Images

To perform a contrast enhancement of a color image it is necessary to calculate the histogram of the lightness and then handle it as in the case of a grayscale image. The calculation of the LUT for the transformation of the lightness can be made in the same way as before either with the piecewise linear rule with discard areas or with histogram equalization. However, to change the intensities of the color channels a new procedure should be used: It is necessary to calculate for each pixel the relation of the transformed lightness to the original one and then multiply each of the three intensities R, G, and B by this relation. For example, the transformed red channel for a pixel P is:

$$RT = RO \cdot LiT/LiO$$

where RT and LiT are the transformed red intensity and lightness, whereas RO and LiO are the original value of the red intensity and of the lightness for the pixel P. In this way all three intensities can be changed proportionally and the hue remains unchanged, whereby the contrast increases.

Manually Controlled Contrast Enhancement

Some photographs have a rather inhomogeneous lightness originating from an inhomogeneous illumination of the photographed object. This drawback of a photograph can be mostly corrected by the histogram equalization method, which is in general a good contrast enhancement method. However, sometimes it is necessary to correct the contents of the LUT while seeing the result.

Some suggested image processing programs (e.g., Photoshop) contain a tool that permits making the graph of the LUT a Bézier curve, which is a smooth curve with a continuous derivative. This is, however, a bad idea because the function realized by the LUT must not be smooth. It must be continuous and, what is much more important, monotonically increasing. The last condition is not always fulfilled for Bézier curves. If the function of the LUT is not monotonically increasing, the resulting image can be hardly distorted.

It is much simpler to define the function of the LUT as a piecewise linear monotonically increasing line like that shown in Figure 3-10.

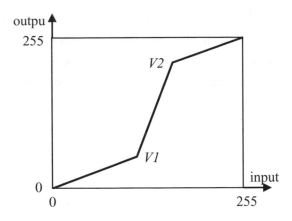

Figure 3-10. *Piecewise linear function of the LUT*

The break points *V1* and *V2* can be defined by mouse clicks. The transformed image must be shown immediately after the definition of the break points.

We have developed the Windows Forms project WFpiecewiseLinear implementing this process. The form of the running project is shown in Figure 3-11.

Figure 3-11. *Example of the form of the running project WFpiecewiseLinear*

The form contains two buttons. When the user clicks Open image, he or she can choose an image. The image will be shown in the left picture box. Simultaneously a copy of the image appears in the right picture box. The histogram of the image appears in the lower left corner of the form with a blue line showing the graph of the function of the LUT.

The user can now click to two points near the line. The line changes in such a way that its break points lie at the clicked points. The LUT changes correspondingly, and the user can observe the choice of the image in the right picture box. As soon as the user is satisfied with the appearance of the image, he or she can click Save result. Then the user can choose the name and save the resulting image. The type of the saved image can be either Bmp or Jpg.

As explained in the previous section, to calculate the new intensities of the color channels it is necessary to calculate by means of a LUT the new lightness of the pixels, then to multiply each of the old color intensities by the new lightness and divide it by the old lightness. This procedure must be performed for each pixel of the image. Due to the multiplication and the division, it takes too much time, and the transformed image appears with a delay.

To make the calculation of the transformed image faster we have developed a method that uses a bigLUT. This is an LUT of $2^{16} = 65,536$ values of the new intensity of a color channel. As an argument for this table we use an integer whose lower valued byte is the old color intensity and the second byte is the old value of the lightness (bytes 3 and 4 are not used) taken from the previously prepared gray value version of the original image. Each of the 65,536 values of the new color intensity is equal to the product of the old color intensity with the value of LUT divided by the old lightness. These values are calculated only once at the time of the definition of the bigLUT. During the run of the project only the argument must be calculated for each pixel. The new intensity is simply read from the bigLUT. Here is the code of the method calculating the bigLUT:

```
int[] bigLUT = new int[65536];

private void makeBigLUT(int[] LUT)
{ for (int colOld = 0; colOld < 256; colOld++)  // old color intensity
    { for (int lightOld = 1; lightOld < 256; lightOld++) //old lightness
        { int colNew = colOld * LUT[lightOld] / lightOld;
          int arg = (lightOld << 8) | colOld;
          bigLUT[arg] = colNew;
        }
    }
}
```

Next is the source code of the most important parts of the project. The first part starts when the Open image button is clicked. This part opens the image, produces the bitmap origBmp, defines three objects of the class CImage, and fills the object origIm with the contents of the origBmp. The software WindowsForms suggests the access to the pixels of a bitmap by the method GetPixels, which is rather slow. We have developed a faster method, BitmapToGrid, which uses the method LockBits of the class Bitmap. However, BitmapToGrid should not be used for indexed Bitmaps with 8 bits per pixel because these bitmaps contain a color palette and the values of the pixels are always defined by the values of the palette. Therefore the method BitmapToGrid becomes too slow for 8-bit indexed bitmaps. For such bitmaps we use the standard method with GetPixel.

In addition, the first part of our project converts the original image origIm to the grayscale image origGrayIm with the method ColorToGrayMC using our method MaxC for calculating the lightness of color pixels. It also calculates the histogram of origGrayIm, draws the histogram in pictureBox3, calculates the standard LUT containing the values of the piecewise linear curve (with no contrast enhancement), and draws the line representing the function of the standard LUT. It also defines the image contrastIm as the resulting image, makes its copy in the bitmap ContrastBmp by means of the fast method GridToBitmap similar to the previously mentioned method BitmapToGrid, and displays ContrastBmp in pictureBox2.

```csharp
private void button1_Click(object sender, EventArgs e) // Open image
{
  OpenFileDialog openFileDialog1 = new OpenFileDialog();
  if (openFileDialog1.ShowDialog() == DialogResult.OK)
  {
    try
    {
      origBmp = new Bitmap(openFileDialog1.FileName);
      pictureBox1.Image = origBmp;
    }
    catch (Exception ex)
    {
      MessageBox.Show("Error: Could not read file from disk. Original
      error: " +
        ex.Message);
    }
```

```
}
width = origBmp.Width;
height = origBmp.Height;

origIm = new CImage(width, height, 24);
origGrayIm = new CImage(width, height, 8);  // grayscale version of origIm
contrastIm = new CImage(width, height, 24);

if (origBmp.PixelFormat == PixelFormat.Format8bppIndexed)
{
  progressBar1.Visible = true;
  Color color;
  int y2 = height / 100 + 1, nbyte = 3;
  for (int y = 0; y < height; y++) //=====================
  {
    if (y % y2 == 1) progressBar1.PerformStep();
    for (int x = 0; x < width; x++) //==================
    {
      int i = x + width * y;
      color = origBmp.GetPixel(i % width, i / width);
      for (int c = 0; c < nbyte; c++)
      {
        if (c == 0) origIm.Grid[nbyte * i] = color.B;
        if (c == 1) origIm.Grid[nbyte * i + 1] = color.G;
        if (c == 2) origIm.Grid[nbyte * i + 2] = color.R;
      }
    } //========= end for ( int x... ==================
  } //========== end for ( int y... ==================
  progressBar1.Visible = false;
}
else BitmapToGrid(origBmp, origIm.Grid);

// Calculating the histogram:
origGrayIm.ColorToGrayMC(origIm, this);
for (int gv = 0; gv < 256; gv++) histo[gv] = 0;
for (int i = 0; i < width * height; i++) histo[origGrayIm.Grid[i]]++;
MaxHist = 0;
```

```
for (int gv = 0; gv < 256; gv++) if (histo[gv] > MaxHist) MaxHist = histo[gv];
MinGV = 255;
MaxGV = 0;
for (MinGV = 0; MinGV < 256; MinGV++)
  if (histo[MinGV] > 0) break;
for (MaxGV = 255; MaxGV >= 0; MaxGV--)
  if (histo[MaxGV] > 0) break;

// Drawing the histogram:
Graphics g = pictureBox3.CreateGraphics();
SolidBrush myBrush = new SolidBrush(Color.LightGray);
Rectangle rect = new Rectangle(0, 0, 256, 256);
g.FillRectangle(myBrush, rect);

Pen myPen = new Pen(Color.Red);
Pen greenPen = new Pen(Color.Green);
for (int gv = 0; gv < 256; gv++)
{
  int hh = histo[gv]*255/MaxHist;
  if (histo[gv] > 0 && hh < 1) hh = 1;
  g.DrawLine(myPen, gv, 255, gv, 255 - hh);
  if (gv == MinGV || gv == MaxGV)
    g.DrawLine(greenPen, gv, 255, gv, 255 - hh);
}

// Calculating the standard LUT:
int[] LUT = new int[256];
int X = (MinGV + MaxGV) / 2;
int Y = 128;
for (int gv = 0; gv < 256; gv++)
{
  if (gv <= MinGV) LUT[gv] = 0;
  if (gv > MinGV && gv <= X) LUT[gv] = (gv - MinGV) * Y / (X - MinGV);
  if (gv > X && gv <= MaxGV) LUT[gv] = Y + (gv - X) * (255 - Y) / (MaxGV - X);
  if (gv >= MaxGV) LUT[gv] = 255;
}
```

```
// Drawing the standard curve:
int yy = 255;
Pen myPen1 = new Pen(Color.Blue);
g.DrawLine(myPen1, 0, yy, MinGV, yy);
g.DrawLine(myPen1, MinGV, yy, X, yy - Y);
g.DrawLine(myPen1, X, yy - Y, MaxGV, 0);
g.DrawLine(myPen1, MaxGV, 0, yy, 0);

// nbyte = 3;   origIm and contrastIm are both 24-bit images
for (int i = 0; i < nbyte * width * height; i++) contrastIm.Grid[i] =
(byte)LUT[(int)origIm.Grid[i]];

ContrastBmp = new Bitmap(width, height, PixelFormat.Format24bppRgb);
progressBar1.Visible = true;
GridToBitmap(ContrastBmp, contrastIm.Grid);
pictureBox2.Image = ContrastBmp;
progressBar1.Visible = false;
} //**************** end Open image ***********************************
```

The method BitmapToGrid for quickly copying the contents of a bitmap to the image of the class CImage" was described in Chapter 2. The method GridToBitmap is similar, so I do not present it here.

The part of the project that serves to control the shape of LUT allows the user to click twice in pictureBox3, which contains the image of the histogram, thus defining the knick points of the piecewise linear curve of the LUT. This part uses the integer variables cntClick, X1, Y1, X2, and Y2 defined in Form1. The variable cntClick counts the clicks but its value 3 is immediately replaced by 1 so that it can take only the values 1 and 2.

When cntClick is equal to 1, then the coordinates X1 and Y1 of the first knick point V1 (Figure 3-11) are defined by the click point. The first branch of the piecewise linear curve from the starting point of the histogram until the point (X1, Y1) is calculated.

When cntClick is equal to 2, then the coordinates X2 and Y2 of the second knick point V2 (Figure 3-11) are defined. The user should set this point in such a way that X2 is greater than X1 and Y2 is greater than Y1. If it happens that X2 is less than X1, then X2 is set to X1 + 1; similarly Y2. Thus the piecewise linear curve always remains monotonic. The second branch of the piecewise linear curve from the point point (X1, Y1) until the point (X2, Y2) and the third branch from the point (X2, Y2) until the end point of the histogram is calculated. Then the LUT bigLUT is calculated as explained earlier, and the contrasted image is calculated and displayed in pictureBox2.

Here is the code of the part calculating the LUT and simultaneously displaying the resulting image.

```
private void  pictureBox3_MouseDown(object sender, MouseEventArgs e)
// making new LUT and the resulting image
{
  int nbyte = 3;
  Graphics g = g2Bmp;  //pictureBox3.CreateGraphics();
  SolidBrush myBrush = new SolidBrush(Color.LightGray);
  Rectangle rect = new Rectangle(0, 0, 256, 256);

  cntClick++;
  if (cntClick == 3) cntClick = 1;
  int oldX = -1, oldY = -1;

  if (cntClick == 1)
  {
    X1 = e.X;
    if (X1 < MinGV) X1 = MinGV;
    if (X1 > MaxGV) X1 = MaxGV;
    Y1 = 255 - e.Y; // (X, Y) is the clicked point in the graph of the LUT
    if (X1 != oldX || Y1 != oldY) //----------------------------------------
    {
      // Calculating the LUT for X1 and Y1:
      for (int gv = 0; gv <= X1; gv++)
      {
        if (gv <= MinGV) LUT[gv] = 0;
        if (gv > MinGV && gv <= X1) LUT[gv] = (gv - MinGV) * Y1 /
        (X1 - MinGV);
        if (LUT[gv] > 255) LUT[gv] = 255;
      }
    }
    oldX = X1;
    oldY = Y1;

  }
```

```
if (cntClick == 2)
{
  X2 = e.X;
  if (X2 < MinGV) X2 = MinGV;
  if (X2 > MaxGV) X2 = MaxGV;
  if (X2 < X1) X2 = X1 + 1;
  Y2 = 255 - e.Y; // (X2, Y2) is the second clicked point in the graph of
  the LUT
  if (Y2 < Y1) Y2 = Y1 + 1;

  if (X2 != oldX || Y2 != oldY) //----------------------------------------
  {
    // Calculating the LUT for X2 and Y2:
    for (int gv = X1 + 1; gv < 256; gv++)
    {
      //if (gv <= MinGV) LUT[gv] = 0;
      if (gv > X1 && gv <= X2) LUT[gv] = Y1 + (gv - X1) * (Y2 - Y1) /
      (X2 - X1);
      if (gv > X2 && gv <= MaxGV)
                                  LUT[gv] = Y2 + (gv - X2) * (255 - Y2) /
                                  (MaxGV - X2);
      if (LUT[gv] > 255) LUT[gv] = 255;
      if (gv >= MaxGV) LUT[gv] = 255;
    }
  }
  oldX = X2;
  oldY = Y2;
}

Pen myPen1 = new Pen(Color.Blue);
makeBigLUT(LUT);

// Drawing the curve for LUT:
g.FillRectangle(myBrush, rect);

Pen myPen = new Pen(Color.Red);
g.DrawLine(myPen, MinGV, 255, MinGV, 250);
for (int gv = 0; gv < 256; gv++)
```

```
{
  int hh = histo[gv] * 255 / MaxHist;
  if (histo[gv] > 0 && hh < 1) hh = 1;
  g.DrawLine(myPen, gv, 255, gv, 255 - hh);
}

int yy = 255;
g.DrawLine(myPen1, 0, yy-LUT[0], MinGV, yy-LUT[0]);
g.DrawLine(myPen1, MinGV, yy - LUT[0], X1, yy - LUT[X1]);
g.DrawLine(myPen1, X1, yy - LUT[X1], X2, yy - LUT[X2]);
g.DrawLine(myPen1, X2, yy - LUT[X2], MaxGV, 0);
g.DrawLine(myPen1, MaxGV, 0, 255, 0);

// Calculating 'contrastIm':
int[] GV = new int[3];
int arg, colOld, colNew;
for (int i = 0; i < nbyte * width * height; i++) contrastIm.Grid[i] = 0;
progressBar1.Visible = true;
int y3 = 1 + nbyte * width * height / 100;

for (int y = 0, yn=0; y < width * height; y += width, yn+=nbyte * width)
//======
{
  if (y % y3 == 1) progressBar1.PerformStep();
  for (int x = 0, xn=0; x < width; x++, xn+=nbyte)
  {
    int lum = origGrayIm.Grid[x + y];
    for (int c = 0; c < nbyte; c++)
    {
      colOld = origIm.Grid[c + xn + yn]; // xn + yn = nbyte*(x + width * y);
      arg=(lum << 8) | colOld;
      colNew = bigLUT[arg];
      if (colNew > 255) colNew = 255;
      contrastIm.Grid[c + xn + yn] = (byte)colNew;
    }
  }
} //================ end for (int y = 0 ... =====================
```

```
progressBar1.Visible = false;

// Calculating "ContrastBmp":
GridToBitmap(ContrastBmp, contrastIm.Grid);
pictureBox2.Image = ContrastBmp;
pictureBox3.Image = BmpPictBox3;
progressBar1.Visible = false;
} //**************** end pictureBox3_MouseDown *********************
```

There is also a small part of the code for saving the resulting image. It uses the dialog SaveFileDialog. If the user wants to save the resulting image into the file of the input original image, some additional operations are necessary. The name OpenImageFile of the input file must be determined and saved in the program part Open image. In addition, a provisional file named tmpFileName must be defined. The resulting image is saved in the file tmpFileName. Then the following method must be called:

```
File.Replace(tmpFileName, OpenImageFile,
      OpenImageFile.Insert(OpenImageFile.IndexOf("."), "BuP"));
```

This method copies the contents of tmpFileName to the input file OpenImageFile, deletes tmpFileName, and saves the old contents of the input file into a new file whose name is produced by inserting the string BuP into OpenImageFile before the . character. Here is the code for this part of the project.

```
private void button2_Click(object sender, EventArgs e)  // Save result
{
  SaveFileDialog dialog = new SaveFileDialog();
  dialog.Filter =
      "Image Files(*.BMP;*.JPG;*.GIF)|*.BMP;*.JPG;*.GIF|All files
      (*.*)|*.*";
  if (dialog.ShowDialog() == DialogResult.OK)
  {
    string tmpFileName;
    if (dialog.FileName == OpenImageFile)
    {
      tmpFileName = OpenImageFile.Insert(OpenImageFile.IndexOf("."), "$$$");
      if (dialog.FileName.Contains("jpg"))
            ContrastBmp.Save(tmpFileName, ImageFormat.Jpeg); // saving tmpFile
      else ContrastBmp.Save(tmpFileName, ImageFormat.Bmp);
```

```
    origBmp.Dispose();
    File.Replace(tmpFileName, OpenImageFile,
                  OpenImageFile.Insert(OpenImageFile.IndexOf("."), "BuP"));
    origBmp = new Bitmap(OpenImageFile);
    pictureBox1.Image = origBmp;
  }
  else
  {
    if (dialog.FileName.Contains("jpg"))
          ContrastBmp.Save(dialog.FileName, ImageFormat.Jpeg);
    else ContrastBmp.Save(dialog.FileName, ImageFormat.Bmp);
  }
  MessageBox.Show("The result image saved under " + dialog.FileName);
 }
} //***************** end Save result *****************************
```

Figure 3-12 shows an example of contrast enhancement obtained with the described project. The project can be used for contrast enhancement of both color and grayscale images.

Figure 3-12. *An example of contrast enhancement with the project*
WFpiecewiseLinear

The project WFpiecewiseLinear can be found in the source codes for this book.

CHAPTER 4

Shading Correction with Thresholding

Some photographs are not homogeneously light because the photographed object was not homogeneously illuminated. Fine details in the dark area of such photographs are hardly recognizable. We suggest a method to improve the quality of such images.

A known method used for correcting digital photographs taken by automatic devices installed on space probes on other planets uses the subtraction of the local mean lightness from the lightness of the pixels of the original image:

$$GVnew[x, y] = GVold[x, y] - Mean[x, y] + Const$$

where $GVold[x, y]$ is the lightness of the pixel with coordinates (x, y), $Mean[x, y]$ is the mean lightness in the neighborhood of the pixel (x, y), $Const$ is a value of lightness not depending on the coordinates, and $GVnew$ is the lightness of the pixels of the resulting image.

This method gives mostly sufficient results. However, I suggest a slightly different method. Consider the lightness $L(x, y)$ of the light reflected from a surface with reflectance $R(x, y)$ illuminated by a light source producing an illumination $I(x, y)$:

$$L(x, y) = R(x, y) \cdot I(x, y) \cdot \cos\varphi$$

where φ is the angle between the direction of the falling light and the normal to the surface. If we have an estimate $E(x, y)$ of the illumination of the surface and we are interested in knowing the reflectance $R(x, y)$ of the surface and we suppose $\cos\varphi = 1$, then we could obtain a function providing a value proportional to the reflectance $R(x, y)$ by dividing the observed lightness $L(x, y)$ by $E(x, y)$ and not by subtracting $E(x, y)$ from $L(x, y)$.

© Vladimir Kovalevsky 2019
V. Kovalevsky, *Modern Algorithms for Image Processing*, https://doi.org/10.1007/978-1-4842-4237-7_4

The illumination $I(x, y)$ is mostly a function slowly changing its value as the coordinates x and y change while the reflectance $R(x, y)$ of the surface changes rapidly. Therefore an estimate of the illumination can be obtained by calculating the mean value of $L(x, y)$ in the neighborhood of each point (x, y). In the case of digital photography, the lightness of the pixels of a digital photo is proportional to $L(x, y)$ and we are interested in the function $R(x, y)$. Therefore, to obtain a function proportional to $R(x, y)$, we should calculate $E(x, y)$ as the local mean of the lightness of the photo and divide $L(x, y)$ by $E(x, y)$. It is also possible to get an estimation of $R(x, y)$ by subtracting $E(x, y)$ from $L(x, y)$. This is correct if all the values $L(x, y)$, $R(x, y)$, $I(x, y)$, and $E(x, y)$ are proportional to the logarithm of the corresponding physical values. However, it sometimes gives good results with usual values of $L(x, y)$, $R(x, y)$, $I(x, y)$, and $E(x, y)$. Therefore we use in our projects both subtraction and division. The user can compare the results and choose the best one.

I present here the project WFshadingBin performing shading correction (see our software in the Internet) and the thresholding of the shading-corrected image.

The local mean of the given image can be calculated by means of the method Averaging described in Chapter 2. However, modern digital photos are large. Most photos contain more than $1,000 \cdot 1,000 = 10^6$ pixels. The size of the window in which the mean should be calculated for the shading correction of typical images must have a size of at least $100 \cdot 100 = 10,000$ pixels. The Averaging method would be too slow for this size. It is better to use a method providing fast averaging, like FastAverageM, described in Chapter 2. The width of the averaging window is specified by the tool numericUpDown1 with label Window as a part of the width of the image. This is more convenient for users who generally do not know the size of the processed image.

On the other side, for shading correction of photographs of drawings we need a window of the local averaging that has a width a little greater than the width of the lines in the drawing. The latter width is generally between four and nine pixels. This can be less than 1 percent of the width of the image, which can be as large as 2,000 pixels. Therefore we have decided to specify the width of the averaging window in per mille of the width of the image.

Even for color images, we only need the local mean of the lightness, not that of the color channels. Therefore we must transform a color image into a grayscale image containing in its pixels the lightness of the trio (R, G, B). The method ColorToGrayMC performs this transformation while computing for each pixel of a color image the value

$$Lightness = \max(R*0.713, G, B*0.527)$$

calculated with our method MaxC (see Chapter 3). Then it is possible to use the method FastAverageM to calculate the local mean value of a grayscale image.

I next describe the project WFshadingBin. The form for this project is shown in Figure 4-1.

Figure 4-1. *Form for the project WFshadingBin after shading correction*

It contains five picture boxes, four buttons, and two tools of the type numericUpDown. The first button, Open image starts the first part of the project, which is similar to the first part of the project WFpiecewiseLinear with the difference that here seven images—OrigIm, SigmaIm, SubIm, DivIm, GrayIm, MeanIm, and BinIm—are defined. The image SigmaIm contains the results of filtering the original image by means of the sigma filter. The images are used to perform the shading correction by means of subtraction and division and the thresholding of the images SubIm and DivIm. The thresholding is described in the next section.

The Shading correction button starts the corresponding part of the project. It contains the method CorrectShading presented here.

```csharp
public void CorrectShading()
{
  int c, i, x, y;
  bool ROWSECTION = false; // used to show the values of images in one row.
  int[] color = {0, 0, 0};
  int[] color1 = {0, 0, 0};
  int Lightness=(int)numericUpDown2.Value;
  int hWind = (int)(numericUpDown1.Value * width / 2000);
  MeanIm.FastAverageM(GrayIm, hWind, this); // uses numericUpDown1
  progressBar1.Visible = true;
  progressBar1.Value = 0;
  int[] histoSub = new int[256];
  int[] histoDiv = new int[256];
  for (i = 0; i < 256; i++) histoSub[i] = histoDiv[i] = 0;
  byte lum =  0;
  byte lum1 = 0;
  int jump = height / 17; // width and height are properties of Form1
  for (y = 0; y < height; y++) //=========================================
  {
    if (y % jump == jump - 1) progressBar1.PerformStep();
    for (x = 0; x < width; x++)
    {                                  // nbyteIm is member of 'Form1'
      for (c = 0; c < nbyteIm; c++) //====================================
      {
        color[c] = Round(SigmaIm.Grid[c + nbyteIm * (x + width * y)] *
        Lightness / (double)MeanIm.Grid[x + width * y]); // Division
        if (color[c] < 0) color[c] = 0;
        if (color[c] > 255) color[c] = 255;
        DivIm.Grid[c + nbyteIm * (x + width * y)] = (byte)color[c];

        color1[c] = SigmaIm.Grid[c + nbyteIm * (x + width * y)] +
        Lightness - MeanIm.Grid[x + width * y]; // Subtraction
```

```
      if (color1[c] < 0) color1[c] = 0;
      if (color1[c] > 255) color1[c] = 255;
      SubIm.Grid[c + nbyteIm * (x + width * y)] = (byte)color1[c];
    } //=============== end for (c... ===============================
    if (nbyteIm == 1)
    {
      lum = (byte)color[0];
      lum1 = (byte)color1[0];
    }
    else
    {
      lum = SigmaIm.MaxC((byte)color[2], (byte)color[1], (byte)color[0]);
      lum1 = SigmaIm.MaxC((byte)color1[2], (byte)color1[1], (byte)
      color1[0]);
    }
    histoDiv[lum]++;
    histoSub[lum1]++;
  }
} //============== end for (y... ===================================
// Calculating  MinLight and MaxLight for 'Div':
int MaxLightDiv, MaxLightSub, MinLightDiv, MinLightSub, Sum = 0;
for (MinLightDiv = 0; MinLightDiv < 256; MinLightDiv++)
{
  Sum += histoDiv[MinLightDiv];
  if (Sum > width * height / 100) break;
}
Sum = 0;
for (MaxLightDiv = 255; MaxLightDiv >= 0; MaxLightDiv--)
{
  Sum += histoDiv[MaxLightDiv];
  if (Sum > width * height / 100) break;
}

// Calculating  MinLight and MaxLight for 'Sub':
Sum = 0;
for (MinLightSub = 0; MinLightSub < 256; MinLightSub++)
```

```
  {
    Sum += histoSub[MinLightSub];
    if (Sum > width * height / 100) break;
  }
  Sum = 0;
  for (MaxLightSub = 255; MaxLightSub >= 0; MaxLightSub--)
  {
    Sum += histoSub[MaxLightSub];
    if (Sum > width * height / 100) break;
  }
  // Calculating  MinLight and MaxLight for 'Sub':
  Sum = 0;
  for (MinLightSub = 0; MinLightSub < 256; MinLightSub++)
  {
    Sum += histoSub[MinLightSub];
    if (Sum > width * height / 100) break;
  }
  Sum = 0;
  for (MaxLightSub = 255; MaxLightSub >= 0; MaxLightSub--)
  {
    Sum += histoSub[MaxLightSub];
    if (Sum > width * height / 100) break;
  }

  // Calculating LUT for 'Div':
  byte[] LUT = new byte[256];
  for (i = 0; i < 256; i++)
    if (i <= MinLightDiv) LUT[i] = 0;
    else
      if (i > MinLightDiv && i <= MaxLightDiv)
        LUT[i] = (byte)(255 * (i - MinLightDiv) / (MaxLightDiv -
        MinLightDiv));
      else LUT[i] = 255;

  // Calculating LUTsub for 'Sub':
  byte[] LUTsub = new byte[256];
```

```
for (i = 0; i < 256; i++)
  if (i <= MinLightSub) LUTsub[i] = 0;
  else
    if (i > MinLightSub && i <= MaxLightSub)
      LUTsub[i] = (byte)(255 * (i - MinLightSub) / (MaxLightSub -
      MinLightSub));
    else LUTsub[i] = 255;

// Calculating contrasted "Div" and "Sub":
for (i = 0; i < 256; i++) histoDiv[i] = histoSub[i] = 0;
jump = width * height / 17;
for (i = 0; i < width * height; i++) //===================================
{
  if (i % jump == jump - 1) progressBar1.PerformStep();
  for (c = 0; c < nbyteIm; c++)
  {
    DivIm.Grid[c + nbyteIm * i] = LUT[DivIm.Grid[c + nbyteIm * i]];
    SubIm.Grid[c + nbyteIm * i] = LUTsub[SubIm.Grid[c + nbyteIm * 1]];
  }

  if (nbyteIm == 1)
  {
    lum = DivIm.Grid[0 + nbyteIm * i];
    lum1 = SubIm.Grid[0 + nbyteIm * i];
  }
  else
  {
    lum = SigmaIm.MaxC(DivIm.Grid[2 + nbyteIm * i],
    DivIm.Grid[1 +  nbyteIm * i],
      DivIm.Grid[0 + nbyteIm * i]);
    lum1 = SigmaIm.MaxC(SubIm.Grid[2 + nbyteIm * i],
    SubIm.Grid[1 +  nbyteIm * i],
      SubIm.Grid[0 + nbyteIm * i]);
  }
  histoDiv[lum]++;
  histoSub[lum1]++;
```

```
} //=============== end for (i = 0; ... ===============================

// Displaying the histograms and the row sections:
Graphics g1 = pictureBox4.CreateGraphics();
Graphics g = pictureBox5.CreateGraphics();
Graphics g0 = pictureBox1.CreateGraphics();
int MaxHisto1 = 0, SecondMax1 = 0;
int MaxHisto = 0, SecondMax = 0;
for (i = 0; i < 256; i++)
{
  if (histoSub[i] > MaxHisto1) MaxHisto1 = histoSub[i];
  if (histoDiv[i] > MaxHisto) MaxHisto = histoDiv[i];
}
for (i = 0; i < 256; i++) if (histoSub[i] != MaxHisto1 && histoSub[i] >
SecondMax1) SecondMax1 = histoSub[i];
MaxHisto1 = SecondMax1 * 4 / 3;
for (i = 0; i < 256; i++) if (histoDiv[i] != MaxHisto && histoDiv[i] >
SecondMax) SecondMax = histoDiv[i];
MaxHisto = SecondMax * 4 / 3;
Pen redPen = new Pen(Color.Red), yellowPen = new Pen(Color.Yellow),
                   bluePen = new Pen(Color.Blue), greenPen = new
                   Pen(Color.Green);
SolidBrush whiteBrush = new SolidBrush(Color.White);
Rectangle Rect1 = new Rectangle(0, 0, 256, 200);
g1.FillRectangle(whiteBrush, Rect1);
Rectangle Rect = new Rectangle(0, 0, 256, 200);
g.FillRectangle(whiteBrush, Rect);
for (i = 0; i < 256; i++)
{
  g1.DrawLine(redPen, i, pictureBox4.Height - histoSub[i] * 200 /
  MaxHisto1, i, pictureBox4.Height);
  g.DrawLine(redPen, i, pictureBox5.Height - histoDiv[i] * 200 /
  MaxHisto, i, pictureBox5.Height);
}
for (i = 0; i < 256; i += 50)
{
```

```
    g1.DrawLine(greenPen, i, pictureBox4.Height - 200, i, pictureBox4.Height);
    g.DrawLine(greenPen, i, pictureBox5.Height - 200, i, pictureBox5.
    Height);
  }
  if (ROWSECTION)
  {
    y = height * 10 / 19;
    g0.DrawLine(redPen, marginX, marginY + (int)(y * Scale1),
      marginX + (int)(width * Scale1), marginY + (int)(y * Scale1));
    int xold = marginX, xs = 0;
    int yd = 0, ydOld = 256 - DivIm.Grid[0 + width * y];
    int ys = 0, ysOld = 256 - SubIm.Grid[0 + width * y];
    int yg = 0, ygOld = 256 - GrayIm.Grid[0 + width * y];
    int ym = 0, ymOld = 256 - MeanIm.Grid[0 + width * y];
    for (x = 1; x < width; x++)
    {
      xs = marginX + (int)(x * Scale1);
      yd = 256 - DivIm.Grid[x + width * y];
      ys = 256 - SubIm.Grid[x + width * y];
      yg = 256 - GrayIm.Grid[x + width * y];
      ym = 256 - MeanIm.Grid[x + width * y];
      g0.DrawLine(redPen, xold, ymOld, xs, ym);
      g0.DrawLine(yellowPen, xold, ydOld, xs, yd);
      //g0.DrawLine(bluePen, xold, ysOld, xs, ys);
      xold = xs;
      ydOld = yd;
      ysOld = ys;
      ygOld = yg;
      ymOld = ym;
    }
    g0.DrawLine(bluePen, marginX, 256 - Threshold,
    marginX + (int)(width * Scale1, 256 - Threshold);
  }
} //************* end CorrectShading *********************************
```

The method `FastAverageM` obtains the parameter `hWind` from the tool `numericUpDown1` with the label `Window in per mille to Width`. The method calculates the local mean of the grayscale image `GrayIm`. Note that to obtain good results in the case of photographs of drawings it is sometimes necessary to choose rather small values of `Window`. Still better results can be obtained with the project `WFshadBinImpulse` described later.

The contents of the shading-corrected images `SubIm` and `DivIm` are calculated in the loops with the variables `y` and `x`.

As you can see, the method `CorrectShading` calculates the image with corrected shading in two ways. The first way consists of the division of the values of the original image `OrigIm` by the local mean lightness saved in the image `MeanIm` and in multiplication with the value `Lightness`, which is manually specified by means of the tool `numericUpDown2`. The second way consists of subtracting the local mean lightness saved in `MeanIm` from the original image `OrigIm` and adding `Lightness`. It is important to use both methods because experiments have shown that the results of the division method are not always better than those of the subtraction method. The method `CorrectShading` calculates two images, `DivIm` and `SubIm`, in the two ways just described. Both results are shown to the user, and he or she can decide which of the two results should be saved.

The quality of the corrected images depends on two parameters: `Window` and `Lightness`. It is possible to change these parameters by means of the tools with the corresponding labels and to immediately see the results. The parameter `Lightness` specifies the mean lightness of the image. The parameter `Window` defines the size of the gliding window in which the mean lightness of the original image is calculated. This parameter must be chosen so that it is approximately equal to the size of the spots in the original image occurring due to the inhomogeneous lightness. For example, the optimal value of the window for the image shown in Figure 4-1 earlier is about 200 pixels. This value should be set in per mille of the width of the image. In this case 200 pixels make 500 per mille from the width = 400. The user must define `Window=500`. The view of the form after shading correction is shown in Figure 4-1.

When the user is satisfied with the results of shading correction he or she can either save the image `SubIm` or the image `DivIm`, or threshold these images. The process for thresholding is described next.

Thresholding the Images

The commonly used method of choosing the optimal threshold for thresholding grayscale images consists of using the gray value corresponding to the histogram minimum as the threshold. The justification is as follows: The histogram of an image with two regions, each having a constant gray level, looks like two columns. If noise is present, the histogram looks like two hills with a valley in between (Figure 4-2).

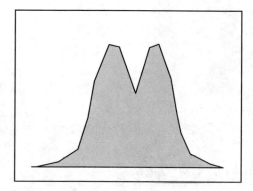

Figure 4-2. *Example of a histogram of an image with two regions*

The optimal threshold corresponds to the local minimum of the histogram, but not always to the global minimum. Therefore, it is necessary to restrict the area of the search for the minimum to guarantee that at least some predefined portion of the image will be black or white. For example, if you want at least 5 percent of the image to be black, you must find such a gray value *minGV* that 5 percent of the histogram area is to the left of *minGV*. Only minima to the right of *minGV* must be considered. Similarly, the choice of *maxGV* can guarantee that at least the desired portion of the area is white.

Sometimes the histogram has more than one local minimum and the deepest one is not always the one corresponding to your desired outcome. It is appropriate in that case to display small binary images for the thresholds corresponding to all local minima and to choose the best one.

Another possibility is to produce a multilevel image, with each level corresponding to a space between two thresholds. Levels corresponding to the gray values less than the first and greater than the last threshold must also be provided. This means that the lightness equal to 0 and the lightness equal to 255 should also be considered thresholds. Producing a multilevel image means that the image is quantized: All pixels with the lightness between thresholds T_i and T_{i+1} obtain the value $(T_i + T_{i+1})/2$. To make the search for the local minima more certain, it is necessary to smooth the histogram because it can have many very small local minima due to noise. Figure 4-3 shows an example of an image with four levels and the results of thresholding with three different thresholds corresponding to the local minima of the histogram.

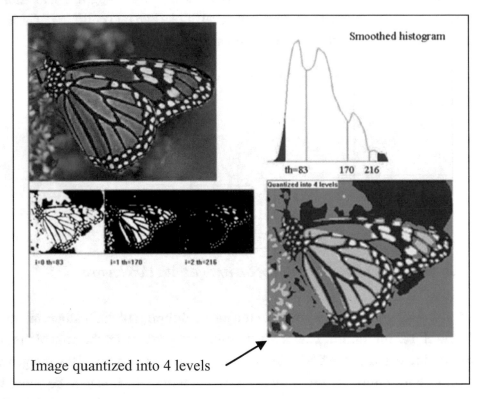

Figure 4-3. Choice among three threshold candidates

Many different methods of choosing the optimal threshold are suggested, but I suggest another approach: Our project suggests the possibility of manually changing the threshold and immediately seeing the result. Thus the user can choose the result that seems optimal.

Some images to be thresholded have strong shading, which means that the local average lightness changes gradually from one part of the image to another. If the light side of the darker area is brighter than the dark side of the lighter area then there exists no constant threshold separating these two areas. In such cases the shading correction is very useful. The procedure of shading correction was already described. As you already know, there are two methods of shading correction: It is possible to use either subtraction or division by the local mean value. The user can choose between thresholding the result of the shading correction with subtraction or with division. Our project WFshadingBin performs thresholding after shading correction. It shows the histograms of the shading-corrected images. The user can choose the threshold by clicking the histogram (e.g., in a local minimum) and immediately sees the result. The chosen threshold is shown in the histogram as a vertical blue line. Figure 4-4 shows the form of the project WFshadingBin again.

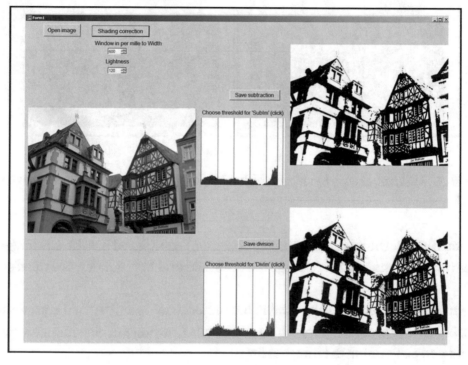

Figure 4-4. *The form of the project* WFshadingBin

The thresholded image sometimes contains dark spots in a homogeneous white area. If this happens, the Window parameter must be increased.

This project can be used for correcting poorly illuminated photographs of drawings. In such cases the best size of the averaging window can be very small, for example six or nine pixels. This is less than 1 percent of the width, which is usually greater than 1,000 pixels. Therefore we have decided to define the size of the averaging window in this project in per mille rather than in percent of the width of the image.

The results of the thresholding with the WFshadingBin project are quite satisfactory. Figure 4-5a shows the result obtained for the image presented on Wikipedia.en in the article "Otsu's Method," describing a rather complicated method developed by a Japanese scientist Nobuyuki Otsu for choosing the optimal threshold. Figure 4-5b shows the result obtained by Otsu's method.

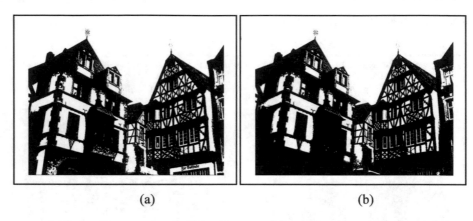

(a)   (b)

Figure 4-5. *Wikipedia image thresholded by (a) WFshadingBin, and (b) Otsu's method*

As you can see, the results are similar. However, our method has the advantage that the user can easily and quickly change the threshold and immediately see the resulting image.

The method CorrectShading used in our project was described in the previous section. Here we present the part of the source code drawing the blue line showing the threshold and performing the thresholding.

```
private void pictureBox5_MouseClick(object sender, MouseEventArgs e)
// Thresholding DivIm
{
  Threshold = e.X;
  Graphics g = pictureBox5.CreateGraphics();
  Pen bluePen = new Pen(Color.Blue);
  g.DrawLine(bluePen, Threshold, 0, Threshold, pictureBox5.Height);
  progressBar1.Visible = true;
  progressBar1.Value = 0;
  int nbyte = DivIm.N_Bits / 8;
```

```
int jump = height / 100;
for (int y = 0; y < height; y++)
{
  if (y % jump == jump - 1) progressBar1.PerformStep();
  for (int x = 0; x < width; x++)
  {
    int i = x + width * y;
    if (nbyte == 1)
    {
      if (DivIm.Grid[i] > Threshold) BinIm.Grid[i] = 255;
      else BinIm.Grid[i] = 0;
    }
    else
    {
      if (DivIm.MaxC(DivIm.Grid[2 + 3*i], DivIm.Grid[1 + 3*i],
                              DivIm.Grid[0 + 3*i]) > Threshold)
                              BinIm.Grid[i] = 255;
      else BinIm.Grid[i] = 0;
    }
    Div_Bitmap.SetPixel(x, y, Color.FromArgb(BinIm.Grid[i],
                                             BinIm.Grid[i],
                                             BinIm.Grid[i]));
  }
}
pictureBox3.Image = Div_Bitmap;
Threshold = -1;
} //**************** end pictureBox5_MouseClick *********************
```

The project WFshadingBin is especially effective in improving photographs of historical images. Figure 4-6 is one more example of processing the photograph of a fragment of a historical image.

(a)   (b)

Figure 4-6. *(a) Original image, and (b) processed image*

CHAPTER 5

Project
WFshadBinImpulse

We have also developed the project WFshadBinImpulse where the procedures of shading correction, thresholding, and suppression of impulse noise are combined. This combination is especially useful for processing images of photographs of old drawings (refer to Figure 2-8). The form of this project is shown in Figure 5-1.

Figure 5-1. *The form of the project* WFshadBinImpulse

Clicking Open image starts the usual part of the project with the dialog OpenFileDialog. Also seven images of the class CImage—OrigIm, SigmaIm, GrayIm, MeanIm, ShadIm, BinIm, and ImpulseIm—are defined in this part of the project.

The user should specify the kind of the image by choosing one of four options: Drawing with dark lines, or Drawing with light lines, No drawing Div, or No drawing Sub. Starting values of the parameters Window in per mille of Width, Lightness, Threshold, and the parameter of suppressing impulse noise will be set automatically according to the choice of these options. The user can correct these values by means of the corresponding numericUpDown tools. Window will be specified as a part of the width of the original image in per mille as previously explained. The specification in per mille of the width of the image rather than directly in pixels is necessary because the optimal width of the window depends on the size of the image, but users usually do not know how big the image is.

After the user has specified the type of image, he or she should click Shading. For the shading correction, the local mean lightness of the image is calculated by the method FastAverageM described previously. Then the images SubIm and DivIm are calculated by the CorrectShading method described in Chapter 4. The shading-corrected image is shown in the picture box at the right. The user can correct the proposed values of the parameters to obtain the best possible corrected image.

The CorrectShading method also draws the histograms of the shading-corrected image. The user can specify the threshold by clicking the histogram. The thresholded image is shown immediately.

Suggested values of the parameters of the methods used for suppressing impulse noise are also set automatically. The user should nevertheless test some values for these parameters.

If the image is a drawing, the user should draw in pictureBox1 (the original image) small rectangles around the parts of the image where small spots (e.g., the eyes of people) should not be eliminated. The user should click with the mouse the upper left und lower right corners of the rectangles. The rectangles appear in a blue color. It is possible to define these rectangles anew after the suppression of impulse noise has been run. It is possible to draw up to six rectangles. The doubled maximum number of the rectangles called maxNumber is defined at the beginning of Form1.

If the user is satisfied with the results of shading correction and of thresholding then he or she can start the suppression of impulse noise seen as small black and white spots in the thresholded image by clicking Impulse noise. If the user is not satisfied with the obtained results, he or she can try to change the values of Delete dark and Delete light by means of the corresponding `numericUpDown` tools. These values specify the maximum number of pixels in the spots that should be deleted.

If the user is satisfied with the final results, then he or she can save the result. It is necessary to click Save result, choose the correct directory, and specify the name of the file for the resulting image with the extension `.bmp` or `.jpg`.

PART II

Image Analysis

CHAPTER 6

Edge Detection

Among the known methods of edge detection are simple gradient filters containing some kind of smoothing of the image. The Sobel filter is a common example. It is defined by two matrices with weights as shown in Figure 6-1.

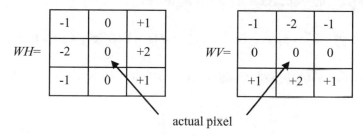

Figure 6-1. Weights of Sobel filter

The filter calculates two sums SH and SV of products of the gray values in a gliding 3×3 neighborhood of the actual pixel with corresponding weights WH and WV shown in Figure 6-1 and returns the sum of the absolute values $|SH| + |SV|$. Pixels in which this value is greater than a given threshold belong to the edge. The results are generally unsatisfactory because the edges are too thick.

Other known methods of edge detection are the zero crossing of the Laplacian Kimmel (2003) and the Canny (1986) filter. I present in what follows a comparison of these methods with our new rather simple and efficient method.

Laplacian Operator

An efficient method of edge detection is that of zero crossing of the Laplacian. The Laplacian operator is defined in mathematics as the sum of the second partial derivatives:

$$\text{Lap}(F(x, y)) = \nabla^2 F(x, y) = \partial^2 F / \partial x^2 + \partial^2 F / \partial y^2.$$

© Vladimir Kovalevsky 2019
V. Kovalevsky, *Modern Algorithms for Image Processing*, https://doi.org/10.1007/978-1-4842-4237-7_6

Because a digital image is not differentiable, it is necessary to replace the derivatives by finite differences.

Definition 1: The expression $D_1(x, \Delta x, F) = F(x + \Delta x) - F(x)$ is called the *first difference of F(x)* with respect to x and with the increment Δx.

Definition 2: The expression $D_n(x, \Delta x, F) = D_1(x, \Delta x, D_{n-1}(x, F(x)))$ with $n > 1$ is called the *nth difference of F(x)* with respect to x and with the increment Δx. The second partial differences with respect to x and y are equal to

$$D_2(x, \Delta x, F) = F(x - \Delta x, y) - 2 \cdot F(x, y) + F(x + \Delta x, y)$$

$$D_2(y, \Delta y, F) = F(x, y - \Delta y) - 2 \cdot F(x, y) + F(x, y + \Delta y)$$

and the finite Laplacian with $\Delta x = \Delta y = 1$ is equal to

$$\nabla^2 F(x, y) = F(x - 1, y) + F(x + 1, y) - 4 \cdot F(x, y) + F(x, y - 1) + F(x, y + 1).$$

It can be calculated in digital images with the filter shown in Figure 6-2.

	+1	
+1	-4	+1
	+1	

Figure 6-2. *The filter for calculating the finite Laplacian*

An application of this filter to a digital image with the gray values $F(x, y)$ yields the following value:

$$\nabla^2 F(x, y) = F(x - 1, y) + F(x + 1, y) - 4 \cdot F(x, y) + F(x, y - 1) + F(x, y + 1) \quad (6.1)$$

Equation 6.1 can be rewritten as follows:

$$\nabla^2 F(x, y) = F(x - 1, y) + F(x + 1, y) + F(x, y - 1) + F(x, y) + F(x, y + 1) - 5 \cdot F(x, y)$$

$$= 5 \cdot M(x, y) - 5 \cdot F(x, y) = 5 \cdot (M(x, y) - F(x, y)) \quad (6.2)$$

where $M(x, y)$ is the mean value of $F(x, y)$ of the five pixels in the neighborhood of the pixel with coordinates (x, y). It is also possible to calculate the finite Laplacian in the pixel $P = (x, y)$ by subtracting the gray value of P from the local mean value in the neighborhood of *P*. It is appropriate to use the fast averaging filter (Chapter 2) when using a greater neighborhood.

The Method of Zero Crossing

The method of zero crossing is based on detecting locations where the Laplacian changes its sign. Consider the cross-section through a row of a digital grayscale image shown in Figure 6-3.

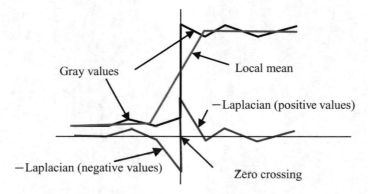

Figure 6-3. *Cross-section through a row of a digital image*

The Laplacian has positive values on one side of an edge and negative values on its other side. The absolute values of Laplacian near the edge are great as compared with its values on locations far away from the edge. It is more practical using the negative value of Laplacian—that is, the value $(F(x, y) - \text{mean value})$ instead of the value $(\text{mean value} - F(x, y))$—because these values are greater at greater gray values.

Locations at which the Laplacian changes its sign are called *zero crossings*. Some of these locations correspond to the location of the edge. A zero crossing always lies between two pixels. These indications of the location of an edge are therefore always quite thin.

Are Zero Crossings of Laplacian Closed Curves?

One advantage of the Laplacian put forward in some textbooks on image processing is that the edges produced by Laplacian are always closed lines. However, this is true only if we threshold the values of Laplacian; for example, if we replace the positive values of the

Laplacian by 1 and the negative ones by 0. The fact that the boundaries of sets of pixels with the value 1 in such an image are closed curves is, however, the advantage of binary images and not that of Laplacian. Such edges are shown in Figure 6-4b. Most edges in an image of the Laplacian binarized with a threshold equal to 0 are irrelevant.

(a)   (b)

Figure 6-4. *(a) Original image, and (b) Laplacian binarized with threshold 0; edges are shown as white lines*

As you can see, the overwhelming majority of the white lines in Figure 6-4b are completely meaningless and cannot be used as edges. These are the so-called irrelevant zero crossings.

Figure 6-5 shows an explanation for the irrelevant zero crossings of the Laplacian. The black lines shows the gray values of the original image. The green line represents the local mean value of the gray values, and the red line is the Laplacian. Red arrows show the irrelevant zero crossings. The values of the Laplacian at these locations are small, whereas at the relevant crossing the absolute value of the Laplacian is great.

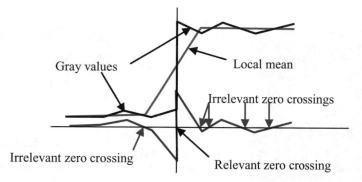

Figure 6-5. *Irrelevant zero crossings of the Laplacian (red arrows)*

We explain in the next section how to eliminate the irrelevant zero crossings.

How to Eliminate Irrelevant Crossings

Irrelevant crossings can be distinguished from the relevant ones by means of two thresholds: Only transitions from a Laplacian value greater than a positive threshold to a Laplacian value less than a negative threshold should be recognized as relevant edges. Most irrelevant edges disappear, but some relevant ones are interrupted due to the noise in the image. The image should be filtered to reduce the noise, for example, with the simplest averaging filter (Chapter 2). The image should be filtered two times: with a small and with a greater gliding window. The differences between these two filtered images can then be regarded as a good approximation of the Laplacian.

Consider Figure 6-6b, which shows as a blue line the gray values in one row of the image. The Laplacian values are shown as a green line. The black line is the x axis; red lines show the thresholds used to distinguish between relevant and irrelevant zero crossings. A zero crossing is relevant if it lies between two such pixels that one of them has a Laplacian value greater than the positive threshold and the other pixel has a Laplacian value less than the negative threshold.

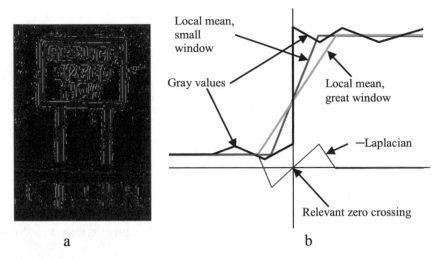

Figure 6-6. *(a) Edges found with two thresholds (white lines), and (b) explanation*

Figure 6-7 explains how the irrelevant zero crossings can be eliminated.

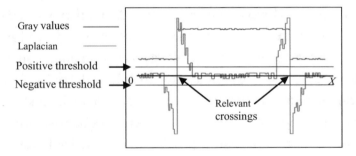

Figure 6-7. *An example of the values of the Laplacian*

Noise Reduction Before Using the Laplacian

When using the averaging filter for noise reduction, the edges become blurred. As a result, the difference between the positive and negative values of Laplacian becomes small; Laplacian values change gradually. This makes it difficult to distinguish between relevant and irrelevant zero crossings. We suggest using the sigma filter (Chapter 2) instead of averaging with a small window. Then the edges remain precipitous; the absolute amounts of the Laplacian become larger.

Black lines in Figure 6-8a show the gray values filtered with averaging with a small window. In Figure 6-8b, the black line represent the gray values filtered with the sigma filter. For both, green lines represent the local mean values with the greater window and red lines show the Laplacian values.

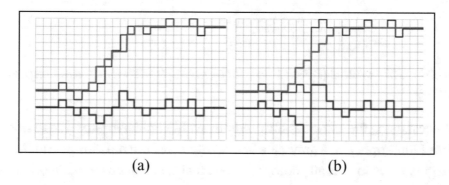

(a)   (b)

Figure 6-8. *The gray and Laplacian values after filtering with (a) averaging, and (b) sigma filter*

Blur During the Digitization and Extreme Value Filter

Even an ideal edge can become somewhat blurred during the digitization of an image. The reason for this is that the boundary between a light and a dark area in an image projected to the set of light-sensitive elements (e.g., CCD, charge-coupled devices, electronic light sensors used in various devices including digital cameras) can fall occasionally near the center of an element, as shown in Figure 6-9.

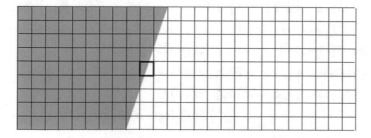

Figure 6-9. *The CCD matrix illuminated by a dark and a light area*

This element obtains a light amount, which we call the *middle value,* lying between the values that are proper for the light and dark areas. The corresponding pixel is located in the middle of the edge and the Laplacian obtains a small value or even a zero value. A gap in the detected edge occurs, as illustrated in Figure 6-10.

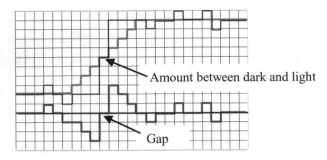

Figure 6-10. *Gray values (black line), local mean (green line), and Laplacian (red line)*

We suggest using the extreme value filter to avoid Laplacian gaps due to middle values. This filter applied to a grayscale image calculates the maximum and the minimum gray value in a small gliding window. It also calculates the differences between the gray value in the central pixel and the maximum and minimum values and decides which of these two values is closer to the central value. The closer value is assigned to the central pixel in the output image. The edges become sharp and the Laplacian gaps disappear. Here is the source code of the extreme filter for grayscale images.

```
int CImage::ExtremVar(CImage &Inp, int hWind)
{ N_Bits=8; width=Inp.width; height=Inp.height;
  Grid=new unsigned char[width*height];
  int hist[256];
  for (int y=0; y<height; y++) // =================================
  { int gv, y1, yStart=__max(y-hWind,0), yEnd=__min(y+hWind,height-1);
    for (int x=0; x<width; x++) //=============================
    { if (x==0) //-----------------------------------------------------
      { for (gv=0; gv<256; gv++) hist[gv]=0;
        for (y1=yStart; y1<=yEnd; y1++)
        for (int xx=0; xx<=hWind; xx++)
                           hist[Inp.Grid[xx+y1*width]]++;
      }
      else
      { int x1=x+hWind, x2=x-hWind-1;
        if (x1<width)for (y1=yStart; y1<=yEnd; y1++)
            hist[Inp.Grid[x1+y1*width]]++;
        if (x2>=0)
```

```
        for (y1=yStart; y1<=yEnd; y1++)
        { hist[Inp.Grid[x2+y1*width]]--;
            if (deb && hist[Inp.Grid[x2+y1*width]]<0) return -1;
        }
     } //--------------- end if (x==0) ----------------------------------
     int gMin=0, gMax=255;
     for (gv=gMin; gv<=gMax; gv++)
       if (hist[gv]>0) { gMin=gv; break; }
     for (gv=gMax; gv>=0; gv--)
       if (hist[gv]>0) { gMax=gv; break; }
     if (Inp.Grid[x+width*y]-gMin<gMax-Inp.Grid[x+width*y])
        Grid[x+width*y]=gMin;
     else Grid[x+width*y]=gMax;
   } //=============== end for (int x... ================
 } //=============== end for (int y... ================
 return 1;
} //****************** end ExtremVar *********************
```

Here is the source code of the universal extreme method for color and grayscale images.

```
public int ExtremLightUni(CImage Inp, int hWind,Form1 fm1)
/* The extreme filter for color or grayscale images with variable hWind.
The filter finds in the (2*hWind+1)-neighborhood of the actual pixel (x,y)
the color "Color1" with minimum and the color "Color2" with the maximum
lightness. "Color1" is assigned to the output pixel if its lightness
is closer to the lightness of the central pixel than the lightness of
"Color2". --*/
{
 byte[] CenterColor = new byte[3], Color = new byte[3], Color1 =
  new byte[3], Color2 = new byte[3];
  int c, k, nbyte = 3, x;
  if (Inp.N_Bits == 8) nbyte = 1;
  for (int y = 0; y < height; y++) // =====================================
  {
    if (y % jump == jump - 1) fm1.progressBar1.PerformStep();
```

```
for (x = 0; x < width; x++) //========================================
{
  for (c = 0; c < nbyte; c++) Color2[c] = Color1[c] = Color[c] =
                            CenterColor[c] = Inp.Grid[c + nbyte *
                            (x + y * width)];
  int MinLight = 1000, MaxLight = 0;
  for (k = -hWind; k <= hWind; k++) //===============================
  {
    if (y + k >= 0 && y + k < height)
      for (int i = -hWind; i <= hWind; i++) //==========================
      {
        if (x + i >= 0 && x + i < width) // && (i > 0 || k > 0))
        {
          for (c = 0; c < nbyte; c++)
                    Color[c] = Inp.Grid[c + nbyte * (x + i + (y + k)
                    * width)];
          int light;
          if (nbyte == 3) light= MaxC(Color[2], Color[1], Color[0]);
          else light = Color[0];
          if (light < MinLight)
          {
            MinLight = light;
            for (c = 0; c < nbyte; c++) Color1[c] = Color[c];
          }
          if (light > MaxLight)
          {
            MaxLight = light;
            for (c = 0; c < nbyte; c++) Color2[c] = Color[c];
          }
        }
      } //=============== end for (int i... =======================
  } //=================== end for (int k... =======================
```

```
    int CenterLight = MaxC(CenterColor[2], CenterColor[1],
    CenterColor[0]);
    int dist1 = 0, dist2 = 0;
    dist1 = CenterLight - MinLight;
    dist2 = MaxLight - CenterLight;
    if (dist1 < dist2)
      for (c = 0; c < nbyte; c++)  Grid[c + 3 * x + y * width * 3] =
      Color1[c]; // Min
    else
      for (c = 0; c < nbyte; c++)  Grid[c + 3 * x + y * width * 3] =
      Color2[c]; // Max

  } //================= end for (int x... ==========================
 } //==================== end for (int y... ==========================
 //fm1.progressBar1.Visible = false;
 return 1;
} //********************** end ExtremLightUni *************************
```

Consider an example of edges detected by the Laplacian zero crossing method (threshold = 10) after using the sigma filter and the extreme value filter. Figure 6-11 shows the gray values of the original image (Figure 6-11a) and the images after successive steps of processing the image with the filters: the image processed with the sigma filter (Figure 6-11b), with the extreme value filter (Figure 6-11c), and the Laplacian with edges (Figure 6-11d). Positive Laplacian values are shown in red, negative values in blue, and zero crossings as white lines.

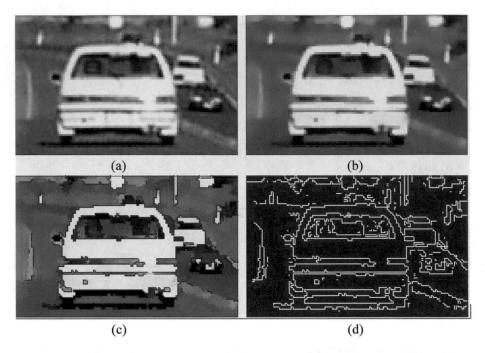

Figure 6-11. *Example of edge detection with Laplacian zero crossing: (a) original image, (b) sigma filtered, (c) extreme filtered, and (d) Laplacian with edges (white lines)*

As you can see, the edge detection is rather successful. However, there are some gaps in the edges as explained in the next section.

Fundamental Errors of the Method of Zero Crossing in the Laplacian

Laplacian has a fundamental property that the sequences of its zero crossings must have gaps in the neighborhood of points where three or four sequences meet. Figure 6-12 provides an example. Figure 6-12 shows an artificial image (a), the edges detected by the method of zero crossing (b), the desired ideal edges (c), and the values of the sign of the Laplacian (d). The red pixels are the pixels with positive values of the Laplacian and the blue pixels are those with negative values. Zero crossings are shown in Figure 6-12d as white lines.

a   b

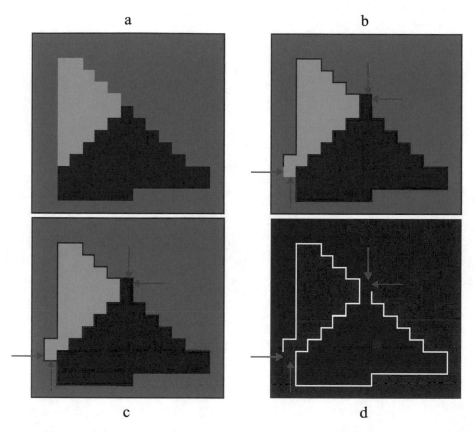

c   d

Figure 6-12. *(a) Artificial image with noise, σ = 5; (b) zero crossings over the image after sigma and extreme filtering; (c) ideal edges; and (d) zero crossings over the Laplacian (red are positive values)*

Notice the missing pieces of the edges occurring due to fundamental errors in Figure 6-12 marked by green arrows. These are considered fundamental errors because it is impossible to eliminate them. These errors occur because the Laplacian is the difference between the local mean and the actual gray value. A zero crossing lies between a pixel with a positive value and one with a negative value of the Laplacian. One of these pixels has a gray value greater than the local mean and the other one a gray value less than the local mean. If, however, there are more than two different gray values in the gliding window, then the local mean can lie only between two of gray values. There can be no zero crossing for the third gray value. The edge therefore has a gap. Due to these gaps, the edges produced by means of Laplacian zero crossings contain no crotches.

These errors are very important because edges are often used to produce polygons representing boundaries of areas with a constant color. Missing crotches make these polygons incomplete, as they do not describe the boundaries of regions correctly.

CHAPTER 7

A New Method of Edge Detection

As shown in the example of Figure 6-11, the implementation of the sigma and extreme value filters improves the quality of the Laplacian zero crossings and thus also the quality of edges. It is important to stress that these two filters improve the quality of the image so strongly that it becomes possible to apply the simplest method of edge detection. This is the *binarization of the gradient* of the gray values:

$$\text{Grad}_x(x, y) = GV(x, y) - GV(x - 1, y)$$

$$\text{Grad}_y(x, y) = GV x, y) - GV(x, y - 1).$$

Here $GV(x, y)$ is the gray value of the pixel (x, y). The values of $|\text{Grad}_x(x, y)|$ and $|\text{Grad}_y(x, y)|$ must be compared with a threshold. If the value of $|\text{Grad}_x(x, y)|$ is greater than the threshold, then a small piece of the edge lies between the pixels (x, y) and $(x - 1, y)$. Similarly for the value of $|\text{Grad}_y(x, y)|$: If this value is greater than the threshold, then the edge runs between the pixels (x, y) and $(x, y - 1)$.

In the case of color images we use the color difference of the pixels (x_1, y_1) and (x_2, y_2). We call this method the binarized gradient. This is the sum of absolute values of the differences of the intensities of the color channels of the pixels:

$$\text{DifColor} = \sum |\text{color}(i, x_1, y_1) - \text{color}(i, x_2, y_2)| / 3$$

where $\text{color}(i, x_1, y_1)$ is the intensity of the ith color channel of the pixel (x_1, y_1) and similarly for $\text{color}(i, x_2, y_2)$.

Figure 7-1 shows an example of the comparison of the results of edge detection with Laplacian zero crossing (a) and the binarized gradient (b). You can see that the images are pretty much the same.

© Vladimir Kovalevsky 2019
V. Kovalevsky, *Modern Algorithms for Image Processing*, https://doi.org/10.1007/978-1-4842-4237-7_7

(a)   (b)

Figure 7-1. *Laplacian zero crossing (a) and the binarized gradient (b)*

Compare the location indicated by the green arrows: The edges found by means of binarized gradient do not have the gaps that occur in zero crossing edges due to the fundamental errors of the zero crossing method. The further processing of the edges becomes more precise when using color differences.

Means for Encoding the Edges

Encoding the edges is no trivial problem: If, for example, a pair of pixels (x, y) and $(x - 1, y)$ with a great color difference is found, then a pixel indicating the location of the edge must be labeled in the image containing the edges. Suppose that we decide to label the pixel (x, y) in the image with the edges. In the case of the pixel pair (x, y) and $(x, y - 1)$ we decide to label the pixel (x, y). Then in the three cases with different edge elements shown in Figure 7-2 and the threshold equal to 40, one and the same pixels, namely the shaded ones, will be labeled, and there will be no possibility to distinguish among these three cases.

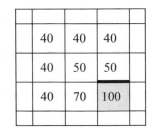

Figure 7-2. *Three images with different edges*

If we decide to label the other pixel of a pair of adjacent pixels with a great color difference then the same situation will take place in the case of the other images. The only possible way to solve this problem consists in introducing another structure for encoding the edges, namely a structure containing different elements for pixels and for the edge element lying between two adjacent pixels. This structure is known as an abstract cell complex (ACC; see Kovalevsky, 1989, 2008).

The Idea of an Abstract Cell Complex

We consider here the digital plane as a two-dimensional cell complex rather than a set of pixels (see Figure 7-3). Thus our digital plane contains cracks and points besides the pixels, which are considered as small squares. *Cracks* are the sides of these squares; *points* are end points of the cracks and therefore corners of the pixels. Points are zero-dimensional cells, cracks are one-dimensional cells, and pixels are two-dimensional cells.

Figure 7-3. *Example of a small two-dimensional complex containing the crack boundary of the shaded subset*

Considering the plane as an abstract cell complex has many advantages: There are no more connectivity paradoxes as described in Chapter 8, a boundary of a subset becomes a thin curve with a zero area, the boundary of a region and that of its complement are the same, and so on. The definition and the processing of digital curves and especially that of digital straight lines becomes simpler and clearer. The most important advantage from the point of view of economical encoding and exact reconstruction of images is the ability to fill the interior of crack boundaries by an extremely simple and fast algorithm (refer to Kovalevsky, (1990)) that cannot be applied when representing boundaries as sets of pixels.

The rest of this section contains a short summary of the topological notions important for this presentation. Please refer to Kovavlevsky (2008) for more details and topological foundations. The reader acquainted with cell complexes may skip the rest of this section.

There is a bounding relation imposed on the cells: A cell of a lower dimension may bound some cells of a higher dimension. Refer back to the example of a small two-dimensional complex shown in Figure 7-3. The pixels are represented as interiors of squares, cracks as the sides of the squares, and points (i.e., the 0 cells) are end points of the cracks and simultaneously the corners of the pixels.

Now let us introduce some notions that we will need in the sequel. A *boundary crack* of a subset *S* of a complex is a crack separating a pixel belonging to *S* from another pixel not belonging to *S*. The boundary cracks of the shaded subset in Figure 7-3 are drawn as bold lines. The *boundary* (also known as a *crack boundary*) of a subset *S* is the set of all boundary cracks of *S* and all end points of these cracks. A boundary contains no pixels and is therefore a thin set with an area of zero. A connected subset of a boundary is called a *boundary curve*. For the notion of connectedness, please refer to Kovalevsky (1989).

We consider the digital plane a *Cartesian two-dimensional complex;* that is, as a Cartesian product of two one-dimensional complexes that are the coordinate axes of the plane. The *x* coordinate is the number of a row; the *y* coordinate is the line number. We use here the coordinate system of computer graphics; that is, the positive *x* axis runs from left to right and the positive *y* axis runs from top to bottom.

For saving the `detected` edges we need a special kind of ACC: the `Cartesian two-dimensional ACC.` Using such an ACC it becomes possible to introduce coordinates of cells. Exactly as in the case of digital images the *x* coordinate is the number of a column and the *y* coordinate is the number of a row.

We use for digital images the usual coordinates where *x* changes from 0 to *width* – 1 and *y* from 0 to *height* – 1. We call these coordinates *standard.* The coordinates of cells in an ACC representing an image of *width* × *height* pixels have a greater area: The *x* coordinate changes from 0 to 2*width* and *y* from 0 to 2*height*. Thus the size of the ACC representing an image of *width* × *height* pixels has the size of (2*width* + 1) × (2*height* + 1) cells. We call the coordinates of cells in the image representing the ACC of a given digital image *combinatorial coordinates.* We call the image containing an ACC an *image in combinatorial coordinates.*

Notice that both combinatorial coordinates x and y of a pixel are odd, whereas the x coordinate of a vertical crack is even and its y coordinate is odd. In the case of a horizontal crack it is the opposite: Its x coordinate is odd and its y coordinate is even. Both combinatorial coordinates of a point are even.

In some of our projects we process the detected edges. For example, for analyzing the shape of objects it is rather convenient to approximate the detected edges by polygons. To find the polygons we must trace the edges. It is much simpler and more convenient to trace edges in an image in combinatorial coordinates than in a usual image containing only pixels. In our projects the image in combinatorial coordinates is called `CombIm`.

A Simple Method of Encoding Edges

This method uses an image `CombIm` that contains the cell complex whose sizes correspond to the size of the processed image: The width of `CombIm` is equal to 2*width + 1 and its height is equal to 2*height + 1 where width and height are the sizes of the processed image. The addition of + 1 is necessary to have place for the points at the right hand and at the bottom boundaries of `CombIm`, which are sometimes important for processing.

The method `LabelCells` reads the image processed by the extreme filter one row after another and tests for each pixel (x, y) whether the absolute difference of the color of the pixel (x, y) and the color of one of its adjacent pixels $(x - 1\ y)$ and $(x, y - 1)$ is greater than the given threshold. The threshold can be defined by the user who should know that under low thresholds the number of edge cracks becomes large and the probability that some part of the edge becomes thick is also large. The correct value of the threshold should be found by experimenting.

If the absolute value of the color difference of the pixels (x, y) and $(x - 1, y)$ is greater than the threshold, then the vertical crack lying between these pixels obtains the label 1. Similarly, if the color difference of the pixels (x, y) and $(x, y - 1)$ is greater than the threshold, then the corresponding horizontal crack is labeled 1.

The labels of both points incident to a crack will be simultaneously increased. If a point is incident to many cracks (there can be up to four incident cracks) the label of the point becomes increased many times. Finitely, the value of a point's label becomes equal to the number of cracks incident to this point. This information can be used during the processing of the encoded edges.

Here is the source code of the LabelCells method.

```
public void LabelCells(int th, CImage Image3)
{
  int difH, difV, nbyte, NXB = Image3.width, x, y;
  byte Lab = 1;
  if (Image3.N_Bits == 24) nbyte = 3;
  else nbyte = 1;
  for (x = 0; x < width * height; x++) Grid[x] = 0;

  byte[] Colorh = new byte[3];
  byte[] Colorp = new byte[3];
  byte[] Colorv = new byte[3];

  for (y = 0; y < height; y += 2)
    for (x = 0; x < width; x += 2) // through all points
      Grid[x + width * y] = 0;

  for (y = 1; y < height; y += 2)
    for (x = 1; x < width; x += 2) // through the right and upper pixels
    {
      if (x >= 3) //-- vertical cracks: abs.dif{(x/2, y/2)-((x-2)/2, y/2)}
      -------
      {
        for (int c = 0; c < nbyte; c++)
        {
          Colorv[c] = Image3.Grid[c + nbyte *((x-2)/2)+nbyte*NXB*(y/2)];
          Colorp[c] = Image3.Grid[c + nbyte * (x / 2) + nbyte *NXB*(y/2)];
        }
        if (nbyte == 3) difV = ColorDifAbs(Colorp, Colorv);
        else difV = Math.Abs(Colorp[0] - Colorv[0]);
        if (difV < 0) difV = -difV;
        if (difV > th)
        {
          Grid[x - 1 + width * y] = Lab; // vertical crack
          Grid[x - 1 + width * (y - 1)]++; // point above the crack;
          Grid[x - 1 + width * (y + 1)]++; // point below the crack
```

```
    }
} //-------------------- end if (x>=3) -------------------------
if (y >= 3) //--- horizontal cracks: abs.dif{(x/2, y/2)-(x/2,
(y-2)/2)} ---
{
  for (int c = 0; c < nbyte; c++)
  {
    Colorh[c] = Image3.Grid[c + nbyte *(x/2)+nbyte*NXB*((y-2)/2)];
    Colorp[c] = Image3.Grid[c + nbyte * (x / 2) + nbyte *NXB*(y/2)];
  }
  if (nbyte == 3) difH = ColorDifAbs(Colorp, Colorh);
  else difH = Math.Abs(Colorp[0] - Colorh[0]);
  if (difH > th)
  {
    Grid[x + width * (y - 1)] = Lab; // horizontal crack
    Grid[x - 1 + width * (y - 1)]++; // point left of crack
    Grid[x + 1 + width * (y - 1)]++;  // point right of crack
  }
} //--------------------- end if (y>=3) -------------------------
} //================= end for (x=1;... ====================
} //***************** end LabelCells ***********************
```

Improvements of the Method of Binarized Gradient

The simplest version of the method of binarized gradients has a drawback: The edges produced with a small threshold for the difference of the gray values or colors are sometimes too thick. This happens if the image is blurred at some locations, creating ramps of the intensities. In cases when the width of the ramp is greater than four pixels (which happens seldom) the usually used extreme filter with a window of 5×5 pixels (the parameter hWind in the preceding source codes is equal to 2) cannot completely remove the ramp. Then the edge can be blurred.

To eliminate this problem we have developed an improved version of the method LabelCells that we call LabelCellsSign. The goal of this method is similar to the goal of Canny's (1986) No-maximum suppression method, but the implemented solution is quite different.

Let us first consider the notion of the gradient as applied to digital images. One cannot use the classical notion of the gradient defined (in the two-dimensional case) as a vector with two components that are the derivatives of the intensity with respect to the coordinates x and y, because a digital image is not a Euclidean space. It is necessary to replace the derivatives by finite differences: the derivative of the intensity I of a color with respect to x by $I(x + 1, y) - I(x, y)$ and the derivative of the intensity I with respect to y by $I(x, y + 1) - I(x, y)$. The intensity $I(x, y)$ is a property of the pixel (x, y) where x is the number of the column and y is the number of the row. However, the differences $I(x + 1, y) - I(x, y)$ and $I(x, y + 1) - I(x, y)$ cannot be assigned to a pixel, because each of them is defined for a pair of pixels. In this case the notion of an ACC becomes very useful: Each of the two differences can be assigned to the corresponding crack (one-dimensional cell) lying between the pixels of a pair. The gradient should then be assigned to the point (zero-dimensional cell) incident to both cracks.

Consider first the case of a grayscale image. It is necessary to calculate for each location in the image the gradient of the gray value, label locations where the absolute value of the gradient is greater than the threshold defined for edge detection, find the connected subset of labeled locations lying along a line parallel to the gradient, and find the location in this subset where the absolute value of the gradient reaches the maximum. This location belongs to the edge.

It is clear that at the location where the absolute value of the gradient reaches the maximum, its components being equal to differences of the gray values in adjacent pixels also reach the maximum. We are interested in cracks belonging to the edge. Therefore it is not necessary to use the complicated procedure of looking for the locations in a connected subset along the direction of the gradient. It is sufficient to test all pairs of adjacent pixels in a row to find the pairs where the difference of the gray values is greater than the threshold and to look for the maximum of the difference among these pairs. In this way the vertical cracks of the edge will be found. The horizontal cracks of the edge can be found in a similar way by testing pairs of adjacent pixels in a column.

However, the direction of the gradient or the sign of the differences of the gray values should be considered. If we consider only the absolute values, then the cases denoted in Figure 7-4 by red and green arrows cannot be distinguished, and a single maximum of the absolute value will be found. However, there must be two edges found in this case because there are two ramps: one ramp with decreasing lightness above the dark strip and another one with increasing lightness below it. Thus we must consider the sign of the differences of the gray values and look for the maximum of positive differences and for the minimum of negative ones.

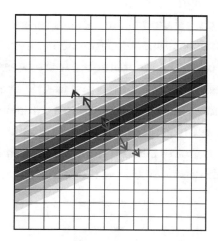

Figure 7-4. *Example of gradients of the lightness in a grayscale image*

Let us consider the method LabelCellsSign first for the case of grayscale images, although it is also applicable to color images.

The method implements some kind of a finite-state machine. It uses a variable State with values that correspond to different states of the method. At the start of the method State obtains the value zero.

The method belongs to the class CImage and is called as CombIm. LabelCellsSign(threshold, InputImage) where InputImage is the image calculated by the extreme filter. CombIm is the image containing the cell complex used for encoding the edges. Therefore its sizes are (as in the case of the method LabelCells described earlier) 2*width + 1 and 2*height + 1 where width and height are the sizes of the InputImage.

The method LabelCellsSign uses two pairs of for loops whose variables x and y are scanning all locations of two-dimensional cells of the ACC contained in the image CombIm destined to save the edges.

The first pair of loops serves for the detection of vertical cracks. The outside loop with the variable y runs through all odd values from 1 to height - 1. The inside loop with the variable x starts with the value x = 3 because it uses the value x - 2, which must remain in the area of the image CombIm. The calculation of the difference difV of the colors of two adjacent pixels ((x - 1) / 2, y / 2) and (x / 2, y / 2) (x and y are coordinates in the image CombIm) of the input image stands at the beginning of the x loop. In the case of a grayscale image it is calculated directly, by subtraction. However, in the case of color images it is calculated with the method ColorDifSign, which is explained later. Unlike the method LabelCells, the difference is calculated here not as an absolute value, but with a sign.

The variable Inp shows the relation of the color difference of the two pixels mentioned earlier to the Threshold specified for edge detection: Inp is equal to 1 if the difference is greater than Threshold and it is equal to 0 elsewhere. The variables State and Inp compose the control variable Contr, equal to 3*State + Inp controling the switch instruction. The variable xStartP contains the value of x where the sequence of color differences greater than Threshold starts. Similarly, the variable xStartM contains the value of x where the sequence of color differences less than the negative threshold -Threshold starts. Here is the pseudo-code of the switch instruction.

```
switch (Contr)
{
  case 4: if (x > xStartP && difV > maxDif)
            { maxDiv = difV;
              xopt = x;
            }
            break;
  case 3: label the vertical crack at (xopt - 1, y) and its end points;
            State = 0;
            break;

  case 2: label the vertical crack at (xopt - 1, y) and its end points;
            minDif = difV;
            xStartM = x;
            State = -1;
            break;
  case 1: maxDiv = difV; xopt = x; xStartP = x;
            State = 1;
            break;
  case 0: break;
```

```
case -1: maxDiv = difV; xopt = x; xStartP = x;
               State = -1;
               break;
case -2: label the vertical crack at (xopt - 1, y) and its end points;
               maxDif = difV;
               xStartP = x;
               State = 1;
case -3: label the vertical crack at (xopt - 1, y) and its end points;
               State = 0;
               break;
case -4: if (x > xStartM && difV < minDif)
               { minDiv = difV;
                 xopt = x;
               }
               break;
} //::::::::::::::::::::: end switch ::::::::::::::::::::::::::::::::.:::::
```

At the beginning of a line the variables State, Inp, and Contr are equal to 0. If Inp becomes the value 1 then Contr also becomes 1 and in case 1: the maximum maxDif is set to difV, xopt and xStartP are set to x, and State is set to 1. The value xStartP is the start's coordinate of the sequence of cracks where the color difference is greater than Threshold. If Inp remains 1 then Contr becomes 4 because State == 1 and the maximum of difV is calculated along the sequence of cracks where Inp remains 1.

If Inp changes to 0 then Contr becomes 3 and a vertical crack is labeled at the maximum position xopt - 1. This is the only position in the sequence of pixels with difV greater than Threshold where a vertical crack is labeled. Thus the sequence of vertical cracks becomes thin at the running value of y.

The labeling of horizontal cracks and their end points takes place in the second pair of for loops where the outer loop is an x loop and the inner one is a y loop. The switch instruction looks similar to that for vertical cracks, but the variable difV is replaced by difH, xopt is replaced by yopt, xStartP is replaced by yStartP, and xStartM is replaced by yStartM. Here is the source code of the method LabelCellsSign:

```
public int LabelCellsSign(int th, CImage Extrm)
{
  int difH, difV, c, maxDif, minDif, nByte, NXB = Extrm.width, x, y, xopt, yopt;
  int Inp, State, Contr, xStartP, xStartM, yStartP, yStartM;
  if (Extrm.N_Bits == 24) nByte = 3;
  else nByte = 1;
  for (x = 0; x < width * height; x++) Grid[x] = 0;
  byte[] Colorp = new byte[3], Colorh = new byte[3], Colorv = new byte[3];
  maxDif = 0; minDif = 0;
  for (y = 1; y < height; y += 2) //====== vertical cracks ==============
  {
    State = 0;
    xopt = -1;
    xStartP = xStartM = -1;
    for (x = 3; x < width; x += 2)   //===============================
    {
      for (c = 0; c < nByte; c++)
      {
        Colorv[c] = Extrm.Grid[c + nByte * ((x - 2) / 2) + nByte*NXB*(y / 2)];
        Colorp[c] = Extrm.Grid[c + nByte * (x / 2) + nByte * NXB * (y / 2)];
      }
      if (nByte == 3) difV = ColorDifSign(Colorp, Colorv);
      else difV = Colorp[0] - Colorv[0];
      if (difV > th) Inp = 1;
      else
        if (difV > -th) Inp = 0;
        else Inp = -1;

      Contr = State * 3 + Inp;
      switch (Contr) //::::::::::::::::::::::::::::::::::::::::::::::::::::::::
      {
        case 4:
          if (x > xStartP && difV > maxDif)
          {
            maxDif = difV;
            xopt = x;
```

```
    }
    break;
  case 3:
    Grid[xopt - 1 + width * y] = 1; // vertical crack
    Grid[xopt - 1 + width * (y - 1)]++; // point above
    Grid[xopt - 1 + width * (y + 1)]++; // point below
    State = 0;
    break;
  case 2:
    Grid[xopt - 1 + width * y] = 1; // vertical crack
    Grid[xopt - 1 + width * (y - 1)]++; // point above
    Grid[xopt - 1 + width * (y + 1)]++; // point below
    minDif = difV;
    xopt = x;
    xStartM = x;
    State = -1;
    break;
  case 1: maxDif = difV; xopt = x; xStartP = x; State = 1; break;
  case 0: break;
  case -1: minDif = difV; xopt = x; xStartM = x; State = -1; break;
  case -2:
    Grid[xopt - 1 + width * y] = 1;       // vertical crack
    Grid[xopt - 1 + width * (y - 1)]++; // point above
    Grid[xopt - 1 + width * (y + 1)]++; // point below
    maxDif = difV;
    xopt = x;
    xStartP = x;
    State = 1;
    break;
  case -3:
    Grid[xopt - 1 + width * y] = 1;       // vertical crack
    Grid[xopt - 1 + width * (y - 1)]++; // point above
    Grid[xopt - 1 + width * (y + 1)]++; // point below
    State = 0;
    break;
```

113

```
        case -4:
          if (x > xStartM && difV < minDif)
          {
            minDif = difV;
            xopt = x;
          }
          break;
      }  //::::::::::::::::::::::: end switch ::::::::::::::::::::::::::::::::
    } //=============== end for (x=3;... =====================
  } //=============== end for (y=1;... =====================

  for (x = 1; x < width; x += 2) //=== horizontal cracks ================
  {
    State = 0;
    minDif = 0; yopt = -1; yStartP = yStartM = 0;
    for (y = 3; y < height; y += 2)   //===============================
    {
      for (c = 0; c < nByte; c++)
      {
        Colorh[c] = Extrm.Grid[c + nByte * (x / 2) + nByte*NXB*((y - 2) / 2)];
        Colorp[c] = Extrm.Grid[c + nByte * (x / 2) + nByte * NXB * (y / 2)];
      }
      if (nByte == 3) difH = ColorDifSign(Colorp, Colorh);
      else difH = Colorp[0] - Colorh[0];
      if (difH > th)
        Inp = 1;
      else
        if (difH > -th) Inp = 0;
        else Inp = -1;
      Contr = State * 3 + Inp;
      switch (Contr) //::::::::::::::::::::::::::::::::::::::::::::::::::::::::
      {
        case 4:
          if (y > yStartP && difH > maxDif)
          {
```

```
      maxDif = difH;
      yopt = y;
   }
   break;
case 3:
   Grid[x + width * (yopt - 1)] = 1;      // horizontal crack
   Grid[x - 1 + width * (yopt - 1)]++; // left point
   Grid[x + 1 + width * (yopt - 1)]++; // right point
   State = 0;
   break;
case 2:
   Grid[x + width * (yopt - 1)] = 1;        // horizontal crack
   Grid[x - 1 + width * (yopt - 1)]++; // left point
   Grid[x + 1 + width * (yopt - 1)]++; // right point
   yopt = y;
   State = -1;
   break;
case 1: maxDif = difH; yopt = y; yStartP = y; State = 1; break;
case 0: break;
case -1: minDif = difH; yopt = y; yStartM = y; State = -1; break;
case -2:
   Grid[x + width * (yopt - 1)] = 1;        // horizontal crack
   Grid[x - 1 + width * (yopt - 1)]++; // left point
   Grid[x + 1 + width * (yopt - 1)]++; // right point
   yopt = y;
   State = 1;
   break;
case -3:
   Grid[x + width * (yopt - 1)] = 1; // horizontal crack
   Grid[x - 1 + width * (yopt - 1)]++; // left point
   Grid[x + 1 + width * (yopt - 1)]++; // right point
   State = 0;
   break;
```

```
    case -4:
      if (y > yStartM && difH < minDif)
      {
        minDif = difH;
        yopt = y;
      }
      break;
  }  //::::::::::::::::::::::: end switch :::::::::::::::::::::::::::::::
  } //=============== end for (y=3;... ====================
  } //=============== end for (x=1;... ====================
  return 1;
} //******************** end LabelCellsSign *********************
```

We explained earlier how this method works in the case of grayscale images. Let us now explain its functioning in the case of color images.

We should first consider the notion of a gradient as applied to color digital images. First of all, in the case of a color image there is not a single gradient, but rather three gradients each for one of the three primary colors: red, green, and blue. Each of these gradients is defined by two differences of the intensities of the corresponding colors in adjacent pixels: the x component as $I(x + 1, y) - I(x, y)$ and the y component as $I(x, y + 1) - I(x, y)$ where I is the intensity of one of the primary colors. The intensity $I(x, y)$ is a property of the pixel (x, y) where x is the number of the column and y is the number of the row. However, a difference $I(x + 1, y) - I(x, y)$ or $I(x, y + 1) - I(x, y)$ cannot be assigned to a pixel, because a difference is defined for a pair of pixels. In this case the notion of an ACC is very useful: Each of the two differences can be assigned to one of two corresponding cracks (one-dimensional cells) lying between the pixels of a pair. The gradient should then be assigned to the point (zero-dimensional cell) incident to both cracks.

According to the correct idea of Canny (1986), it is necessary to find the maximum of the absolute value of the gradient. In the case of a color image it is necessary to decide which combination of the values of the three color gradients or their components should be used to correctly represent the change in the color. One possibility is to use, instead of the difference of the gray values, as we have done in the case of grayscale images, the sum of the three absolute values of the differences of the three primary colors. However, as in the case of grayscale images, the sum must have a sign. If we take the sum of the signed differences of the intensities of the colors, the differences of different primary colors could have different signs and compensate for each other so that their sum becomes small. Our investigations have shown that the three color gradients near a location of an edge in a color image have very different directions so that they really can compensate for each other in a sum.

We have decided to use the sum of the absolute differences assigned with the sign of the difference of the lightness. This is realized by the ColorDifSign method, shown here.

```
int ColorDifSign(byte[] Colp, byte[] Colh)
{
  int Dif = 0;
  for (int c = 0; c < 3; c++) Dif += Math.Abs(Colp[c] - Colh[c]);
  int Sign;
  if (MaxC(Colp[2], Colp[1], Colp[0])-MaxC(Colh[2], Colh[1], Colh[0])>0)
                                                          Sign = 1;
  else Sign = -1;
  return (Sign * Dif) / 3;
}
```

In this code, MaxC( ) is the method described in Chapter 3 returning the lightness of the color of a pixel.

For the purpose of investigating the functioning of the method LabelCellsSign we have developed in the project WFdetectEdges1 a tool displaying the changing lightness in a line of the image ExtremIm, the relation of the color differences to the threshold of the edge detection, and the detected vertical cracks of the edge. The user can click a point in the right picture box. Then an enlarged section of the clicked line starting with the clicked point appears in the third picture box below. In each of the upper picture boxes a horizontal line appears showing the line section displayed in the lower box. Figure 7-5 shows the form of the project WFdetectEdges1 as an example.

The lower curve in Figure 7-5 shows the lightness in a line of the image SigmaIm. The color differences with an absolute value greater than the threshold are shown in the upper curve as color vertical lines. The red lines show the positive differences and the green lines show the negative ones. Both red and green lines show the positions of detected vertical cracks of the edge.

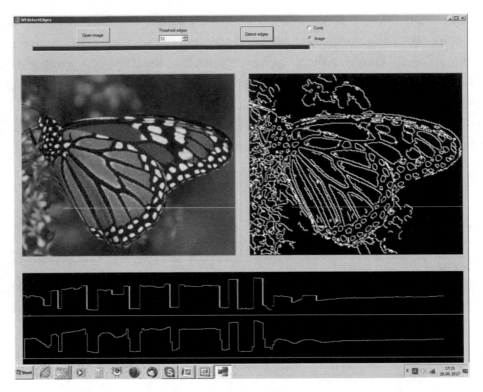

Figure 7-5. *The form of the project* `WFdetectEdges1`

Figure 7-6 shows the cell complex with the edges of a fragment of the image of Figure 7-5. This is the representation of the edges by the method `DrawComb` described later. Edges shown in Figure 7-5 and in Figure 7-6 were produced by means of the method `LabelCellsSign` finding the maximum absolute color difference in a color ramp, which is a narrow strip between two homogeneous areas. The color in this strip changes rapidly. As you can see, the method works well.

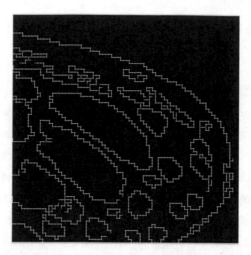

Figure 7-6. *The detected edges in a fragment of the image of Figure 7-5*

However, using our method `ExtremLightUni` with a relatively high size of the gliding window that must be greater than the width of the ramp produces mostly narrow edges appearing as a thin line inside the ramp. Therefore a simpler method, `LabelCells`, described earlier, can be successfully used.

To demonstrate the success of our method of edge detection we have copied the images from the article "Canny Edge Detector" from Wikipedia and applied our method to the color image from that article. Figure 7-7 shows a fragment of this image (a), the edges detected by our method (b), and the edges detected by the Canny edge detector.

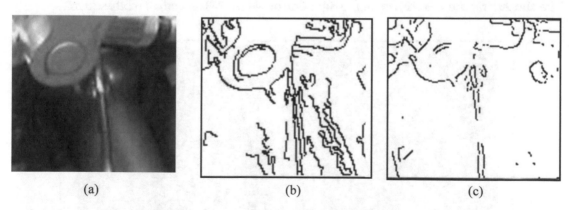

(a)   (b)   (c)

Figure 7-7. *(a) Fragment of the image, (b) edges detected by our method, and (c) edges detected by the Canny edge detector*

Further Improvements of the Method of Binarized Gradient

The edges calculated by the method LabelCellsSign are always thin and very fine. However, due to the inhomogeneous structure of some images there are often small pieces of the edge present that can unnecessarily disturb the further processing of the edges. Therefore we have developed the method CleanCombNew, which consists of three parts. Part 1 transforms each structure of four cracks that looks like a square into a corner consisting of two cracks; Part 2 deletes single cracks incident to a crotch point that have an incident end point; and Part 3 deletes components of the edge with a number of contained cells that is less than a predefined threshold. This threshold is a parameter of CleanCombNew.

The code for Parts 1 and 2 is simple, so we do not explain it. However, the code for Part 3 is rather complicated. Before explaining it, I should mention that we have developed a method DrawComb that displays an enlarged fragment of CombIm representing the cracks as short white lines and the points as small color rectangles. The color is red for an end point that can be detected as a point incident with a single crack. The color is green for a point incident with two cracks, yellow for the case of three cracks, and violet for four incident cracks. The location of the fragment can be chosen by the user by means of clicking in the right picture box with the mouse. The click point specifies the location of the left upper corner of the fragment. The size of the fragment is standard; it is chosen in such a way that the enlarged fragment fits in the window of the left picture box. Figure 7-8 shows an example. The chosen fragment is shown on the right side of Figure 7-8 as a small white square.

Figure 7-8. *A fragment of the edge represented by* DrawComb

The third part of the method `CleanCombNew` must find connected components of the edge and count their cells. The notion of connected components is well known from graph theory. Notice that an edge represented as a cell complex is a graph with vertices as points and edges that are cracks. A connected component of an edge is its subset in which for any two elements there exists an incidence path containing these elements, and an incidence path is a sequence a_1, a_2, a_3, ... a_n in which any two adjacent elements are incident. An edge of a graph is incident to its end points and these end points are incident to the edge.

Finding connected components of the edge is handled by the well-known *breadth-first search method*. This is an algorithm for traversing a graph. It starts at some arbitrary vertex of the graph and explores the neighbor vertex first, before moving to the next-level neighbors.

The search for the starting point is made in the method `CleanCombNew` in a pair of `for` loops where the variables x and y take only even values. Note that any point in our cell complex has both even coordinates.

Points that were not used before are searched. Used points obtain the highest bit 7 labeled (label 128). When a not used point with the label 1, 3, or 4 has been found, the method `ComponClean` is started. It works with a copy of the grid of the image `CombIm` because `ComponClean` labels some cells in the grid that it uses, and these labels would disturb the further use of `CombIm`. The method `ComponClean` traces by means of its subroutine `Trace` all cells of a component and counts them. As long as the number of counted cells is less than the threshold `Size` being a parameter of `CleanCombNew`, the coordinates of the cells are saved in the array `Index` as the value x + width * y. After all cells of a component are scanned, its number is compared with `Size`: If it is less than `Size` then the saved cells are deleted. Figure 7-9 shows an example of edges before and after the use of `CleanCombNew`.

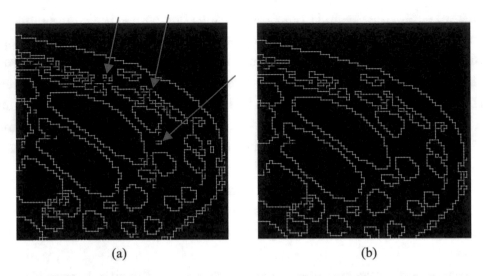

(a)   (b)

Figure 7-9. *Edges (a) before and (b) after using* CleanCombNew *with the parameter* Size = 21

The Edge Detector of Canny

The well-known edge detector of Canny (1986) calculates the gradient of the gray values $G(x, y)=|Sobel.X| + |Sobel.Y|$ with the Sobel filter (Chapter 6), calculates the direction of the edge (as a multiple of 45°), and deletes all candidates on the edge that do not have the local maximum of the absolute value $|G(x, y)|$ of the gradient. This is the procedure of *nonmaximum suppression* (NMS): If the pixel (x, y) has the value $|G(x, y)|$ and its neighbor, which does not lie in the direction of the edge, has a greater value, then this value is set equal to zero. After that a special procedure is applied: It uses two thresholds $T_1 < T_2$. The image is scanned until a pixel is found for which the value of $|G(x, y)|$ is greater than T_2. This pixel lies on the edge. This edge is traced in two directions, and all pixels with a value greater than T_1 are labeled as belonging to the edge. After this last step the algorithm is finished.

Figure 7-10 compares the results of the Canny algorithm with those of our binarized gradient. As you can see, the binarized gradient provides much more detail and it is simpler than the Canny algorithm.

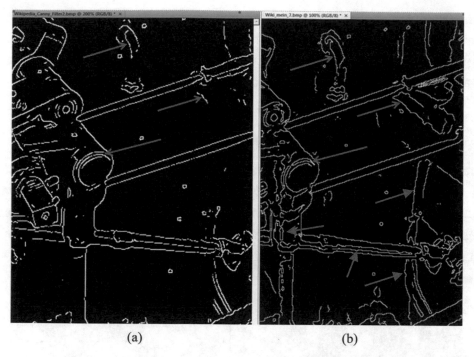

(a)   (b)

Figure 7-10. *Results of (a) the Canny algorithm, and (b) the binarized gradient*

Edges in Color Images

Both the method of zero crossing of Laplacian and the Canny algorithm demand that a color image should be converted to a grayscale image. However, after this conversion some edges in the color image disappear. This occurs if two adjacent areas have different colors but the same lightness.

The binarized gradient can detect true color edges between two areas with the same lightness but different colors. For this purpose one needs the sigma filter and the extreme filter suitable for color images. The sigma filter for color images was described in Chapter 2. The extreme filter for color images has a special feature: Instead of finding the maximum and the minimum of the gray values in the small gliding window, it must find two colors with the maximum difference. Difference between two colors is the sum of the squares of differences of the color channels red, green, and blue. The central pixel in the output image obtains that of the two most different colors that has the smaller difference from the color of the central pixel of the input image.

Our edge detector uses, as described previously, the `ColorDifSign` method calculating the color difference between two adjacent pixels $P_1(Red_1, Green_1, Blue_1)$ and $P_2(Red_2, Green_2, Blue_2)$ as the sum of the absolute differences of the color channels provided with the sign of the difference of lightness:

$$ColorDifSign =$$

$$signof(light_2 - light1)*(|Red_2 - Red_1|+|Green_2 - Green_1| + |Blue_2 - Blue_1|).$$

The edge lies between two pixels if their color difference is positive and is greater than a predefined threshold or it is negative and is less than (-threshold). The advantage of our method can be seen on edges between two areas with different colors and equal intensities, as on edges in Figure 7-11 between the red flower and a green leaf having almost the same lightness. Note the locations indicated by the arrows. As you can see, many edges are missing in Figure 7-11d.

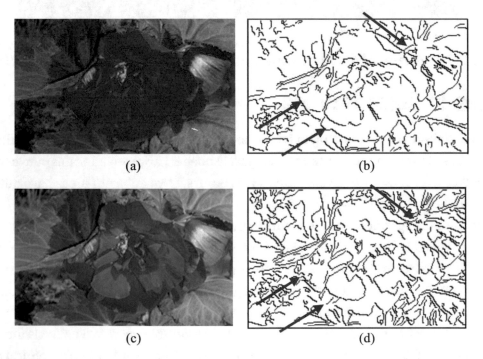

(a)　　　　　　　(b)

(c)　　　　　　　(d)

Figure 7-11. *(a) Original image; (b) edges of the color image; (c) original converted to gray values; (d) edges of the grayscale image*

Conclusions

Our edge detector (improved binarized gradient) provides better results than the well-known Canny algorithm. Our method also detects edges in color images with more precision than methods using differences of gray values.

CHAPTER 8

A New Method of Image Compression

We suggest a new method of image compression based on edge detection. The idea is based on the supposition that important information in an image is located in pixels lying near the edges. All other pixels contain only a homogeneous distribution of colors that can by reconstructed by solving numerically a partial differential equation with the methods of finite differences. We use here edge detection with the method described in the previous chapter. We represent edges as an ACC, described in Chapter 7. This representation has advantages because an element of the edge is defined by the difference of colors of two adjacent pixels. Thus an element of the edge belongs to neither of these two pixels, but rather to a space element lying between these pixels. Such a space element does not exist in a digital image; however, it exists in an ACC. This is the one-dimensional cell called the crack, whereas pixels are two-dimensional cells. The ends of a crack are zero-dimensional cells called points. When considering pixels as small squares, cracks are the sides of these squares; points are their corners and the end points of the cracks.

The edges make up a network of thin lines that are sequences of cracks and points where each line segment is either a closed curve or a sequence starting and ending either at an end point or at a branching point where three or four line segments meet (Figure 8-1).

© Vladimir Kovalevsky 2019
V. Kovalevsky, *Modern Algorithms for Image Processing*, https://doi.org/10.1007/978-1-4842-4237-7_8

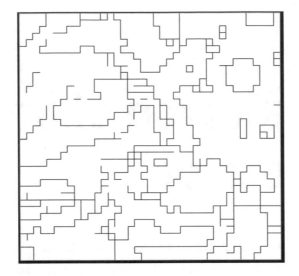

Figure 8-1. *Example of edges*

This structure can be described with the so-called cell list. The idea of a cell list is based on the representation of an image as an ACC (refer to Kovalevsky (1989, 2008)).

Using a Cell Complex for the Encoding of Boundaries

Considering a digital image as an ACC brings advantages by encoding boundaries of subsets: A boundary represented as a sequence of cracks and points becomes a thin curve with a zero area; the boundary of a region and that of its complement are the same. The definition and the processing of digital curves and especially that of digital straight lines becomes simpler and clearer. The most important advantage from the point of view of economical encoding and exact reconstruction of images is the ability to fill the interior of crack boundaries using an extremely simple and fast algorithm that cannot be applied when representing boundaries as sets of pixels.

A short summary of the topological notions important for this presentation was presented in Chapter 7. Please refer to Kovalevsky (2008) for more details and topological foundations.

We often need Euclidean coordinates to discuss problems of digitizing analog images. To remain in the frame of cell complexes we suggest considering Euclidean coordinates as rational numbers with a relatively large denominator. This corresponds to any computer model because the floating point variables in computers are rational numbers with large denominators. For encoding the edges in a cell complex we use an image of the size (2*width + 1)*(2*height + 1), where width*height is the size of the original image. We call this image an image in combinatorial coordinates or CombIm because the numbers of columns and of rows in this image considered as coordinates specify the positions of cells of all dimensions (zero, one, and two). It is more convenient to find cells of different dimensions and to trace edges in this image than in a usual image containing only pixels. Both coordinates of a pixel in combinatorial coordinates are odd; a crack has one odd and one even coordinate; and a point has both even coordinates. Compare Figure 8-2.

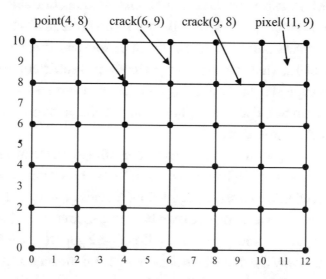

Figure 8-2. *Combinatorial coordinates of cells of dimensions zero, one and two*

An edge consists of sequences of cracks and points. An edge contains no pixels. A crack of the edge lies between two pixels of different colors. The colors of both pixels incident to the crack of an edge have a difference greater than a predefined threshold.

The set of edges of an image consists of lines, which are connected sequences of cracks and points. A line can be closed; in that case it contains no end points and no branch points. Each point of a closed line is incident to two cracks. A nonclosed line starts and ends at a point that is incident to one, three, or four, but not two cracks. Each of the interior points of a line is incident to exactly two cracks (Figure 8-3).

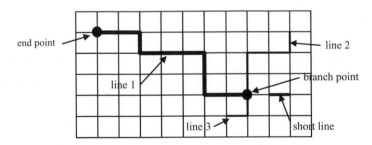

Figure 8-3. *Examples of a line (bold segments), a branch point, and a short line*

To completely describe the edge of an image one needs only a list of lines. To reconstruct an image it is sufficient to know the colors of pixels incident to the cracks of each line. However, these colors are almost constant along one side of a line. If there were great changes of colors in the set of pixels lying at one side of a line, then there would also be edge cracks perpendicular to the line; however, there are no such cracks. Because the colors at one side of a line change slowly, it is sufficient to save for each side of a line colors in one pixel at the beginning and one at the end of a line. All other colors at one side of a line can be calculated by means of an interpolation between these colors at the beginning and at the end of a line.

To perform this interpolation one needs to know the exact location of all elements of the line, which can be specified by the coordinates of the starting point and by the sequence of the directions of all cracks of the line. A crack of an oriented line (i.e., it is specified which point is the starting one) can have one of four directions: Direction 0 goes to the right, direction 1 goes downward, direction 2 goes to the left, and direction 3 goes upward. In this way the edge lines of an image and the adjacent colors can be encoded very sparingly. Also colors at the borders of the image are necessary for the reconstruction. It is enough to know only the colors at the four edges of a rectangular image. All other colors at the borders can be calculated by an interpolation. Colors at the cracks of the edge crossing the sequence of border pixels can also be regarded during this interpolation.

After interpolating the colors at the sides of lines and those at the borders, there remains a large set of pixels lying in the areas between the lines that remain empty after all the interpolations. The colors in these pixels can be approximately calculated by linear interpolation along the rows and along the columns of the image. This interpolation must start at a color at the border or at a line and can be continued along a row until an already present color appears. A similar interpolation can be done along the columns. Then each pixel obtains two colors: one from the interpolation along the rows and another from the interpolation along the columns. These two colors are averaged. After these interpolations, the distribution of colors is not quite homogeneous. It can be made more homogeneous by smoothing by means of a digital solution of the Laplacian partial differential equation. The reconstructed image looks very similar to the original one after this kind of smoothing.

Description of the Project `WFcompressPal`

The form of the running project is shown in Figure 8-4.

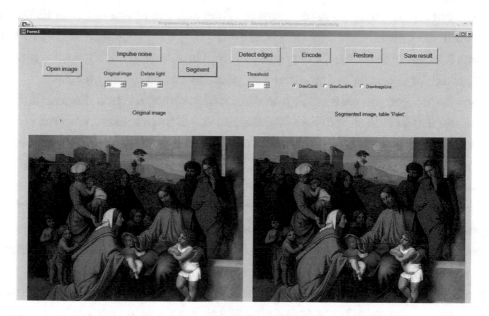

Figure 8-4. *The form of the running project `WFcompressPal`*

When the user clicks Open image, he or she can choose an image that will be opened as the original image `OrigBmp` and displayed in the left picture box. Eight working images are defined in this block of the project. The `OrigBmp` must be transformed to the working image `OrigIm`. The software `WindowsForms` suggests the access to the pixels of a bitmap by the method `GetPixels`, which is rather slow. We have developed a faster method, `BitmapToImage`, which uses the method `LockBits` of the class `Bitmap` for color images. However, if the original image is an image with 8 bits per pixel, it means that the opened image is an indexed one. The method `LockBits` should not be used for indexed bitmaps with 8 bits per pixel because these bitmaps contain a color palette and the values of the pixels are always defined by the values of the palette. Therefore the `LockBits` method is too slow for 8-bit indexed bitmaps. For such bitmaps we use the standard method `GetPixel`. All working images besides `EdgeIm` and `MaskIm` will be defined as 24-bit images. The images `EdgeIm` and `MaskIm` are always 8-bit images.

Now the user can decide whether to suppress the impulse noise. This procedure is also useful when the original image contains no impulse noise because removing small spots with lightness that differs from the lightness of surrounding pixels makes the image more homogeneous and the quality of the image for human perception remains unchanged. Making the image more homogeneous increases the compression rate.

If the user decides to use the suppression of impulse noise, he or she can change the maximum size of the spots to be removed while and the values of the tools with the labels Delete dark and Delete light. It is possible to skip this procedure simply by setting the values for Delete dark and Delete light to zero. The user can click Impulse noise. The methods used for suppressing impulse noise were described in Chapter 2.

Now it is necessary to perform segmentation of the image. When the user clicks Segment, the image with suppressed impulse noise will be processed with the sigma filter suppressing the Gaussian noise (Chapter 2) and with the extreme value filter increasing the color difference between adjacent pixels (Chapter 6). The result of processing with the extreme value filter is saved in the image `ExtremIm`. Then in the case of a color image a color palette `Palet` of 256 colors representing the colors of the processed image will be calculated and an indexed image `Pal` with this palette is created. The image `SegmentIm` is a true color image obtained by converting the indexed image `Pal` to a true color image. It is shown in the right picture box.

The calculation of the palette is performed with the method `MakePalette`. This method creates an array `Palette` containing 256 colors provided with color numbers, called `indices`. The colors of `Palette` approximately represent all colors appearing in the original image.

The method `MakePalette` first specifies a three-dimensional cube in the space with coordinate axes that correspond to the color channels RED, GREEN, and BLUE. The cube has the sizes

$$[Min[c], Max[c]], c = 0, 1, 2$$

where `Min[c]` is the minimum value of the color channel c appearing in the image and `Max[c]` is the maximum value. Thus this three-dimensional cube of colors contains all colors appearing in the image. The cube of colors is subdivided into $10 \times 10 \times 10 = 1,000$ small cubes. The position of a small cube in the color cube is specified by three coordinates iComp[c], c = 0, 1, 2. Each of the numbers iComp[c] can take values from 0 to 9. The three numbers iComp[c], c = 0, 1, 2 are calculated for each pixel of the image by dividing three values of the channels (RED, GREEN, and BLUE) of the pixel's color by values Div[c] depending on the predefined values MaxComp[3]={9, 9, 9}. The three numbers iComp[c] specify the value index, which can have a value between 0 and 999. The index specifies the position of the small cube to which the color of the pixel belongs. The index has the value:

$$index = \sum_{c=0}^{2} iComp[c]\,"Weight[c];$$

and the values Weight[c] depending on MaxComp are calculated in the method MakePalette. The method MakePalette calculates for each small cube the number of pixels of the original image with color that lies in the small cube.

The number of nonempty small cubes specifies the number of colors in the palette. We want this number to fall between 200 and 255. If it is below 200 then the value of MaxComp[1] (for the green color channel) is increased. Therefore the number of small cubes is increased and with it also the number of active palette elements. If the mentioned number falls over the maximum of 255 (we reserve one value of the palette for the index 0 as being (0, 0, 0)), then MaxComp[1] is decreased. Thus the number of active small cubes obtains a value between 200 and 255. In the case of small images this control process does not work. It is interrupted when MaxComp[1] is greater than 20 and the number of active palette elements in this case can lie outside of the desired interval.

The method MakePalette calculates for each nonempty small cube the average value of all colors belonging to this cube. Also the standard deviation of colors (this part of the code is omitted in the following text version) is calculated. The standard deviation is of interest only to give an idea of how exactly the calculated palette represents the colors of the original image.

The mean values are used as the values of the palette. The nonempty small cubes are counted and the value of the count is the number of new indexes of the colors (or color numbers) used in the palette. The palette is saved as an array. MakePalette creates a palette image Pal. The color indexes are copied from the image Pal into the pixels of the image Comb. Here is the source code of MakePalette.

```
public int MakePalette(CImage Img, int[] Palet, Form1 fm1)
// Produces a palette of 256 elements optimally representing colors of the
image "Img"
{
  bool deb = false;
  int MaxN = 1000, ResIndex = 10000;
  int[] Sum = new int[3 * MaxN];
  int[] nPix = new int[MaxN]; // "nPix[Index]" is number of pixels with index
  double[] Mean = new double[3 * MaxN];
  int[] SumO = new int[3 * ResIndex];
  int[] nPixO = new int[ResIndex];
  int c, i, jump, nIndex, n, MaxIndex;
  int[] iChan = new int[3], Div = new int[3], Weight = new int[3];
  int[] NumbInterv = { 11, 12, 9 };

  // Computing minimum and maximum of the color channels:
  int[] Min = { 256, 256, 256 }, Max = { 0, 0, 0 };
  fm1.progressBar1.Visible = true;
  fm1.progressBar1.Step = 1;
  if (Img.width * Img.height > 300) jump = Img.width * Img.height / 20;
  else jump = 3;
  for (i = 0; i < Img.width * Img.height; i++) //========================
  {
    if (i % jump == jump - 1) fm1.progressBar1.PerformStep();
    for (c = 0; c < 3; c++)
    {
      if (Img.Grid[3 * i + c] < Min[c]) Min[c] = Img.Grid[3 * i + c];
      if (Img.Grid[3 * i + c] > Max[c]) Max[c] = Img.Grid[3 * i + c];
    }
  } //============================== end for (i... =============

  int nIndexMin = 228, nIndexMax = 255;
  nIndex = 0;
  // Changing NumbInterv[] to get nIndex between nIndexMin and nIndexMax:
  do //====================================================
  {
```

```
Weight[0] = 1;
Weight[1] = NumbInterv[0] + 1;
Weight[2] = NumbInterv[0] + Weight[1] * NumbInterv[1] + 1;
for (i = 0; i < ResIndex; i++) SumO[i] = 0;
for (i = 0; i < 3 * MaxN; i++) //==================
{
  Sum[i] = 0;
  Mean[i] = 0.0;
  nPix[i / 3] = 0;
} //================== end for (i ... ===========
for (c = 0; c < 3; c++)
{
  Div[c] = (int)(0.5 + (double)(Max[c] - Min[c]) / (double)
  NumbInterv[c]);
  if (Div[c] == 0) Div[c] = 1;
  if ((Max[c] - Min[c]) / Div[c] > NumbInterv[c]) NumbInterv[c]++;
}
MaxIndex = Weight[0] * NumbInterv[0] + Weight[1] * NumbInterv[1] +
                                      Weight[2] * NumbInterv[2];

int maxIndex = 0;
if (MaxIndex >= ResIndex)
{ MessageBox.Show("MakePalette, Overflow: MaxIndex=" +
  MaxIndex + " > ResIndex=" + ResIndex + "; return -1.");
  return -1;
}
for (i = 0; i < ResIndex; i++) nPixO[i] = 0;
int Index = 0;
for (i = 0; i < Img.width * Img.height; i++) //========================
{
  Index = 0;
  for (c = 0; c < 3; c++)
  {
    iChan[c] = (Img.Grid[3 * i + c] - Min[c]) / Div[c];
    Index += Weight[c] * iChan[c];
  }
```

```
  if (Index > maxIndex) maxIndex = Index;

  if (Index > ResIndex - 1)
  {
    MessageBox.Show("MP, Overflow: Index=" + Index + " too great;
    return -1.");
    return -1;
  }
  for (c = 0; c < 3; c++) Sum0[3 * Index + c] += Img.Grid[3 * i + c];
  nPix0[Index]++;
} //================ end for (i = 0; ... ============================
nIndex = 0;
for (i = 0; i <= MaxIndex; i++) if (nPix0[i] > 0) nIndex++;
int minInd = 0, maxInd = 0;
if (nIndex < nIndexMin)
{
  if (NumbInterv[0] <= NumbInterv[1] && NumbInterv[0] <= NumbInterv[2])
            minInd = 0;
  else
    if (NumbInterv[1] <= NumbInterv[0] && NumbInterv[1] <= NumbInterv[2])
        minInd = 1;
    else
      if (NumbInterv[2] <= NumbInterv[0] && NumbInterv[2] <= NumbInterv[1])
        minInd = 2;
  NumbInterv[minInd]++;
}
if (nIndex > nIndexMax)
{
  if (NumbInterv[0] >= NumbInterv[1] && NumbInterv[0] >= NumbInterv[2])
                maxInd = 0;
  else
    if (NumbInterv[1] >= NumbInterv[0] && NumbInterv[1] >= NumbInterv[2])
            maxInd = 1;
    else
      if (NumbInterv[2] >= NumbInterv[0] && NumbInterv[2] >= NumbInterv[1])
            maxInd = 2;
```

```
      NumbInterv[maxInd]--;
   }
   if (nIndex >= nIndexMin && nIndex <= nIndexMax || NumbInterv[1] > 20)
   {
     if (deb)
     MessageBox.Show("MakePalette: nIndex=" + nIndex + " is OK. break.");
     break;
   }
} while (nIndex > nIndexMax || nIndex < nIndexMin); //====================

int[] NewIndex = new int[MaxIndex];
if (MaxIndex > 300) jump = MaxIndex / 20;
else jump = 3;
for (i = n = 0; i < MaxIndex; i++) //=====================================
{
   if (i % jump == jump - 1) fm1.progressBar1.PerformStep();
   if (nPix0[i] > 0) //----------------------------------------------------
   {
     n++;
     if (n > MaxN - 1)
     {
       MessageBox.Show("MP: Overflow in Sum; n=" + n + "< MaxN=" + MaxN);.
       return -1;
     }
     NewIndex[i] = n;
     nPix[n] = nPix0[i];
     for (c = 0; c < 3; c++)
     {
       Sum[3 * n + c] = Sum0[3 * i + c];
       if (nPix[n] > 0) Mean[3 * n + c] = (double)(Sum[3 * n + c]) /
       (double)(nPix[n]);
       else Mean[3 * n + c] = 0;
     }
   } //----------------------- end if (nPix0... ----------------------
} //===================== end for (i... =========================
int MaxNewIndex = n;
```

```
if (Img.width * Img.height > 300) jump = Img.width * Img.height / 20;
else jump = 3;
// Putting NewIndex into "this.Grid":
for (i = 0; i < Img.width * Img.height; i++) //===========================
{
  if (i % jump == jump - 1) fm1.progressBar1.PerformStep();
  int Index = 0;
  for (c = 0; c < 3; c++)
  {
    iChan[c] = (Img.Grid[3 * i + c] - Min[c]) / Div[c];
    Index += Weight[c] * iChan[c];
  }
  if (Index >= MaxIndex) Index = MaxIndex - 1;
  Grid[i] = (byte)NewIndex[Index];
  if (Grid[i] == 0) Grid[i] = (byte)MaxNewIndex;
} //=============== end for (i=0; ... ===============================

// Calculating "Palet" and "this.Palette":
byte R = 0, G = 0, B = 0;
jump = MaxNewIndex / 20;
for (n = 0; n <= MaxNewIndex; n++)
{
  if (n % jump == jump -1) fm1.progressBar1.PerformStep();
  if (n > 0)
  {
    if (Mean[3 * n + 2] < 255.0) R = (byte)Mean[3 * n + 2];
    if (Mean[3 * n + 1] < 255.0) G = (byte)Mean[3 * n + 1];
    if (Mean[3 * n + 0] < 255.0) B = (byte)Mean[3 * n + 0];
    Palet[n] = RGB(R, G, B);
  }
  else
  {
    Palet[n] = 0;
  }

}
```

```
return 1;
} //****************** end MakePalette ******************************
```

Now the edge detection can be performed. The user can choose the threshold for the edge detection, which specifies the value of the minimum difference between the colors of two adjacent pixels at which the crack between these pixels will be labeled as belonging to the edge. The user can either tip a new value into the small window of the tool `numericUpDown` under the label Threshold or click one of two small arrows at the right side of this setting to increase or decrease the value. The user should consider that under a higher threshold a smaller amount of edge elements will be produced. This leads to a higher compression rate, but also to lower quality of the restored image.

The part of the project designed to detect edges defines the one byte per pixel image `CombIm` with combinatorial coordinates (see Chapter 7) and a greater size (2*width + 1)*(2*height + 1). This is necessary because the representation of cracks and points in an image of standard size is difficult. The image `CombIm` will contain the cell complex representing the detected edges. The description of the cell complex can be found in Chapter 7. The method `LabelCellsSign` tests each pair of adjacent pixels of the image `ExtremIm`. If the color difference of the pixels is greater than the threshold, the crack between these pixels is labeled with 1. This means that the element of the image `CombIm` corresponding to this crack obtains the value 1. Simultaneously the labels of the end points of the crack will be increased and thus obtain a label equal to the number of cracks incident with this point. Examples of labels of points are shown in Figure 8-5.

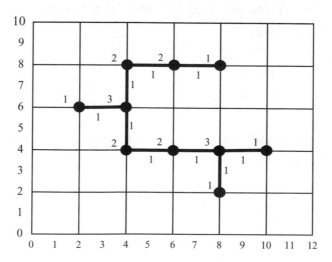

Figure 8-5. *Labels of cells of dimensions zero and one*

As already mentioned, the palette indexes are copied from the image Pal produced by MakePalette into the pixels of the image Comb. In the case of a grayscale image, gray values are copied from Image3, which was processed by the ExtremVar method.

Now the part Encode can be started. When the user clicks Encode, the method SearchLin is started using the image CombIm as its parameter. This method looks at all points of CombIm and calls the method ComponLin for each point labeled with 1, 3, or 4 in the least valuable bits of the corresponding byte. These are either end points of the edge lines or branch points. All lines of a connected component are traced and encoded by the method ComponLin called by SearchLin. The labels of all points encountered during the tracing are deleted.

After SearchLin has processed all points with labels 1, 3, or 4, it looks for points with nondeleted label 2. These points belong to a component that has no end and no branch points. Such a component is a closed curve.

Here is the code for SearchLin.

```
public int SearchLin(ref CImage Comb, Form1 fm1)
{ int Lab, rv, x, y;
  for (x=0; x<MaxByte; x++) Byte[x]=0;
  if (Step[0].Y < 0)  x = Step[0].Y;
  fm1.progressBar1.Value = 0;
  int y1 = Comb.nLoop * CNY / Comb.denomProg;
  for (y=0; y<CNY; y+=2)
  {
    if ((y % y1) == 0) fm1.progressBar1.PerformStep();
    for (x=0; x<CNX; x+=2)
    { Lab=Comb.Grid[x+CNX*y] & 3;
      if (Lab==1 || Lab==3)
      { rv=ComponLin(Comb.Grid, x, y);
        if (rv<0)
        { MessageBox.Show("SearchLin, Alarm! ComponLin returned " + rv);
          return -1;
        }
      }
    }
  }
}
```

```
// Starting the search for loops:
for (y=0; y<CNY; y+=2)
for (x=0; x<CNX; x+=2)
{ Lab=Comb.Grid[x+CNX*y] & 3;
  if (Lab==2)
  { rv=ComponLin(Comb.Grid, x, y);
    if (rv<0)
    { MessageBox.Show("SearchLin, Alarm! ComponLin returned " + rv);
      return -1;
    }
  }
}
nByte++;
return nByte;
} //******************** end SearchLin ******************************
```

The method ComponLin traces and encodes each whole component; that is, a connected part of the edge. This method is designed to trace a connected graph, as a connected component of the edge is a connected graph with vertices that are the points and with edges that are the lines. As is well known, traversing or searching a tree or a graph data structure can be done by the breadth-first algorithm using a first-in-first-out data structure called *queue*.

ComponLin puts the starting point of a component into the queue. When getting a point from the queue, it tests all four cracks incident to this point. If one of these cracks ends at an end point or at a branch point, then it is considered a short line consisting of a single crack. It will be immediately encoded in the data structure CListLines of which ComponLin is a method.

If a crack ends at a point with label 2 then the method TraceLin is started. This method traces a long line, saves the color indexes or the gray values at the sides of the line, and saves the directions of all cracks of the line. When TraceLin returns and the processed image is a color one, then the method FraqInds is started, which calculates the most frequent indexes in two halves of the line and assigns them to the stored code of the line. In the case of a grayscale image AverageGrays is started, which calculates the average gray values in the two halves of the line. The average gray values are then assigned to the code of the line.

Here is the code for the methods TraceLin and ComponLin:

```
public int TraceLin(byte[] CGrid, int X, int Y, ref iVect2 Pterm, ref int
dir)
/* This method traces a line in the image "Comb" with combinatorial
coordinates, where the cracks and points of the edges are labeled: bits 0,
1 and 2 of a point contain the label 1 to 4 of the point. The label indicates
the number of incident edge cracks. Labeled bit 6 indicates that the point
already has been put into the queue; labeled bit 7 indicates that the point
should not be used any more. The crack has only one label 1 in bit 0. This
method traces the edge from one end or branch point to another while changing
the parameter "dir". ----------*/
{ bool atSt_P=false, BP=false, END=false;
    int rv = 0;
    iVect2  Crack, P=new iVect2(0,0), PixelP, PixelN, StartPO;
    int iShift=-1, iCrack=0, Lab;
    P.X=X; P.Y=Y;
    StartPO=P;
    if (nLine2==0) nByte=0;
    else nByte=Line2[nLine2-1].EndByte+1;

    int[] Shift={0,2,4,6};
    while(true) //=================================================
    { Crack=P+Step[dir];
       P=Crack+Step[dir];
       Lab=CGrid[P.X+CNX*P.Y]&3;
       switch(Lab)
       { case 1: END=true; BP=false; rv=1; break;
          case 2: BP=END=false; break;
          case 3: BP=true; END=false; rv=3; break;
       }
       PixelP=Crack+Norm[dir];
       PixelN=Crack-Norm[dir];
       IndPos[iCrack]=CGrid[PixelP.X+CNX*PixelP.Y];
       IndNeg[iCrack]=CGrid[PixelN.X+CNX*PixelN.Y];
```

```
    if (Lab==2) CGrid[P.X+CNX*P.Y]=0;
    iShift++;
    iCrack++;
    if (iShift==4)
    { iShift=0;
        if (nByte<MaxByte-1) nByte++;
      else
        { return -1;
        }
    }
  Byte[nByte] |= (byte)(dir << Shift[iShift]);

  if (P.X == StartP0.X && P.Y == StartP0.Y) atSt_P = true;
  else atSt_P = false;
    if (atSt_P)
    { Pterm=P;
        rv=2;
        break;
    }

  if (!BP && !END) //-------------------------------------------
    { Crack=P+Step[(dir+1)%4];
        if (CGrid[Crack.X+CNX*Crack.Y]==1)
        {   dir=(dir+1)%4;
        }
        else
        {   Crack=P+Step[(dir+3)%4];
          if (CGrid[Crack.X+CNX*Crack.Y]==1)
          { dir=(dir+3)%4;
          }
        }
    }
    else
    { Pterm=P;
        break;
    } //----------------- end if (!BP && !END) --------------------
} //=========== end while =====================================
```

```
    Line2[nLine2].EndByte=nByte;
    Line2[nLine2].nCrack=(ushort)iCrack;

    return rv;
} //************** end TraceLin ***************************************

public int ComponLin(byte[] CGrid, int X, int Y)
/* Encodes in "CListLines" the lines of the edge component with the point
(X, Y) being a branch or an end point. Puts the starting point 'Pinp' into
the queue and starts the 'while' loop. It tests each labeled crack incident
with the point 'P' fetched from the queue. If the next point of the crack
is a branch or an end point, then a short line is saved. Otherwise the
method "TraceLin" is called. "TraceLin" traces a long line, saves the color
indices at the sides of the line and ends at the point 'Pterm' with the
direction 'DirT'. Then the method "FreqInds" assigns the most frequent
from the saved color indices to the line. If the point 'Pterm' is a branch
point then it is put to the queue. "ComponLin" returns when the queue is
empty.    ---------------*/
{ int dir, dirT;
   int   LabNext, rv;
   iVect2 Crack, P, Pinp, PixelN, PixelP, Pnext, Pterm=new iVect2(0, 0);
   Pinp=new iVect2(X,Y); // comb. coord.

   pQ.Put(Pinp);
   while(pQ.Empty()==false) //======================================
   { P=pQ.Get();
      for (dir=0; dir<4; dir++) //===================================
      {   Crack=P+Step[dir];
         if (Crack.X<0 || Crack.X>CNX-1 || Crack.Y<0 || Crack.Y>CNY-1 )
         continue;
         if (CGrid[Crack.X+CNX*Crack.Y]==1) //--------------------------
         { PixelP=Crack+Norm[dir]; PixelN=Crack-Norm[dir];
            Pnext=Crack+Step[dir];
            LabNext=CGrid[Pnext.X+CNX*Pnext.Y] & 3; //Ind0
            if (LabNext==1 || LabNext==3)
            {
```

```
    Line1[nLine1].x = (ushort)(P.X / 2); Line1[nLine1].y =
    (ushort)(P.Y / 2);
     Line1[nLine1].Ind0=CGrid[PixelN.X+CNX*PixelN.Y];
     Line1[nLine1].Ind1=CGrid[PixelP.X+CNX*PixelP.Y];
     if (nLine1>MaxLine1-1)
    {
      MessageBox.Show("ComponLin: Overflow in Line1; return -1");
      return -1;
    }
}
if (LabNext==3) pQ.Put(Pnext);
if (LabNext==2) //-----------------------------------------------
{ Line2[nLine2].x=(ushort)(P.X/2);
   Line2[nLine2].y=(ushort)(P.Y/2); //transf. to standard
   coordinates
   dirT=dir;
   rv=TraceLin(CGrid, P.X, P.Y, ref Pterm, ref dirT);
   if (nBits3==24) FreqInds(nLine2);
   else AverageGray(nLine2);
   if (rv<0)
   {
       return -1;
   }
   if (nLine2>MaxLine2-1)
   { return -1;
   }
   else    nLine2++;
   if ((CGrid[Pterm.X+CNX*Pterm.Y] & 64)==0) // '64'= label for
   visited;
   {
       if (rv==3) //--------------------------------------------
       { CGrid[Pterm.X+CNX*Pterm.Y] |=64;
          pQ.Put(Pterm);
       }
   } //-------- end if  ((CGrid[Pterm.X... ---------------------
```

```
        } // ---------- end if (LabNest==2) ---------------------------
        if ((CGrid[P.X+CNX*P.Y]&3)==1) break;
      } //-------------- end if (CGrid[Crack.X ...==1) ----------------
    } //========== end for (dir ... ===================================
    CGrid[P.X+CNX*P.Y]=0;
  } //============ end while =========================================
  return 1;
} //************** end ComponLin ************************************
```

When SearchLin returns and the codes of all lines are saved in the object List of the class CListLines, an object LiCod of the class CListCode is created. This class is a short version of the class CListLines. It contains only the information necessary to reconstruct the image. The method Transform copies the necessary information from List to LiCod and transforms the data into a sequence of bytes contained in the array ByteNew. This transformation is necessary to avoid using the method Serialize for saving the code on the disk because Serialize produces a disk file sometimes ten times longer than the file produced by the system method Write. The method Serialize can thus destroy the compression, and therefore we do not use it.

The following is the code for Transform.

```
public int Transform(int nx, int ny, int nbits, int[] Palet, CImage Comb,
CListLines L, Form1 fm1)
// Transforms the provisional list "L" to an object of the class
"CListCode".
{ int i, ib, il, nCode=0;
  width=nx; height=ny; nBits=nbits;
  nCode+=3*4;
  nLine1=L.nLine1; nLine2=L.nLine2; nByte=L.nByte;
  nCode+=3*4;
  nCodeAfterLine2 = nCode;
  Palette=new int[256];
  for ( i=0; i<256; i++) Palette[i]=Palet[i]; nCode+=256*4;
  Corner[0]=Comb.Grid[1+(2*width+1)*1]; // this is a gray value or a
  palette index
  Corner[1]=Comb.Grid[2*width-1+(2*width+1)*1];
  Corner[2]=Comb.Grid[2*width-1+(2*width+1)*(2*height-1)];
```

```
Corner[3]=Comb.Grid[1+(2*width+1)*(2*height-1)];
nCode+=4;
int il1=Comb.nLoop*nLine1/Comb.denomProg;

for (il = 0; il < nLine1; il++)
{
  Line1[il] = L.Line1[il];
  if (((il + 1) % il1) == 0) fm1.progressBar1.PerformStep();
}

nCode += nLine1*6; // "6" is the sizeof(CCrack);

int il2 = Comb.nLoop * nLine2 / Comb.denomProg;

for (il = 0; il < nLine2; il++)
{ Line2[il]=L.Line2[il];
  if (((il + 1) % il2) == 0) fm1.progressBar1.PerformStep();
}
nCode += nLine2 * 14; // sizeof(CLine);

int il3 = Comb.nLoop * nByte / Comb.denomProg;
for (ib = 0; ib < nByte; ib++)
{ Byte[ib]=L.Byte[ib];
  if (((ib + 1) % il3) == 0) fm1.progressBar1.PerformStep();
}
nCode += nByte;

// The following code is necessary to avoid "Serialize":
ByteNew = new byte[nCode+4];
for (int ik = 0; ik < nCode + 4; ik++) ByteNew[ik] = 0;
int j = 0;
ByteNew[j] = (byte)(nCode & 255); j++;
ByteNew[j] = (byte)((nCode >> 8) & 255); j++;
ByteNew[j] = (byte)((nCode >> 16) & 255); j++;
ByteNew[j] = (byte)((nCode >> 24) & 255); j++;

ByteNew[j] = (byte)(nx & 255); j++;
ByteNew[j] = (byte)((nx >> 8) & 255); j++;
ByteNew[j] = (byte)((nx >> 16) & 255); j++;
ByteNew[j] = (byte)((nx >> 24) & 255); j++;
```

```
ByteNew[j] = (byte)(ny & 255); j++;
ByteNew[j] = (byte)((ny >> 8) & 255); j++;
ByteNew[j] = (byte)((ny >> 16) & 255); j++;
ByteNew[j] = (byte)((ny >> 24) & 255); j++;

ByteNew[j] = (byte)(nbits & 255); j++;
ByteNew[j] = (byte)((nbits >> 8) & 255); j++;
ByteNew[j] = (byte)((nbits >> 16) & 255); j++;
ByteNew[j] = (byte)((nbits >> 24) & 255); j++;

ByteNew[j] = (byte)(nLine1 & 255); j++;
ByteNew[j] = (byte)((nLine1 >> 8) & 255); j++;
ByteNew[j] = (byte)((nLine1 >> 16) & 255); j++;
ByteNew[j] = (byte)((nLine1 >> 24) & 255); j++;

ByteNew[j] = (byte)(nLine2 & 255); j++;
ByteNew[j] = (byte)((nLine2 >> 8) & 255); j++;
ByteNew[j] = (byte)((nLine2 >> 16) & 255); j++;
ByteNew[j] = (byte)((nLine2 >> 24) & 255); j++;

ByteNew[j] = (byte)(nByte & 255); j++;
ByteNew[j] = (byte)((nByte >> 8) & 255); j++;
ByteNew[j] = (byte)((nByte >> 16) & 255); j++;
ByteNew[j] = (byte)((nByte >> 24) & 255); j++;

for (int ii = 0; ii < 256; ii++)
{
  ByteNew[j] = (byte)(Palet[ii] & 255); j++;
  ByteNew[j] = (byte)((Palet[ii] >> 8) & 255); j++;
  ByteNew[j] = (byte)((Palet[ii] >> 16) & 255); j++;
  ByteNew[j] = (byte)((Palet[ii] >> 24) & 255); j++;
}

for (int i1 = 0; i1 < 4; i1++) ByteNew[j+i1] = Corner[i1];
j+=4;

for (int i2 = 0; i2 < nLine1; i2++)
```

```
{
   ByteNew[j] = (byte)(L.Line1[i2].x & 255); j++;
   ByteNew[j] = (byte)((L.Line1[i2].x >> 8) & 255); j++;
   ByteNew[j] = (byte)(L.Line1[i2].y & 255); j++;
   ByteNew[j] = (byte)((L.Line1[i2].y >> 8) & 255); j++;
   ByteNew[j] = L.Line1[i2].Ind0; j++;
   ByteNew[j] = L.Line1[i2].Ind1; j++;
}

for (int i3 = 0; i3 < nLine2; i3++)
{
   ByteNew[j] = (byte)(L.Line2[i3].EndByte & 255); j++;
   ByteNew[j] = (byte)((L.Line2[i3].EndByte >> 8) & 255); j++;
   ByteNew[j] = (byte)((L.Line2[i3].EndByte >> 16) & 255); j++;
   ByteNew[j] = (byte)((L.Line2[i3].EndByte >> 248) & 255); j++;
   ByteNew[j] = (byte)(L.Line2[i3].x & 255); j++;
   ByteNew[j] = (byte)((L.Line2[i3].x >> 8) & 255); j++;
   ByteNew[j] = (byte)(L.Line2[i3].y & 255); j++;
   ByteNew[j] = (byte)((L.Line2[i3].y >> 8) & 255); j++;
   ByteNew[j] = (byte)(L.Line2[i3].nCrack & 255); j++;
   ByteNew[j] = (byte)((L.Line2[i3].nCrack >> 8) & 255); j++;
   ByteNew[j] = L.Line2[i3].Ind0; j++;
   ByteNew[j] = L.Line2[i3].Ind1; j++;
   ByteNew[j] = L.Line2[i3].Ind2; j++;
   ByteNew[j] = L.Line2[i3].Ind3; j++;
}

for (int i4 = 0; i4 < nByte; i4++) ByteNew[j + i4] = L.Byte[i4];
j += nByte;
return nCode;
} //************************ end Transform *****************************
```

When the method Transform returns, the message "Image encoded" is shown and the length of the code and the value of the compression rate are presented.

The project WFcompressPal also contains a part called by clicking Restore that is necessary to reconstruct the image from the code. This is required because the user must see whether the quality of the reconstructed image is sufficient. Otherwise the user can specify a lower threshold to obtain finer edges. This will naturally lead to a smaller compression rate. This part of the project is identical with the corresponding part of the project WFrestoreLin described in the next section.

Clicking Save code calls the method WriteCode, which writes the array ByteNew with the code into a file with the extension *.dat.

If the user does not click the buttons in the correct order, he or she gets a warning and an indication of the correct sequence.

The Project WFrestoreLin

This project serves to reconstruct the image from the saved code and to store the image on the disk. The project starts with reading a chosen file with the extension *.dat. The system method Read reads first the length of the code, which makes it possible to allocate the byte array ByteNew and then reads the code into the array ByteNew. The constructor of the class CListCode transforms the bytes of ByteNew into the object LiCod of the class CListCode. This object contains parameters of the image to be reconstructed; the lengths of the arrays Line1, Line2, and Byte; the palette; the palette indexes of the four corners of the image; and these arrays.

When the user clicks Restore, two images are defined with parameters contained in LiCod: RestoreIm to be reconstructed and MaskIm as an auxiliary image. All pixels of both images are set to zero. Then the method Restore reconstructs the image that is displayed in pictureBox1. This method is also used in the project WFcompressPal to reconstruct the encoded image so that the user can assess the quality of the reconstructed image.

The method Restore puts first the indexes or the colors of the corners of the image to corresponding pixels. If the image to be reconstructed is a color one, then Restore transforms the read indexes to colors by means of the palette.

The pixels of the image Mask corresponding to pixels of Image that obtain colors or gray levels are always set to LabMask=250. (This high value is chosen for the possibility to display the contents of Mask at debugging.)

Then Restore reads the array Line1 with codes of short lines and puts the colors or the gray values in the pixels on the sides of the single crack of the short line. A line is a short line if it consists of a single crack. All other lines are long lines. Restore then reads the array Line2 with the codes of long lines and puts colors or gray values in the pixels at the beginning and at the end of each long line. Restore next performs the interpolation of colors or gray values along the sides of long lines to complete its work.

Here is the code for Restore.

```
public int Restore(ref CImage Image, ref CImage Mask, Form1 fm1)
{ int dir, nbyte, x, y;
  byte LabMask=250;
  if (nBits==24) nbyte=3;
  else nbyte=1;

  fm1.progressBar1.Value = 0;
  fm1.progressBar1.Visible = true;
  int denomProg = fm1.progressBar1.Maximum / fm1.progressBar1.Step;
  int Sum = nLine1 + nLine2;
  int i1 = Sum / denomProg;
  for (int i = 0; i < width * height * (nBits / 8); i++) Image.Grid[i] = 0;

  for (int i=0; i<width*height; i++) Mask.Grid[i]=0;
  if (nBits==24)
  { for (int c=0; c<nbyte; c++)
    { Image.Grid[c]=(byte)((Palette[Corner[0]]>>8*(2-c)) & 0XFF); // left below
      Image.Grid[nbyte*(width-1)+c]=
                              (byte)((Palette[Corner[1]]>>8*(2-c)) &
                              0XFF); // right below
      Image.Grid[nbyte*width*height-nbyte+c]=
                                (byte)((Palette[Corner[2]]>>8*(2-c)) &
                                0XFF); // right on top
      Image.Grid[nbyte*width*(height-1)+c]=
                                (byte)((Palette[Corner[3]]>>8*(2-c)) &
                                0XFF); // left on top
    }
  }
  else
  { Image.Grid[0]=Corner[0];
    Image.Grid[width-1]=Corner[1];
    Image.Grid[width*height-1]=Corner[2];
    Image.Grid[0+width*(height-1)]=Corner[3];
  }
```

```
Mask.Grid[0]=Mask.Grid[width-1]=Mask.Grid[width*height-1]=
                                Mask.Grid[width*(height-1)]=LabMask;
// Short lines:
fm1.progressBar1.Value = 0;
for (int il = 0; il < nLine1; il++) //======================================
{
  if ((il % i1) == 0) fm1.progressBar1.PerformStep();
  dir=((Line1[il].x>>14) & 2) | (Line1[il].y>>15);
  x=Line1[il].x & 0X7FFF;       y=Line1[il].y & 0X7FFF;
  if (nBits==24)
  { switch(dir)
    { case 0:
      if (y > 0)
      {
        for (int c = 0; c < nbyte; c++)
        {
          int Index = Line1[il].Ind1;
          byte col = (byte)(Palette[Index] >> 8 * c);
          Image.Grid[nbyte * (x + width * y) + 2 - c] = col;
          Image.Grid[nbyte * (x + width * (y - 1)) + 2 - c] =
                                        (byte)((Palette[Line1[il].
                                        Ind0] >> 8 * c) & 0XFF);
        }
        Mask.Grid[x + width * y] = Mask.Grid[x + width * (y - 1)] =
        LabMask;
      }
      break;
      case 1:
       for (int c = 0; c < nbyte; c++)
       { Image.Grid[nbyte*(x+width*y)+2-c]=(byte)((Palette[Line1[il].
       Ind0]>>8*c) & 0XFF);
            Image.Grid[nbyte*(x-1+width*y)+2-c]=(byte)((Palette
            [Line1[il].Ind1]>>8*c) & 0XFF);
       }
       Mask.Grid[x+width*y]=Mask.Grid[x-1+width*y]=LabMask;
       break;
```

```
case 2:
for (int c = 0; c < nbyte; c++)
{ Image.Grid[nbyte*(x-1+width*y)+2-c]=(byte)((Palette[Line1[il].
Ind0]>>8*c) & 0XFF);
   Image.Grid[nbyte*(x-1+width*(y-1))+2-c]=(byte)((Palette[Line1[il].
   Ind1]>>8*c) & 0XFF);
 }
 Mask.Grid[x-1+width*y]=Mask.Grid[x-1+width*(y-1)]=LabMask;
 break;
case 3:
 for (int c = 0; c < nbyte; c++)
{ Image.Grid[nbyte*(x+width*(y-1))+2-c]=(byte)((Palette[Line1[il].
Ind1]>>8*c) & 0XFF);
   Image.Grid[nbyte*(x-1+width*(y-1))+2-c]=(byte)((Palette[Line1[il].
   Ind0]>>8*c) & 0XFF);
 }
 Mask.Grid[x+width*(y-1)]=Mask.Grid[x-1+width*(y-1)]=LabMask;
 break;
} //::::::::::::::::::::: end switch ::::::::::::::::::::::::::::::::::
}
else
{ switch(dir)
  {  case 0: Image.Grid[x+width*y]=Line1[il].Ind1;
           Image.Grid[x+width*(y-1)]=Line1[il].Ind0;
           Mask.Grid[x+width*y]=Mask.Grid[x+width*(y-1)]=LabMask;
           break;
     case 1: Image.Grid[x+width*y]=Line1[il].Ind0;
           Image.Grid[x-1+width*y]=Line1[il].Ind1;
           Mask.Grid[x+width*y]=Mask.Grid[x-1+width*y]=LabMask;
           break;
     case 2: Image.Grid[x-1+width*y]=Line1[il].Ind0;
           Image.Grid[x-1+width*(y-1)]=Line1[il].Ind1;
           Mask.Grid[x-1+width*y]=Mask.Grid[x-1+width*(y-1)]=LabMask;
           break;
```

```
          case 3: Image.Grid[x+width*(y-1)]=Line1[il].Ind1;
                  Image.Grid[x-1+width*(y-1)]=Line1[il].Ind0;
                  Mask.Grid[x+width*(y-1)]=Mask.Grid[x-1+width*(y-1)]=LabMask;
                  break;
      } //:::::::::::::::::::::::: end switch :::::::::::::::::::::::::::::::::::
      } //------------------ end if (nBits==24) --------------------------
  } //============ end for (il < nLine1 …============================
  int first, last;
  int[] Shift = new int[]{0,2,4,6};
  for (int il=0; il<nLine2; il++) //======================================
  {
    if ((il % i1) == 0) fm1.progressBar1.PerformStep();
    if (il==0) first=0;
    else first=Line2[il-1].EndByte+1;

    last=Line2[il].EndByte;
    x=Line2[il].x;
    y=Line2[il].y;
    int iByte=first, iShift=0;
    iVect2 P = new iVect2(), PixelP = new iVect2(), PixelN = new iVect2();
// comb. coordinates
    byte[] ColN = new byte[3], ColP = new byte[3];
    byte[] ColStartN = new byte[3], ColStartP = new byte[3],
                                    ColLastN = new byte[3], ColLastP =
                                    new byte[3]; // Colors
    for (int c=0; c<3; c++)
          ColN[c]=ColP[c]=ColStartN[c]=ColStartP[c]=ColLastN[c]=ColLastP
          [c]=0;

    if (nBits==24)
    { for (int c=0; c<nbyte; c++)
      { ColStartN[2-c]=(byte)((Palette[Line2[il].Ind0]>>8*c) & 255);
        ColStartP[2-c]=(byte)((Palette[Line2[il].Ind1]>>8*c) & 255);
        ColLastN[2-c]= (byte)((Palette[Line2[il].Ind2]>>8*c) & 255);
        ColLastP[2-c]= (byte)((Palette[Line2[il].Ind3]>>8*c) & 255);
      }
```

```
}
else
{ ColStartN[0]=Line2[il].Ind0;
  ColStartP[0]=Line2[il].Ind1;
  ColLastN[0]=Line2[il].Ind2;
  ColLastP[0]=Line2[il].Ind3;
}
P.X=Line2[il].x; P.Y=Line2[il].y;

int nCrack=Line2[il].nCrack;
int xx, yy;     // Interpolation:
for (int iC=0; iC<nCrack; iC++) //=====================================
{ dir=(Byte[iByte] & (3<<Shift[iShift]))>>Shift[iShift];
  switch(dir) // Standard coordinates
  { case 0: PixelP=P; PixelN=P+Step[3];  break;
    case 1: PixelP=P+Step[2]; PixelN=P;  break;
    case 2: PixelP=P+Step[2]+Step[3]; PixelN=P+Step[2];  break;
    case 3: PixelP=P+Step[3]; PixelN=P+Step[2]+Step[3]; break;
  }
  if (PixelP.Y<0 || PixelN.Y<0 || PixelP.Y>height-1 || PixelN.Y>height-1)
  { MessageBox.Show("Restore: Bad 'PixelP' or 'PixelN'. 'Byte' is bad.
  iByte=" +
    iByte + "; dir=" + dir + "; Byte=" + Byte[iByte]);
  }
  for (int c=0; c<nbyte; c++) //=====================================
  { ColN[c]=(byte)((ColLastN[c]*iC+ColStartN[c]*(nCrack-iC-1))/(nCrack-1));
    ColP[c]=(byte)((ColLastP[c]*iC+ColStartP[c]*(nCrack-iC-1))/(nCrack-1));
  } //=============== end for (c... =============================
  // Assigning colors to intermediate pixels of a line:
  xx=PixelP.X; yy=PixelP.Y;
  if (xx+width*yy>width*height-1 || xx+width*yy<0)
  {
    MessageBox.Show("Restore: Bad 'xx,yy'="+(xx+width*yy)+"; 'Byte' is bad.");
  }

  if (xx+width*yy<width*height && xx+width*yy>=0)
```

```
{ for (int c=0; c<nbyte; c++) Image.Grid[c+nbyte*xx+nbyte*width*yy]
=ColP[c];
   Mask.Grid[xx+width*yy]=LabMask;
}
xx=PixelN.X; yy=PixelN.Y;
if (xx + width * yy > width * height - 1 || xx + width * yy < 0)
return -1;

if (xx+width*yy<width*height && xx+width*yy>=0)
{ for (int c=0; c<nbyte; c++) Image.Grid[c+nbyte*xx+nbyte*width*yy]
=ColN[c];
   Mask.Grid[xx+width*yy]=LabMask;
}
P=P+Step[dir];

iShift++;
if (iShift==4)
{ iShift=0;
   iByte++;
}
} //=============== end for (iC... ===============================
} //=============== end for (il < nLine2 ===========================
Mask.Grid[0]=Mask.Grid[width-1]=Mask.Grid[width*height-1]=
                                          Mask.Grid[width*
                                          (height-1)]=LabMask;

return 1;
} //****************** end Restore ********************************
```

The next method, Image.Smooth( ), belongs to the class CImage and starts as a method of the image RestoreIm. It begins by smoothing the borders of the image. The method is designed to process either a color or a grayscale image. The variable nbyte is set equal to 3 if Image is a color image or to 1 if it is a grayscale image. Thus in the first case three color channels are processed and in the second case only one gray value is handled.

The method interpolates the colors or the gray values between the corners and eventually existing cracks of lines crossing the borders. This is done in four separate parts of the method because the four borders have quite different coordinates.

Smooth then starts the smoothing of areas where the image Mask has zero pixels. It first makes a smoothing along the rows. It follows a row of the image and tests pairs of subsequent pixels in the image Mask. If the actual pixel (x, y) is zero and the previous pixel is nonzero, then the value of xbeg is set to x - 1 and the variable ColorBeg is set to the color (or gray value) of the pixel $(x - 1, y)$ of Image. If both the actual and the previous pixels are zero, the passed pixels are counted. If the actual pixel (x, y) is nonzero and the previous pixel is zero then a segment of the row starting and ending with a zero has been found. The variable ColorEnd is set to the color (or gray value) of the pixel (x, y) of Image and all passed zero pixels are filled with colors (or gray values) interpolated between ColorBeg and ColorEnd.

A similar procedure is then performed along the columns. The interpolation values obtained in this case are averaged with the values saved in the pixels of Image during the smoothing along the rows.

After these two interpolations, the restored image already looks good. It shows only some vertical and horizontal lines that are a little lighter or darker than their surroundings. The method Smooth removes these lines by smoothing the areas where the image Mask has zero values. It implements for this purpose a digital solution of Laplace's partial differential equation. It uses the method described as Simultaneous Over-Relaxation (SOR) in Press, (1990). This method is not the fastest one, but it is very simple and easy to program.

Here is the code for Smooth.

```
public int Smooth(ref CImage Mask, Form1 fm1)
/* Calculates the average colors between "gvbeg" and "gvend" and saves them
in the image "this". This is a digital automation with the states S=1 at
Mask>0 and S=2 at Mask==0, but S is not used. The variable "mpre" has the
value of "Mask" in the previous pixel. --*/
{
  int c, cnt, LabMask = 250, msk, mpre, x, xx, xbeg, xend, ybeg, yend, y,
  yy;
  int[] Col = new int[3], ColBeg = new int[3], ColEnd = new int[3];
  int nbyte;
  if (N_Bits == 24) nbyte = 3;
  else nbyte = 1;
```

```
// Smoothing the borders:
// Border at y=0:
y = 0; cnt = 0; xbeg = 0; mpre = 200;
for (c = 0; c < nbyte; c++) ColBeg[c] = Grid[c];
for (x = 0; x < width; x++) //======================================
{
  msk = Mask.Grid[x + width * y];
  if (mpre > 0 && msk == 0) //-------------------------------------------
  {
    cnt = 1; xbeg = x - 1;
    for (c = 0; c < nbyte; c++) ColBeg[c] = Grid[nbyte * (x - 1 + width * y) + c];
  }
  if (mpre == 0 && msk == 0) //-------------------------------------------
  {
    cnt++;
  }
  if (mpre == 0 && msk > 0) //-------------------------------------------
  {
    cnt++; xend = x;
    for (c = 0; c < nbyte; c++) ColEnd[c] = Grid[nbyte * (x + width * y) + c];
    for (xx = xbeg + 1; xx < xend; xx++) //=============================
    {
      for (c = 0; c < nbyte; c++)  Grid[nbyte * (xx + width * y) + c] =
                         (byte)((ColBeg[c] * (xend - xx) + ColEnd[c]
                         * (xx - xbeg)) / cnt);
      Mask.Grid[xx + width * y] = (byte)LabMask;
    } //=============== end for (xx... ================================
  }
  mpre = msk;
} //=============== end for (x=0; ... ================================

// Border at y=height-1:
y = height - 1; cnt = 0; xbeg = 0; mpre = 200;
for (c = 0; c < nbyte; c++) ColBeg[c] = Grid[nbyte * width * y + c];
for (x = 0; x < width; x++) //======================================
{
```

```
  msk = Mask.Grid[x + width * y];
  if (mpre > 0 && msk == 0) //-----------------------------------------
  {
    cnt = 1; xbeg = x - 1;
    for (c = 0; c < nbyte; c++) ColBeg[c] = Grid[nbyte * (x - 1 + width * y) + c];
  }
  if (mpre == 0 && msk == 0) //-----------------------------------------
  {
    cnt++;
  }
  if (mpre == 0 && msk > 0) //-----------------------------------------
  {
    cnt++; xend = x;
    for (c = 0; c < nbyte; c++) ColEnd[c] = Grid[nbyte * (x + width * y) + c];
    for (xx = xbeg + 1; xx < xend; xx++)
    {
      for (c = 0; c < nbyte; c++)  Grid[nbyte * (xx + width * y) + c] =
                         (byte)((ColBeg[c] * (xend - xx) + ColEnd[c] *
                         (xx - xbeg)) / cnt);
      Mask.Grid[xx + width * y] = (byte)LabMask;
    }
  }
  mpre = msk;
} //=============== end for (x=0; ... ===============================

// Border at x=0
x = 0; cnt = 0; ybeg = 0; mpre = 200;
for (c = 0; c < nbyte; c++) ColBeg[c] = Grid[nbyte * (x + width * 0) + c];
for (y = 0; y < height; y++) //=======================================
{
  msk = Mask.Grid[x + width * y];
  if (mpre > 0 && msk == 0) //-----------------------------------------
  {
    cnt = 1; ybeg = y - 1;
    for (c = 0; c < nbyte; c++) ColBeg[c] = Grid[nbyte * (x + width *
    (y - 1)) + c];
```

```
  }
  if (mpre == 0 && msk == 0) //-------------------------------------------
  {
    cnt++;
  }
  if (mpre == 0 && msk > 0) //--------------------------------------------
  {
    cnt++; yend = y;
    for (c = 0; c < nbyte; c++) ColEnd[c] = Grid[nbyte * (x + width * y)
    + c];
    for (yy = ybeg + 1; yy < yend; yy++)
    {
      for (c = 0; c < nbyte; c++)
      {
        Col[c] = (ColBeg[c] * (yend - yy) + ColEnd[c] * (yy - ybeg)) / cnt;
        Grid[nbyte * (x + width * yy) + c] = (byte)Col[c];
      }
      Mask.Grid[x + width * yy] = (byte)LabMask;
    }
  }
  mpre = msk;
} //=============== end for (y=0; ... ==============================

// Border at x=width-1
x = width - 1; cnt = 0; ybeg = 0; mpre = 200;
for (c = 0; c < nbyte; c++) ColBeg[c] = Grid[nbyte * (x + width * 0) + c];
for (y = 0; y < height; y++) //========================================
{
  msk = Mask.Grid[x + width * y];
  if (mpre > 0 && msk == 0) //------------------------------------------
  {
    cnt = 1; ybeg = y - 1;
    for (c = 0; c < nbyte; c++) ColBeg[c] = Grid[nbyte * (x + width *
    (y - 1)) + c];
  }
  if (mpre == 0 && msk == 0) //-----------------------------------------
```

```
    {
      cnt++;
    }
    if (mpre == 0 && msk > 0) //-------------------------------------
    {
      cnt++; yend = y;
      for (c = 0; c < nbyte; c++) ColEnd[c] = Grid[nbyte * (x + width * y) + c];
      for (yy = ybeg + 1; yy < yend; yy++)
      {
        for (c = 0; c < nbyte; c++)
        {
          Col[c] = (ColBeg[c] * (yend - yy) + ColEnd[c] * (yy - ybeg)) / cnt;
          Grid[nbyte * (x + width * yy) + c] = (byte)Col[c];
        }
        Mask.Grid[x + width * yy] = (byte)LabMask;
      }
    }
    mpre = msk;
} //=============== end for (y=0; ... ==============================

// End smoothing border; Smooth on "x":
fm1.progressBar1.Visible = true;
fm1.progressBar1.Value = 0;
int Sum = height + width + 50 * 10;
int denomProg = fm1.progressBar1.Maximum / fm1.progressBar1.Step;
int i1 = Sum / denomProg;
for (y = 0; y < height; y++) //=====================================
{
  if ((y % i1) == 0) fm1.progressBar1.PerformStep();
  cnt = 0; xbeg = 0; mpre = 200;
  for (c = 0; c < nbyte; c++) ColBeg[c] = Grid[nbyte * width * y + c];
  for (x = 0; x < width; x++) //=====================================
  {
    msk = Mask.Grid[x + width * y];
    if (mpre > 0 && msk == 0) //-------------------------------------
    {
```

```
        cnt = 1; xbeg = x - 1;
        for (c = 0; c < nbyte; c++) ColBeg[c] = Grid[nbyte * (x - 1 + width *
        y) + c];
      }
      if (mpre == 0 && msk == 0) //----------------------------------------
      {
        cnt++;
      }
      if (mpre == 0 && msk > 0) //-----------------------------------------
      {
        cnt++; xend = x;
        for (c = 0; c < nbyte; c++) ColEnd[c] = Grid[nbyte * (x + width *
        y) + c];
        for (xx = xbeg + 1; xx < xend; xx++)
        {
          for (c = 0; c < nbyte; c++)  Grid[nbyte * (xx + width * y) + c] =
                      (byte)((ColBeg[c] * (xend - xx) + ColEnd[c] *
                      (xx - xbeg)) / cnt);
        }
      }
      mpre = msk;
  } //=============== end for (x=0; ... =============================
} //=============== end for (y=0; ... =============================

// Smooth on "y":
for (x = 0; x < width; x++) //=========================================
{
  if ((x % i1) == 0) fm1.progressBar1.PerformStep();
  cnt = 0; ybeg = 0; mpre = 200;
  for (c = 0; c < nbyte; c++) ColBeg[c] = Grid[nbyte * (x + width * 0) + c];
  for (y = 0; y < height; y++) //=======================================
  {
    msk = Mask.Grid[x + width * y];
    if (mpre > 0 && msk == 0) //-----------------------------------------
    {
```

```
      cnt = 1; ybeg = y - 1;
      for (c = 0; c < nbyte; c++) ColBeg[c] = Grid[nbyte * (x + width *
      (y - 1)) + c];
    }
    if (mpre == 0 && msk == 0) //-----------------------------------------
    {
      cnt++;
    }
    if (mpre == 0 && msk > 0) //------------------------------------------
    {
      cnt++; yend = y; for (c = 0; c < nbyte; c++) ColEnd[c] = Grid[nbyte
      * (x + width * y) + c];
      for (yy = ybeg + 1; yy < yend; yy++)
      {
        for (c = 0; c < nbyte; c++)
        { Col[c]= (Grid[nbyte*(x+width*yy)+c]+(ColBeg[c]*(yend-yy) +
                                    ColEnd[c]*(yy-ybeg))/cnt)/2;
          Grid[nbyte * (x + width * yy) + c] = (byte)Col[c];
        }
      }
    }
    mpre = msk;
  } //=============== end for (y=0; ... ==============================
} //================ end for (x=0; ... ==============================

// Solving the Laplace's equation:
int i;
double fgv, omega = 1.4 / 4.0, dMaxLap = 0.0, dTH = 1.0;
double[] dGrid = new double[width * height * nbyte];
double[] Lap = new double[3];
for (i = 0; i < width * height * nbyte; i++) dGrid[i] = (double)Grid[i];

fm1.progressBar1.Visible = false;
fm1.progressBar1.Value = 0;
fm1.progressBar1.Visible = true;
```

```
int it1=10;
for (int iter = 0; iter < 50; iter++) //=================================
{ // Smooth Math.Abs((x-y))%2==0
  if ((iter % it1) == 0) fm1.progressBar1.PerformStep();
  for (y = 1; y < height - 1; y++)
    for (x = 1; x < width - 1; x++)
    {
      if (Mask.Grid[x + width * y] == 0 && Math.Abs((x - y)) % 2 == 0)
        for (c = 0; c < nbyte; c++)
        {
          Lap[c] = 0.0;
          Lap[c] += dGrid[nbyte * (x + width * (y - 1)) + c];
          Lap[c] += dGrid[nbyte * (x - 1 + width * y) + c];
          Lap[c] += dGrid[nbyte * (x + 1 + width * y) + c];
          Lap[c] += dGrid[nbyte * (x + width * (y + 1)) + c];
          Lap[c] -= 4.0 * dGrid[nbyte * (x + width * y) + c];
          fgv = dGrid[nbyte * (x + width * y) + c] + omega * Lap[c];
          if (fgv > 255.0) fgv = 255.0;
          if (fgv < 0.0) fgv = 0;
          dGrid[nbyte * (x + width * y) + c] = fgv;
        }
    }
  // Smooth at Math.Abs((x-y))%2==1
  for (y = 1; y < height - 1; y++)
    for (x = 1; x < width - 1; x++)
    {
      if (Mask.Grid[x + width * y] == 0 && Math.Abs((x - y)) % 2 == 1)
        for (c = 0; c < nbyte; c++)
        {
          Lap[c] = 0.0;
          Lap[c] += dGrid[nbyte * (x + width * (y - 1)) + c];
          Lap[c] += dGrid[nbyte * (x - 1 + width * y) + c];
          Lap[c] += dGrid[nbyte * (x + 1 + width * y) + c];
          Lap[c] += dGrid[nbyte * (x + width * (y + 1)) + c];
          Lap[c] -= 4.0 * dGrid[nbyte * (x + width * y) + c];
```

```
          fgv = dGrid[nbyte * (x + width * y) + c] + omega * Lap[c];
          if (fgv > 255.0) fgv = 255.0;
          if (fgv < 0.0) fgv = 0;
          dGrid[nbyte * (x + width * y) + c] = fgv; //(int)(fgv);
        }
    }

  dMaxLap = 0.0; // Calculating MaxLap:
  for (y = 1; y < height - 1; y++)
    for (x = 1; x < width - 1; x++) //====================================
    {
      if (Mask.Grid[x + width * y] == 0) //--------------------------------
      {
        for (c = 0; c < nbyte; c++) //==============================
        {
          Lap[c] = 0.0;
          Lap[c] += dGrid[nbyte * (x + width * (y - 1)) + c];
          Lap[c] += dGrid[nbyte * (x - 1 + width * y) + c];
          Lap[c] += dGrid[nbyte * (x + 1 + width * y) + c];
          Lap[c] += dGrid[nbyte * (x + width * (y + 1)) + c];
          Lap[c] -= 4.0 * dGrid[nbyte * (x + width * y) + c];
          if (Math.Abs(Lap[c]) > dMaxLap) dMaxLap = Math.Abs(Lap[c]);
        } //================= end for (c=0; =====================
      } //----------------------------- end if (Mask... ---------------
    } //================== end for (x=1; ... ==========================
  int ii;
  for (ii = 0; ii < width * height * nbyte; ii++) Grid[ii] = (byte)dGrid[ii];

  if (dMaxLap < dTH)  break;
  } //==================== end for (iter... =============================
  return 0;
} //******************** end Smooth *********************************
```

CHAPTER 9

Image Segmentation and Connected Components

Image segmentation is an important procedure in image analysis. The following is known about segmentation (refer e.g. to Shapiro (2001):

> *In* computer vision, ***image segmentation*** *is the process of partitioning a* digital image *into multiple segments (sets* of pixels, *also known as super-pixels). The goal of segmentation is to simplify and/or change the representation of an image into something that is more meaningful and easier to analyze.*[1][2] *Image segmentation is typically used to locate objects and* boundaries *(lines, curves, etc.) in images. More precisely, image segmentation is the process of assigning a label to every pixel in an image such that pixels with the same label share certain characteristics.*

There are in the scientific literature a giant number of publications on methods of segmentation. Let us, however, remember that any thresholded image can be considered a segmented one. Also a quantized image, where all the gray values or colors are subdivided in a relatively small number of groups with a single color assigned to all pixels of a group, can be considered segmented. The difficulty of the segmentation problem consists only in the possibility of defining meaningful segments; that is, segments that are meaningful from the point of view of human perception. For example, a segmentation for which we can say, "This segment is a house, this one is the street, this one is a car, and so on," would be a meaningful segmentation. As far as I know, developing a meaningful segmentation is an unsolved problem. We consider in this section segmentation by quantizing the colors of an image into a small number of groups optimally representing the colors of the image.

© Vladimir Kovalevsky 2019

V. Kovalevsky, *Modern Algorithms for Image Processing*, https://doi.org/10.1007/978-1-4842-4237-7_9

Segmentation by Quantizing the Colors

Quantizing the colors is the well-known method of compressing color images: Color information is not directly carried by the image pixel data, but is stored in a separate piece of data called a palette, an array of color elements. Every element in the array represents a color, indexed by its position within the array. The image pixels do not contain the full specification of the color, but only its index in the palette. This is the well-known method of producing indexed 8-bit images.

Our method consists of producing a palette optimal for the concrete image. For this purpose we have developed the method `MakePalette` described in Chapter 8 and successfully used in the project `WFcompressPal`.

Connected Components

We suppose that the segments should be connected subsets of pixels. Connectedness is a topological notion, whereas classical topology considers mostly infinite sets of points where each neighborhood of a point contains an infinite number of points. Classical topology is not applicable to digital images because they are finite.

The notion of connectedness is also used in graph theory. It is possible to consider a digital image as a graph with vertices that are the pixels and an edge of the graph connects any two adjacent pixels. A path is a sequence of pixels in which each pixel besides one at the beginning and one at the end is incident to exactly two adjacent pixels.

It is well known (refer e.g. to Hazewinkel, (2001)) that in an undirected graph, an unordered pair of vertices {x, y} is called connected if a path leads from x to y. Otherwise, the unordered pair is called disconnected.

A connected graph is an undirected graph in which every unordered pair of vertices in the graph is connected. Otherwise, it is called a disconnected graph.

It is possible to apply the notion of connectedness from graph theory to images. One considers two kinds of adjacency: a four adjacency (Figure 9-1a) and an eight adjacency (Figure 9-1b). In the case of Figure 9-1a, both subsets of black pixels and white pixels are disconnected; in the case of Figure 9-1b they are both connected. In both cases there exists a well-known connectedness paradox: Why should the black pixels in Figure 9-1a be disconnected when nothing lies between them? Similarly, why are the black pixels in Figure 9-1b connected in spite of the presence of the path from one white pixel to the other between them?

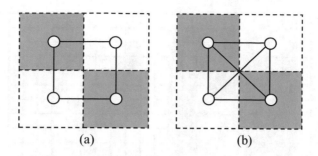

Figure 9-1. *The connectedness paradox: (a) the four adjacency, and (b) the eight adjacency*

Rosenfeld (1970) suggested considering the eight adjacency for black pixels and the four adjacency for white pixels in a binary image. This suggestion solves the problem in the case of binary images, but it is not applicable to multicolor images. The only solution of the connectedness paradox for multicolored images I know of consists of considering a digital image as a cell complex as described in Chapter 7. The connectedness can then be defined correctly and free from paradoxes by means of the EquNaLi rule (refer to Kovalevsky (1989)) specified below.

Two pixels with coordinates (x, y) and (x + 1, y + 1) or (x, y) and (x − 1, y + 1) make up a diagonal pair. A pair of eight adjacent pixels is defined as connected in the theory of ACCs if both pixels have the same color and the lower dimensional cell (one- or zero-dimensional) lying between them also has this color. Naturally, it makes little sense to speak of color of lower dimensional cells because their area is zero. However, it is necessary to use this notion to consistently define connectedness in digital images. To avoid using the notion of colors of low-dimensional cells we suggest replacing color by label when the label of a pixel is equal to its color.

Consider the example of Figure 9-2. Suppose that it is necessary to define the connectedness in such a way that both the white and the black V are connected. This is obviously impossible under any adjacency relation. The aim can be achieved by means of the EquNaLi rule for assigning membership labels (e.g., integers corresponding to colors) to cells of lower dimensions.

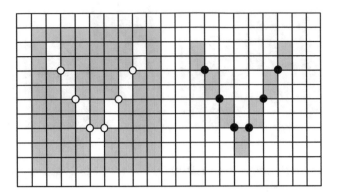

Figure 9-2. *White and black V-shaped regions in one image, both connected due to applying the EquNaLi rule*

The EquNaLi rule for two-dimensional images states that a one-dimensional cell always receives the greatest label (lighter color) of two principal (i.e., two-dimensional) cells incident to it.

The label of a zero-dimensional cell c^0 is defined as follows:

> If the 2×2 neighborhood of c^0 contains exactly one diagonal pair of pixels with equal labels (Equ), then c^0 receives this label. If there is more than one such pair but only one of them belongs to a narrow (Na) stripe, then c^0 receives the label of the narrow stripe. Otherwise c^0 receives the maximum; that is, the lighter (Li) label (i.e., the greater label) of the pixels in the neighborhood of c^0.

The latter case corresponds to the cases when the neighborhood of c^0 contains no diagonal pair with equal labels or it contains more than one such pair and more than one of them belong to a narrow stripe.

To decide whether a diagonal pair in the neighborhood of c^0 belongs to a narrow stripe it is necessary to scan an array of $4 \times 4 = 16$ pixels with c^0 in the middle and to count the labels corresponding to both diagonals. The smallest count indicates the narrow stripe. Examples of other efficient membership rules can be found in Kovalevsky (1989).

It is important for the analysis of segmented images to find and to distinguish all connected components of the image. The problem is finding the maximum connected subsets of the image, each subset containing pixels of a constant color. Then it is necessary to number the components and to assign to each pixel the number of the component it belongs to. Let us call the assigned number a label.

A subset S of pixels of some certain color is called connected if for any two pixels of S there exists a sequence of neighboring pixels in S containing these two pixels. We consider the EquNaLi neighborhood.

To find and to label the components, an image must contain a relatively small number of colors. Otherwise each pixel of a color image could be a maximum connected component. Segmented images mostly satisfy the condition of possessing a small number of colors.

The naive approach involves scanning the image row by row and assigning to each pixel that has no adjacent pixels of the same color in the already scanned subset the next unused label. If the next pixel has in the already scanned subset adjacent pixels of the same color and they have different labels, the smallest of these different labels is assigned to the pixel. All pixels of the already scanned subset having one of these different labels must obtain this smallest label. The replacement might affect in the worst case up to $height^2/2$ pixels, where height is the number of rows in the image. The total number of replacements after the whole image is scanned could then be on the order of $height^3/2$. This number can be very large, so the naive approach is not practical. An efficient method of labeling the pixels of one component is the well-known and widely used method of graph traversal.

The Graph Traversal Algorithm and Its Code

Let us consider now the graph traversal approach. The image is regarded as a graph and the pixels are regarded as vertices. Two vertices are connected by an edge of the graph if the corresponding pixels have equal values (e.g., colors) and are adjacent. The adjacency relation can be the four or eight adjacency. It is easily recognized that the components of the graph correspond exactly to the desired components of the image.

There are at least two well-known methods of traversing all vertices of a component of a graph: the depth-first search and the breadth-first search algorithms. They are rather similar to each other, and we consider here only the breadth-first search. This algorithm was used in our projects containing suppression of impulse noise (Chapter 2). We describe it here in a little more detail.

The breadth-first algorithm employs the well-known data structure called *queue,* also known as first-in-first-out: Values can be put into the queue, and the value put in first will come out of the queue first. The process of the algorithm is as follows.

1. Set the number *NC* of the components to zero.

2. Take any unlabeled vertex *V*, increase *NC*, label *V* with the value *NC* and put *V* into the queue. The vertex *V* is the "seed" of a new component having the index *NC*.

3. Repeat the following instructions, while the queue is not empty:

    3.1. Take the first vertex *W* from the queue.

    3.2. Test each neighbor *N* of *W*. If *N* is labeled, ignore it; otherwise label *N* with *NC* and put it into the queue.

4. When the queue is empty, then the component *NC* is already labeled.

Proceed with Step 2 to find the seed of the next component until all vertices are labeled.

Let us describe the pseudo-code of this algorithm. Given a multivalued array Image[] of N elements and the methods Neighb(i,m) and Adjacent(i,k), the first one returns the index of the mth neighbor of the ith element. The second one returns TRUE if the ith element is adjacent to the kth one and FALSE otherwise. As a result of the labeling each element gets the label of the connected component to which it belongs. The label is saved in an array Label[], which has the same size as Image[]. We assume that all methods have access to the arrays Image and Label and to their size N.

The Pseudo-Code of the Breadth-First Algorithm

Allocate the array Label[N]. All elements of Label must now be initialized with zero, which means that the elements are not yet labeled.

```
for (i=0; i<N; i++) Label[i]=0; // setting all labels to 0
int NC=0; // number of components
for (V=0; V<N; V++) // loop through all elements of the image
{
  if (Label[V]≠0) continue; // looking for unlabeled elements
  NC=NC+1; // index of a new component
  Label[V]=NC; // labeling the element with index V with NC
  PutIntoQueue(V); // putting V into the queue
  while(QueueNotEmpty()) //loop running while queue not empty
```

```
{ W=GetFromQueue();
  for (n=0; n<Max_n; n++) // all neighbors of W ==========
  { N=Neighb(W,n); // the index of the nth neighbor of W
    if (Label[N]==0 AND Adjacent(W,N)==TRUE
                    AND Image[N]==Image[W])
    { Label[N]=NC; // labeling element with index N with NC
      PutIntoQueue(N);
    }
  } // ========= end for (n=0; ... =================
} // =========== end while ========================
} // ============= end for (V =0;... ======================
```

End of the Algorithm

The value Max_n is in this case the maximal possible number of all neighbors of an element of the image regardless of whether it was already visited or not. It is equal to 8. It is necessary to provide the queue data structure with the methods PutIntoQueue(i), GetFromQueue(), and QueueNotEmpty(). The last method returns TRUE if the queue is not empty; otherwise it returns FALSE.

This algorithm labels all pixels of a component containing the starting pixel. To label all components of an image it is necessary to choose the next starting pixel among those not labeled as belonging to an already processed component. This must be repeated until all pixels of the image are labeled.

The Approach of Equivalence Classes

There is another approach to the problem of labeling connected components, that of equivalent classes (EC), which considers labeling all components of an image simultaneously. One of the earliest publications about the approach of EC is that by Rosenfeld and Pfalz (1966). The idea of this algorithm in the case of a two-dimensional image proceeds as follows. The algorithm scans the image row by row two times. It investigates during the first scan for each pixel P the set S of all already visited pixels adjacent to P according to the four or eight adjacency and having the same color as P. If there are no such pixels, then P gets the next unused label. Otherwise P gets the smallest label (the set of labels must be ordered; integers are mostly employed as labels) of the pixels in S. Simultaneously the algorithm declares all labels of the pixels of S as equivalent to the smallest label. For this purpose the algorithm employs an equivalence table, where each column corresponds to one of the employed labels. Equivalent labels are stored in the elements of the column.

When the image has been completely scanned, a special algorithm processes the table and determines the classes of equivalent labels. Each class is represented by the smallest of equivalent labels. The table is rearranged in such a way that in the column corresponding to each label, the label of the class remains. During the second scan each label in the image is replaced by that of the class.

One of the drawbacks of this algorithm is the difficulty of estimating a priori the necessary size of the equivalence table. Kovalevsky (1990) developed an improved version of the EC approach, independent of Gallert and Fisher (1964), called the *root method*. It employs an array L of labels, which has the same number of elements as the number of pixels in the obtained image. This is a substitute for the equivalence table. To explain the idea of the improvement we consider first the simplest case of a two-dimensional binary image, although the algorithm is applicable also in the case of multivalued and multidimensional images without essential changes.

The suggested method is based on the following idea. Each pixel of the image has a corresponding element of the array L of labels. Let us call it the label of the pixel. The array L must be of such a type that it is possible to save in its elements the index x + width*y of each pixel of the image (the type `integer` is sufficient for images of any size). If a component contains a pixel with a label that is equal to the index of this pixel, then this label is called the root of the component.

At the start of the algorithm each element of the array L corresponding to the pixel (x, y) is set equal to the index x+width*y where width is the number of columns of the image. Thus at the start each pixel is considered a component.

The algorithm scans the image row by row. If a pixel has in the previously scanned area no adjacent pixel of the same color, then the pixel retains its label. If, however, the next pixel *P* has adjacent pixels of the same color among the already visited pixels and they have different labels, this means that these pixels belong to different previously discovered components having different roots. These different components must be united into a single component. It is necessary for this purpose to find the roots of these components and to set all these roots and the label of *P* equal to the smallest root. It is important to notice that only the roots are changed, not the values of the labels of the pixels adjacent to *P*. Labels of the pixels will be changed in the second scan. This is the reason this method is so fast. All components that meet at the running pixel get the same root and they are merged into a single component. The labels that are not roots remain unchanged. In the worst case previously mentioned, the replacement could affect only width/2 pixels.

After the first scan, the label of each pixel is pointing to a pixel of the same component with a smaller label. Thus there is a sequence of ever smaller labels ending with the root of the component. During the second scan all labels are replaced by subsequent integer numbers.

The connectedness of subsets must be defined by an adjacency relation. This can be a well-known (n, m) adjacency that is defined only for binary images, or an adjacency relation based on the membership of the cells of lower dimensions in the subsets defined by the method EquNaLi.

It can seem that the array L of labels employed in the root method requires too much memory space: To store the indexes, the number of bits in each element of L must be not less than log2(size), where size is the number of the elements of the image. However, this size of L is necessary for any method of labeling connected components, if the method is supposed to work for any multivalued image. In fact, images exist in which each element is a component. The number of different labels is then equal to the number of the elements of the image. For example, a two-dimensional image with four colors shown in Figure 9-3 has this property under any adjacency relation.

1	2	1	2	1	2	1	2
3	4	3	4	3	4	3	4
1	2	1	2	1	2	1	2
3	4	3	4	3	4	3	4

Figure 9-3. *Example of an image with four colors having as many components as the number of pixels*

If it is known that the number of used labels is smaller than size, then an array L with a smaller number of bits per element can be sufficient for applying the method using an equivalence table. However, this is not important in the case of modern computers, which have ample memory. So, for example, an array of the data type int on a modern computer with a 32-bit processor can be employed for images containing up to 2^{32} elements. Thus a two-dimensional image can have a size of 65,536 × 65,536 pixels and a three-dimensional image a size of 2,048 × 2,048 × 1,024 voxels.

Let us return to the algorithm. It scans the image row by row and investigates for each pixel P the set S of already visited pixels adjacent to P. If there are in S pixels of the same color as that of P and they have different labels, then the algorithm finds the smallest root label of these pixels and assigns it to P and to the roots of all pixels of S. Thus all components that meet each other at the running pixel obtain the same root and are merged into a single component. The labels of pixels that are not roots remain unchanged. In the worst case of a single component, the replacement can affect only width/2 pixels.

Each pixel belongs after the first scan to a path leading to the root of its component. During the second scan the labels of the roots and all other pixels are replaced by subsequent integer numbers.

A simple two-dimensional example is presented in Figure 9-4. Given is a two-dimensional binary array Image[N] of $N = 16$ pixels. Two pixels of the dark foreground are adjacent if and only if they have a common incident 1-cell (four adjacency), whereas pixels of the light background are adjacent if they have any common incident cell (eight adjacency). At the start of the algorithm the labels of all pixels are equal to their indexes (numbers from 0–15 in Figure 9-4a). The pixels with the indexes 0 and 1 have no adjacent pixels of the same color among the pixels visited before. Their labels 0 and 1 remain unchanged. They are the roots. The pixel with the index 2 has the adjacent pixel 1, which has a root of 1. Thus label 2 is replaced by 1. Label 3 remains unchanged after the scanning of the first row. The labels of all pixels are changed according to the preceding rule until the last pixel 15 is reached. This pixel is adjacent to pixels 11 and 14. The label of pixel 11 is pointing to root 3; that of pixel 14 is pointing to pixel 0, which is also a root. Label 0 is smaller than 3. Therefore the label of the root 3 becomes replaced by the smaller label 0 (Figure 9-4b).

During the second run the labels of the roots are replaced by subsequent natural numbers 1 and 2. The labels of all other pixels get the new labels of their roots (Figure 9-4c). The code of the EC algorithm is described later.

0	1	2̶ 1	3
4̶ 0	5̶ 1	6̶ 1	7̶ 3
8̶ 0	9̶ 1	10̶ 1	11̶ 3
12̶ 0	13̶ 0	14̶ 0	15

0	1	2̶ 1	3̶ 0
4̶ 0	5̶ 1	6̶ 1	7̶ 3
8̶ 0	9̶ 1	10̶ 1	11̶ 3
12̶ 0	13̶ 0	14̶ 0	15̶ 0

1	2	2	1
1	2	2	1
1	2	2	1
1	1	1	1

(a) first run   (b) the end of the first run   (c) second run

Figure 9-4. *Illustration of the algorithm for labeling connected components*

The Pseudo-Code of the Root Algorithm

This algorithm can be applied to an image either in a combinatorial or in a standard grid. In a combinatorial grid, where the incidence relation of two cells is defined by their combinatorial coordinates, it is sufficient to assign a value (a color) from the set of values of the pixels to each cell of any dimension. Two *incident* cells having the same value are adjacent and will be assigned to the same component. In a standard grid a method must be given that specifies which grid elements in the neighborhood of a given element e are adjacent to e and thus must be assigned to the same component if they have the same value. In our earlier simple two-dimensional example, we have employed the four adjacency of the foreground pixels and the eight adjacency of the background pixels. In general, the adjacency of principal cells of an n-dimensional complex must be specified by rules specifying the membership of cells of lower dimensions (e.g., by a rule similar to the EquNaLi rule), as the well-known (m, n) adjacency is not applicable to multivalued images. We consider here the pseudo-code for the case of the standard grid.

Given is a multivalued array Image[ ] of N elements and the methods Neighb(i,m) and Adjacent(i,k). The first one returns the index of the mth neighbor of the ith element, and the second one returns TRUE if the ith element is adjacent to the kth one. Otherwise it return FALSE. In the two-dimensional case this can be a method implementing the EquNaLi rule. As a result of the labeling, each element obtains the label of the connected component to which it belongs. The label is saved in another array Label[ ].

The array Label[N] must be the same size as Image[N]. Each element of Label must have at least log2N bits, where N is the number of elements of Image, and must be initialized by its own index:

$$\text{for}(i = 1; i < N; i++) \text{ Label}[i] = i.$$

To make the pseudo-code simpler, we assume that all methods have access to the arrays Image and Label and to their size N.

In the first loop of the algorithm each element of Image gets a label pointing to the root of its component. The value Max_n is the maximum possible number of adjacent elements of an element (pixel or voxel) that have already been visited. It is easily recognized that Max_n is equal to $(3^d - 1)/2$, where d is the dimension of the image. For example, in the two-dimensional case, Max_n is equal to 4 and in the three-dimensional case it is equal to 13.

The Root Algorithm

```
for (i=0; i<N; i++)
{ for (m=0; m<Max_n; m++)
  { k=Neighb(i,m); // the index of the mth adjacent element of i
    if(Adjacent(i,k) AND Image[k] == Image[i]) SetEqu(i, k);
  }
} // end of the first loop
SecondRun();
```

The subroutine SetEqu(i,k) (its pseudo-code is seen next) compares the indexes of the roots of the elements i and k with each other and sets the label of the root with the greater index equal to the smaller index. Thus both roots belong to the same component. The method Root(k) returns the last value in the sequence of indexes where the first index k is that of the given element, the next one is the value of Label[k], and so on, until Label[k] becomes equal to k. The subroutine SecondRun() replaces the value of Label[k] by the value of a component counter or by the root of k depending on whether Label[k] is equal to k or not.

Pseudo-Codes of the Subroutines

```
subroutine SetEqu(i,k)
{ if (Root(i)<Root(k)) Label[Root(k)]=Root(i);
  else Label[Root(i)]=Root(k);
} // end subroutine.

int Root(k)
{ do
  { if (Label[k]==k) return k;
    k=Label[k];
  } while(1); // loop runs until condition Label[k]==k is fulfilled
} // end Root

subroutine SecondRun()
{ count=1;
  for (i=0; i<N; i++)
  { value=Label [i];
    if (value==i )
```

```
    { Label[i]=count; count=count+1;
    }
    else Label[i]=Label[value];
  }
} // end subroutine.
```

The Project WFsegmentAndComp

We have developed a Windows Forms project WFsegmentAndComp segmenting an image and labeling the pixels of its connected components.

It is possible to perform the segmentation in two ways: either by clustering the colors into a relatively small number (e.g., 20) of clusters and assigning to each cluster the average color of all pixels belonging to the cluster, or by converting the color image to a grayscale image, subdividing the full range [0, 255] of the gray values to a small number of intervals, and assigning to each interval the average gray value. The conversion does not cause a loss of information because the labels of the connected components are relatively great numbers having no relation to the colors of the original colors: The set of pixels having a certain color can consist of many components, with each component having another label.

The labeling of connected components is done with both procedures—the breadth-first search and the root method—so that the user can compare the speed of these two procedures. The result of labeling is represented as a color image with an artificial palette with 256 colors and the index of the palette is the result of dividing the label by 256. Figure 9-5 shows the form of the project.

Figure 9-5. *Form of the project* `WFsegmentAndComp`

When the user clicks Open image, he or she can choose an image to be opened. The image will be presented in the left-hand picture box, and five work images will be defined.

The user should then click the next button, Segment. The original image will be converted to a grayscale image. The gray values will be divided by 24 and the integer result of division will be multiplied by 24. In this way the new gray values become multiples of 24 and the scale of the gray values is quantized into 256/24 + 1 = 11 intervals. The segmented image is presented in the right-right picture box.

It is known from experience that the number of components, even of a segmented image, is very large. Among the components are many consisting of a single pixel or few pixels. Such components are of no interest for image analysis. To reduce the number of small components we have decided to suppress impulse noise of the segmented image. This merges many small spots of a certain gray level with the surrounding area and reduces the number of small components.

The user can choose the maximum sizes of dark and light spots to be deleted and click Impulse noise. The image with deleted dark and light spots will be presented instead of the segmented image.

Then the user can click either Breadth First Search or Root method. The labeled images will be shown in false colors; that is, with an artificial palette containing 256 colors. The index of the palette is equal to dividing the label by 256.

The code for suppressing impulse noise was presented in Chapter 2.

Here we present the code of for breadth-first search used for labeling connected components of the segmented image. As already mentioned, this algorithm processes the pixels of one component containing the start pixel. To process all components of the image we have developed the method LabelC, which scans the image and tests whether each pixel is labeled. If it is not, then it is a starting pixel for the next component and the method Breadth_First_Search is called.

All these methods are elements of a special class CImageComp, which differs from the class CImage by the presence of the array Lab for the labels. The properties nLoop and DenomProg are used for the control of the progressBar indicating the progress of the method LabelC.

```
public class CImageComp
{
   public byte[] Grid;
   public int[] Lab;
   public Color[] Palette;
   public int width, height, N_Bits, nLoop, denomProg;
   ... // here are the constructors and the methods
}
```

Here is the code of LabelC.

```
public int LabelC(Form1 fm1)
{ int index, lab=0;
   for (index=0; index<width*height; index++) Lab[index]=0;

   int y1 = nLoop * height / denomProg;
   for (int y=0; y<height; y++) //=========================
   {
      if (y % y1 == 0) fm1.progressBar1.PerformStep();
      for (int x = 0; x < width; x++) //==================
      { index=x+width*y;
         if (Lab[index]==0)
         {  lab++;
```

```
      Breadth_First_Search(index, lab);
    }
  } //================ end for (int x...============
  } //================== end for (int x...=============
  return lab;
} //******************* end LabelC **************************
```

As one can see, the method is very simple: it scans all pixels of the image and checks whether the actual pixel is already labeled. If it is not, then the method Breadth_First_ Search is called.

Here is the code for Breadth_First_Search.

```
public int Breadth_First_Search(int root, int lab)
{ int light, gvP, Index, Len=1000, Nei;
    bool rv;
    iVect2 P = new iVect2(0, 0);
    CQue Q = new CQue(Len);
    light=Grid[root];
    if (Lab[root]==0) Lab[root]=lab;

    Q.Put(root);
    while(!Q.Empty()) //==============================
    { Index=Q.Get();
       gvP=Grid[Index];
       P.Y=Index/width; P.X=Index-width*P.Y;
       for (int n=0; n<8; n++) //=====================
       { Nei=NeighbEqu(Index, n, width, height);
          rv=EquNaliDir(P, n, gvP);
          if (Nei<0) continue;
          if (Grid[Nei]==light && Lab[Nei]==0 && rv)
          {
             Lab[Nei]=lab;
             Q.Put(Nei);
          }
       } //============== end for (n... ==============
    } //================ end while ===================
    return 1;
} //***************** end Breadth_First_Search ************
```

To show the results of component labeling we use a simple palette with 256 colors. The palette is produced by the method MakePalette. Here is its code.

```
public int MakePalette( ref int nPal)
{ int r, g, b;
   byte Red, Green, Blue;
   int ii=0;
   for (r=1; r<=8; r++) // Colors of the palette
   for (g=1; g<=8; g++)
   for (b=1; b<=4; b++)
   { Red=(byte)(32*r);   if (r==8) Red=255;
      Green = (byte)(32 * g);
      if (g == 8) Green = 255;
      Blue= (byte)(64*b);   if (b==4) Blue=255;
      Palette[ii] = Color.FromArgb(Red, Green, Blue);
      ii++;
   }
   nPal=4*ii;
   return 1;
} //**************** end MakePalette *****************
```

The image BreadthFirIm of the class CImageComp contains the labels of the components and the palette. To make the labels visible we transform the image BreadthFirIm to the bitmap BreadthBmp by means of the method LabToBitmap and display this bitmap in the right-hand picture box. Here is the code of LabToBitmap.

```
public void LabToBitmap(Bitmap bmp, CImageComp Image)
{
  if (Image.N_Bits != 8)
  {
    MessageBox.Show("Not suitable  format of 'Image'; N_Bits=" + Image.N_
    Bits);
    return;
  }
  switch (bmp.PixelFormat)
  {
    case PixelFormat.Format24bppRgb: nbyte = 3; break;
```

```
    case PixelFormat.Format8bppIndexed:
        MessageBox.Show("LabToBitmap: Not suitable  pixel format=" + bmp.
        PixelFormat);
        return;
    default: MessageBox.Show("LabToBitmap: Not suitable  pixel format=" +
    bmp.PixelFormat);
        return;
}
Rectangle rect = new Rectangle(0, 0, bmp.Width, bmp.Height);
BitmapData bmpData = bmp.LockBits(rect, ImageLockMode.ReadWrite, bmp.
PixelFormat);

IntPtr ptr = bmpData.Scan0;
int size = bmp.Width * bmp.Height;
int bytes = Math.Abs(bmpData.Stride) * bmp.Height;
byte[] rgbValues = new byte[bytes];
Color color;
int index = 0;
int y1 = nLoop * bmp.Height / 220; // denomProg;
for (int y = 0; y < bmp.Height; y++)
{
  if (y % y1 == 0) progressBar1.PerformStep();
  for (int x = 0; x < bmp.Width; x++)
  {
    color = Image.Palette[Image.Lab[x + bmp.Width * y] & 255];
    index = 3 * x + Math.Abs(bmpData.Stride) * y;
    rgbValues[index + 0] = color.B;
    rgbValues[index + 1] = color.G;
    rgbValues[index + 2] = color.R;
  }
}
System.Runtime.InteropServices.Marshal.Copy(rgbValues, 0, ptr, bytes);
bmp.UnlockBits(bmpData);
} //*********************** end LabToBitmap ***********************
```

The bitmap BreadthBmp shows the components in false colors.

The user can save the image with the labeled components as a color image by clicking Save image of 'Breadth'.

As previously mentioned, I have developed another method for labeling connected components. This method has the advantage of labeling the components not one after another, but rather simultaneously, in parallel. The idea of this method was described earlier. Here we are going to present the code of the important method ComponentE, which is called as a method of the image RootIm when the user clicks Root method.

```
public int ComponentsE(Form1 fm1)
{ /* Labels connected components of "this" in "this->Lab" and returns
      the number of components. Uses the EquNaLi connectedness. --*/
  int Dir, light, i, nComp=0, rv, x1 = 0, y1 = 0;
  bool adjac;
  iVect2 P = new iVect2(0, 0);
  for (int k=0; k<width*height; k++) Lab[k]=k;

  int y2 = nLoop*height / denomProg;;
  for (int y=0; y<height; y++) //=========================================
  { if ((y % y2) == 0) fm1.progressBar1.PerformStep();
    for (int x = 0; x < width; x++) //=====================================
    {  i=x+width*y; // "i" is the index of the actual pixel
      light=Grid[i];
      P.X=x; P.Y=y;
      int nmax;
      if (y==0) nmax=0;
      else nmax=3;
      for (int n=0; n<=nmax; n++) //==== the four preceding neighbors ========
      { switch(n)
        { case 0: x1=x-1; y1=y; break;    // West
          case 1: x1=x-1; y1=y-1; break; // North-West
          case 2: x1=x;   y1=y-1; break; // North
          case 3: x1=x+1; y1=y-1; break; // North-East
        }
        if (x1<0 || x1>=width) continue;
        Dir=n+4;
```

```
        int indN=x1+width*y1;
        int lightNeib=Grid[indN];
        if (lightNeib!=light) continue;
        if ((Dir & 1)==0) adjac=true;
        else
          adjac=EquNaliDir(P, Dir, light);
        if (adjac)
          rv=SetEquivalent(i, indN); // Sets Lab[i] or Lab[indN] equal to
          Root
    } //==================== end for (int n ... ========================
  } //==================== end for (int x ... ========================
} //==================== end for (int y ... ========================
nComp=SecondRun(); // Writes indexes of components from 1 to nComp to
"Comp".
return nComp;  // nComp+1 is the number of indexes
} //*********************** end ComponentsE ***********************
```

The image RootIm of the class CImageComp contains the labels of the components and the palette. As in the case of Breadth_First_Search, the methods MakePalette and LabToBitmap are called to make the labels visible. The image RootIm is transformed to the bitmap RootBmp and the latter is displayed in the right-hand picture box. Then the user can save this image by clicking Save image of 'Root'.

Conclusion

The time complexity of both the root algorithm and the breadth-first algorithm is linear in the number of the elements of the image. Both algorithms can be applied to images of any dimension provided the adjacency relation is defined.

Numerous experiments performed by the author have shown that the runtime of both the root algorithm and the breadth-first algorithm is almost equal. The advantage of the root algorithm is that it tests each element of the image whether it is already labeled or not $(3^d - 1)/2$ times with d equal to 2 or to 3 being the dimension of the image, whereas the breadth-first algorithm tests it 3^d times, which is approximately two times more. The breadth-first algorithm can be directly employed to label only a single component containing a given element of the image, whereas the root algorithm must label all components simultaneously.

CHAPTER 10

Straightening Photos of Paintings

We are sometimes interested in taking photos of paintings shown in an exhibition. If the room is purely illuminated then it is necessary to use a flash. However, if you put the camera directly in front of the painting, the flash reflects in the pane of the painting, and the photo is spoiled. It is necessary to take the photo from the side to avoid the reflection. Then, however, the image of the painting is distorted (Figure 10-1).

Figure 10-1. *Photo of a painting taken from the side*

V. Kovalevsky, *Modern Algorithms for Image Processing*, https://doi.org/10.1007/978-1-4842-4237-7_10

I suggest a project for rectifying such photos. Knowledge of the geometry of central projection would be useful if we knew the distance of the camera from the painting, the direction of the ray from the middle point of the painting to the objective of the camera, and the focal length of the camera. Estimating all these parameters is difficult, especially if a zoom was used during photography because zooming changes the focal length of the camera.

Therefore I suggest a method based on the supposition that the framework of the painting is rectangular. It is then possible to estimate the relation of the width of the framework to its height while using the relation of the length of the left edge of the framework in the photo to the length of its right edge. The relation of the length of the upper edge to the length of the lower edge is also useful.

The suggested project called WFrectify works as follows. It is possible to use .jpg and .bmp images; images in other formats should be converted into one of these formats. This is easy using the program IrfanView, which is free and can be downloaded from the Internet. The form of the project is shown in Figure 10-2.

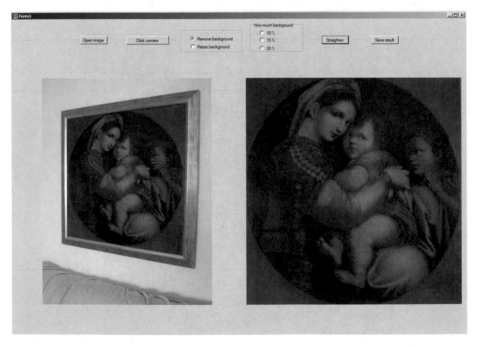

Figure 10-2. *The form of the project WFrectify*

To open an image the user should click Open image and then Click corners. A right angle of two white lines then marks the lower left quarter of the image. The user should then decide whether he or she wants to have the picture with or without the frame. Depending on this decision, the user clicks the lower left corner of either the frame or the image within the frame.

The clicked corner is marked with a small red spot, and the white angle moves to the upper left quarter of the image. The user should click the corresponding corner and so on until all four corners are clicked. Then the marked quadrangle will be displayed with red lines. If the user has clicked a point outside of the angle marked by white lines, a message displays telling the user the correct location of the point, and he or she can close the message and click again.

The middle point of the image `pictureBox1` must be inside of the processed painting. Otherwise it is impossible to correctly click all four corners. In this case the image must be cut, for example, with the program IrfanView, in such a way that the middle point of the whole image lies inside the painting. The coordinates of the four clicked points are saved in the array `Point v[4]`.

The user should decide whether the background outside of the marked quadrangle should be removed or partially retained. Accordingly, he or she should select the option Remove background or Retain background and one of the options to indicate the percentage.

It is then necessary to click Straighten. The straightened image appears in the right-hand picture box. The user can save the resulting image by clicking Save result. The straightened image can be saved as a `.bmp` or `.jpg` file. It is also possible to overwrite an existing image, including the just opened image. Let us explore how the project works.

The Principle of Straightening

To straighten the image we need the width and height of the straightened image. Then we can transform the original image to the straightened one by means of the bilinear transformation or by means of the central projection as explained next.

Experiments have shown that bilinear transformation produces inaccurate results. Different parts of the image are enlarged differently, as shown in Figure 10-3.

Figure 10-3. *Example of an image straightened by means of bilinear transformation*

As seen in Figure 10-3, the rectangles in the left part of the image are drawn up into the width and in the right part into the height. This disadvantage is not noticeable when straightening a painting, because there are no rectangles, but it is still an undesirable distortion of the image. Therefore we have decided not to use bilinear transformation and have developed a method with central transformation, although it was much more difficult.

It is possible to find the necessary parameters of the transformation by means of the well-known equations of the central projection. However, as explained earlier, we need to know the distance from the objective of the camera to the painting and the angles specifying the direction of the optical axis of the camera. There is no way to estimate these parameters. Instead we can use the well-founded assumption that the frame of the painting is a rectangle. We see in the obtained image (Figure 10-1) that the length of the left edge of the frame differs from the length of the right edge. The relation of these lengths as well as the relation of the lengths of the upper and the lower edges can be used to estimate the relations of the distance of the camera from different edges of the painting. These relations can then be used to estimate the parameters of the transformation.

Consider the diagram in Figure 10-4 representing the plane through the objective O of the camera and the points M_0 and M_1 on the left and right edges of the frame in the obtained image (Figure 10-5). We have placed a turned copy (M_0, C, M_1) of the focal plane between the objective and the photographed object (not seen in the diagram) so that the image in that plane is not reversed as the image is in the focal plane.

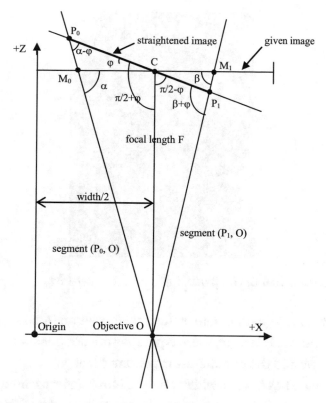

Figure 10-4. *Section of the rays with the plane (M_0, O, M_1)*

To find the parameters of the transformation it is necessary to estimate the parameters of a plane parallel to the plane of the photographed painting because the central projection of the obtained image onto this plane is the desired straightened image. This plane is represented in Figure 10-4 as the line containing the segment (P_0, P_1). The segment (P_0, P_1) is the section of the said plane with the plane (M_0, O, M_1). Important are also the four points clicked by the user at the corners of the frame in the obtained image. These points are vertices of the nonrectangular quadrangle representing the frame in the obtained image (Figure 10-5).

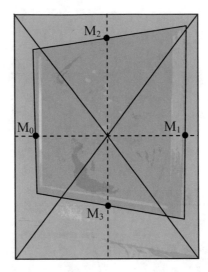

Figure 10-5. *Explanation of the points M_0, M_1, M_2, and M_3*

It is possible to find the parameters of the transformation by solving the corresponding equations. However, these equations are not linear and they are difficult to solve. Therefore we find the parameters trigonometrically.

The obtained image has the size width × height. Most modern cameras have a main focal length (i.e., the focal length without zoom) equal to the width of the light-sensitive matrix. Therefore we suppose that the focal length is equal to the maximum of width and height. We denote the focal length with F. First we calculate the angles α and β (Figure 10-4):

$$\alpha = \arctan(F/(\text{width}/2 - M_0.X)$$

$$\beta = \arctan(F/(M_1.X - \text{width}/2))$$

where width is the width of the obtained image.

The angle φ can be calculated by means of the law of sines from the triangle (P_0, O, C) where C is the center of the obtained image. Its coordinates are (width/2, height/2, F):

$$(P_0 - O)/\sin(\pi/2 + \varphi) = F/\sin(\alpha - \varphi)$$

or

$$(P_0 - O) = F \cdot \sin(\pi/2 + \varphi)/\sin(\alpha - \varphi).$$

Similarly we obtain from the triangle (P_1, O, C):

$$(P_1 - O) = F \cdot \sin(\pi/2 - \varphi)/\sin(\beta + \varphi)$$

and

$$(P_0 - O) = RedY \cdot (P_1 - O)$$

where RedY is the relation $(P_0 - O)/(P_1 - O)$, which is equal to the relation of the length of the right edge to the length of the left edge of the frame in the obtained image.

Therefore, we obtain:

$$F \cdot \sin(\pi/2 + \varphi)/\sin(\alpha - \varphi) = RedY \cdot F \cdot \sin(\pi/2 - \varphi)/\sin(\beta + \varphi).$$

According to the equations $\sin(\pi/2 + \varphi) = \cos(\varphi)$ and $\sin(\pi/2 - \varphi) = \cos(\varphi)$ we obtain:

$$\cos(\varphi)/\sin(\alpha - \varphi) = RedY \cdot \cos(\varphi)/\sin(\beta + \varphi)$$

or after reducing by $\cos(\varphi)$:

$$\sin(\beta + \varphi) = RedY \cdot \sin(\alpha - \varphi).$$

Now we replace $\sin(\beta + \varphi)$ by $\sin \beta \cdot \cos \varphi + \cos \beta \cdot \sin \varphi$ and $\sin(\alpha - \varphi)$ by $\sin \alpha \cdot \cos \varphi - \cos \alpha \cdot \sin \varphi$:

$$\sin \beta \cdot \cos \varphi + \cos \beta \cdot \sin \varphi = RedY \cdot (\sin \alpha \cdot \cos \varphi - \cos \alpha \cdot \sin \varphi).$$

After dividing by $\cos \varphi$ we obtain:

$$\sin \beta \cdot 1 + \cos \beta \cdot tg\, \varphi = RedY \cdot (\sin \alpha \cdot 1 - \cos \alpha \cdot tg\, \varphi)$$

or

$$tg\, \varphi \cdot (\cos \beta + RedY \cdot \cos \alpha) = RedY \cdot \sin \alpha - \sin \beta$$

and

$$tg\, \varphi \cdot = (RedY \cdot \sin \alpha - \sin \beta)/(\cos \beta + RedY \cdot \cos \alpha)$$

or

$$\varphi \cdot = \arctan(RedY \cdot \sin \beta - \sin \alpha)/(\cos \alpha + RedY \cdot \cos \beta).$$

The value of $\varphi \cdot$ allows us to find the parameter CX of the equation of the plane P containing the straightened image:

$$(x - width/2)*CX + (y - height/2)*CY + (z - F) = 0. \qquad (10.1)$$

Because the line (P_0, P_1) is the intersection of P with plane (M_0, O, M_1), CX is approximately equal to $\tan(\varphi)$. This is course estimation, and we present a precise estimation later.

In a similar way we calculate the angle φX in the plane (M_2, O, M_3) where M_2 and M_3 are points of the upper and the lower edges of the frame in the given image with $M_2.X = M_3.X =$ width/2 (see Figure 10-5). The angle φX is similar to the already calculated angle φ which lies in the plane (M^0, O, M^1). The value RedX is the relation of the length of the upper edge to the length of the lower edge of the frame.

$$\varphi X = \arctan(\text{RedX}\cdot\sin \beta X - \sin \alpha X)/(\cos \alpha X + \text{Red}\cdot\cos \beta X).$$

Correspondingly, the estimate of CY is $\tan(\varphi X)$.

Let us now calculate the width of the straightened image. We obtain from the triangle (P_0, O, C) according to the law of sine the length of the segment (P_0, C):

$$|P_0, C| = F\cdot\sin (\pi/2 - \alpha)/\sin(\alpha - \varphi);$$

and from the triangle (P_1, O, C) the length of (P_1, C):

$$|P_1, C| = F\cdot\sin (\pi/2 - \beta)/\sin(\beta + \varphi).$$

The sought value of Width is then equal to:

$$\text{Width} = |P_0, P_1| = |P_0, C| + |P_1, C| =$$

$$F\cdot(\sin (\pi/2 - \alpha)/\sin(\alpha - \varphi) + \sin (\pi/2 - \beta)/\sin(\beta + \varphi)) =$$

$$F\cdot(\cos \alpha/\sin(\alpha - \varphi) + \cos \beta/\sin(\beta + \varphi)).$$

In a similar way we obtain the value of Height while considering the plane (M_2, O, M_3) where M_2 and M_3 are points of the upper and the lower edges of the frame in the given image with $M_2.X = M_3.X =$ width/2 (see Figure 10-5).

$$\text{Height} = F\cdot(\cos \alpha X/\sin(\alpha X - \varphi X) + \cos \beta X/\sin(\beta X + \varphi X))$$

where αX, βX, and φX are angles in the plane (M_2, O, M_3) similar to α, β, and φ calculated in the plane (M_0, O, M_1).

We have calculated the parameters CX and CY of the plane P as

$$CX = \tan(\varphi); CY = \tan(\varphi X).$$

Experiments have shown that these values are approximations. To find exact values of CX and CY we have developed the method `Optimization`, which tests many values of CX and CY in the neighborhood of the previously mentioned approximate values. For each pair of values of CX and CY the method calculates three deviations of the quadruple Q obtained as a central projection of the quadruple V onto the plane P from the desired shape of a rectangle. These deviations are as follows:

194

1. Deviation "dev1" is equal to the projection of a horizontal edge of Q onto its vertical edge. This projection should be equal to zero if Q were a rectangle.

2. Deviation "dev2" is equal to the difference of the lengths of the vertical edges of Q.

3. Deviation "dev3" is equal to the difference of the lengths of the horizontal edges of Q.

The square root of the sum of the squares of these three deviations is the criterion that should be minimized over all tested pairs CX and CY. There are $11 \times 11 = 121$ pairs of values of CX and CY that are tested, and the values of CX and CY change by a step = 0.08. The optimal values of CX and CY corresponding to the minimum of the criterion are tested a second time again in $11 \times 11 = 121$ pairs of values changed with a step = 0.01. The experiments have shown that the minimum of the criterion reaches a value between 1.0 and 10.0 depending on the precision of the vectors v specified by the user who was clicking the corners of the image. This precision of the optimization is sufficient. Even the starting values of CX and CY obtained by trigonometric calculations deliver straightened images that cannot be optically distinguished from ideal images.

After calculating the values of CX and CY the method Rect_Optimal calculates the four points PC[4] which are central projections of the four points v[4] onto the plane P. Then the straightened image ResultIm is defined with the size Width×Height. This image is scanned in two for loops with coordinates X and Y of the pixels. For each pixel (X, Y) the coordinates (xp, yp, zp) of a point lying in the quadruple with the corners PC[4] and corresponding to the pixel (X, Y) are calculated by a bilinear transformation. The point with the coordinates (xp, yp, zp) is centrally projected to the plane of the given image. This projection is a point with coordinates (xf, yf, F). The color of the pixel (xf, yf) of the given image is assigned to the pixel (X, Y) of the straightened image.

A similar method, Rect_Retain, is used to produce the straightened image containing a part of the background around the frame of the painting. This method differs from Rect_Optimal only by the presence of a procedure moving the points PC[4] in the plane P from the centrum C with coordinates (width/2, height/2, F) in such a way that the length of each vector (PC[i], C), I = 0, 1, 2, 3; is multiplied by the parameter Rel, which can be chosen by the user as having the value 1.1, 1.15, or 1.2. As a result of this multiplication, the straightened image includes a narrow strip of the original background around the frame of the painting.

Codes of Most Important Methods

Here is the source code of the most important method, Rect_Optimal.

```
public void Rect_Optimal(Point[] v, bool CUT, ref CImage Result)
// Calculates the corners of the straightened image and then makes a
central projection.
{
  bool deb = false;
  int MaxSize;
  double alphaX, alphaY, betaX, betaY, F, Height, phiX, phiY,
    RedX, RedY, Width, M0X, M1X, M3Y, M2Y;

  M0X = (double)v[1].X + (v[0].X - v[1].X) *((double)height/2 -
                        v[1].Y)/((double)v[0].Y-v[1].Y);
  M1X = (double)v[2].X + (v[3].X - v[2].X) *((double)height/2 -
                        v[2].Y)/((double)v[3].Y-v[2].Y);
  M3Y = (double)v[0].Y + (v[3].Y - v[0].Y) * ((double)width/2 -
                        v[0].X)/((double)v[3].X-v[0].X);
  M2Y = (double)v[1].Y + (v[2].Y - v[1].Y) * ((double)width/2 -
                        v[1].X)/((double)v[2].X-v[1].X);

  RedY = (double)(v[3].Y - v[2].Y) / (double)(v[0].Y - v[1].Y);
  RedX = (double)(v[3].X - v[0].X) / (double)(v[2].X - v[1].X);
  if (width > height) MaxSize = width;
  else MaxSize = height;
  F = 1.0 * (double)(MaxSize);
  alphaY = Math.Atan2(F, (double)(width / 2 - M0X));
  betaY = Math.Atan2(F, (double)(M1X - width / 2));
  phiY=Math.Atan2(RedY*Math.Sin(betaY) -
      Math.Sin(alphaY),Math.Cos(alphaY)+RedY*Math.Cos(betaY));

  alphaX = Math.Atan2(F, (double)(M3Y - height / 2));
  betaX = Math.Atan2(F, (double)(height / 2 - M2Y));
  phiX = Math.Atan2(RedX * Math.Sin(betaX) -
        Math.Sin(alphaX), Math.Cos(alphaX) + RedX * Math.Cos(betaX));
  double P0X = F * Math.Cos(alphaY) / Math.Sin(alphaY - phiY);
  double P1X = F * Math.Cos(betaY) / Math.Sin(betaY + phiY);
```

```
double POY = F * Math.Cos(alphaX) / Math.Sin(alphaX + phiX);
Width = F * (Math.Cos(alphaY) / Math.Sin(alphaY - phiY) +
            Math.Cos(betaY) / Math.Sin(betaY + phiY));
Height = F * (Math.Cos(alphaX) / Math.Sin(alphaX - phiX) +
             Math.Cos(betaX) / Math.Sin(betaX + phiX));
if (Width < 0.0 || Height < 0.0)
{
  MessageBox.Show("The clicked area does not contain the center of the
  image");
  return;
}

double OptCX=0.0;
double OptCY=0.0;
double CX = Math.Tan(phiY);
double CY = Math.Tan(phiX);

Optimization(F, v, CX, CY, ref OptCX, ref OptCY);
CX = OptCX;
CY = OptCY;

CImage Out;
if (CUT)
  Out = new CImage((int)Width, (int)Height, N_Bits);
else
  Out = new CImage(width, height, N_Bits);
Result.Copy(Out, 0);

double A = 0.0, B, C, D, Det, E, G;
double[] xc = new double[4];
double[] yc = new double[4];
double[] zc = new double[4];

for (int i = 0; i < 4; i++)
{
  A = B = C = D = 0.0;
  A = (F / (v[i].X - width / 2) + CX);
  B = CY;
```

```
  C = width / 2 * F / (v[i].X - width / 2) + CX * width / 2 + CY *
      height / 2 + F;
  D = CX;
  E = (F / (v[i].Y - height / 2) + CY);
  G = height / 2 * F / (v[i].Y - height / 2) + CX * width / 2 + CY *
      height / 2 + F;
  Det = A * E - B * D;
  xc[i] = (C * E - B * G) / Det;
  yc[i] = (A * G - C * D) / Det;
  zc[i] = F - CX * (xc[i] - width / 2) - CY * (yc[i] - height / 2);
}

double zz;
double xp, yp, xp0, xp1, yp0, yp1, xf, yf;
for (int Y = 0; Y < Result.height; Y++) //= over the straightened image
{
  xp0 = xc[1] + (xc[0] - xc[1]) * Y / (Result.height - 1);
  xp1 = xc[2] + (xc[3] - xc[2]) * Y / (Result.height - 1);

  for (int X = 0; X < Result.width; X++) //==============================
  {
    yp0 = yc[1] + (yc[2] - yc[1]) * X / (Result.width - 1);
    yp1 = yc[0] + (yc[3] - yc[0]) * X / (Result.width - 1);
    xp = xp0 + (xp1 - xp0) * X / (Result.width - 1);
    yp = yp0 + (yp1 - yp0) * Y / (Result.height - 1);
    zz = F - CX * (xp - width / 2) - CY * (yp - height / 2); // corrected
    xf = width / 2 + (xp - width / 2) * F / (F - CX * (xp - width / 2) -
                                        CY * (yp - height / 2));
    yf = height / 2 + (yp - height / 2) * F / (F - CX * (xp - width / 2) -
                                        CY * (yp - height / 2));

    if ((int)xp >= 0 && (int)xp < width && (int)yp >= 0 && (int)yp <
    height)
      if (N_Bits == 24)
      {
```

```
        for (int ic = 0; ic < 3; ic++)
          Result.Grid[ic+3*X+3*Result.width*Y]=Grid[ic+3*(int)
          xf+3*width*(int)yf];
      }
      else
        Result.Grid[X+Result.width*(Result.height-1-Y)]=Grid[(int)
        xf+width*(int)yf];
    } //================= end for (X... ==============================
  } //================= end for (Y... ==============================
} //******************** end Rect_Optimal *****************************
```

Here is the code for Optimization.

```
private void Optimization(double F, Point[] v, double CX, double CY,
                                     ref double OptCX, ref double OptCY)
{
  bool deb = false;
  double A = 0.0, B, C, D, Det, E, G;
  double[] xc = new double[4];
  double[] yc = new double[4];
  double[] zc = new double[4];

  double[] xopt = new double[4];
  double[] yopt = new double[4];
  double[] zopt = new double[4];

  double dev1, dev2, dev3, Crit;
  double MinCrit = 10000000.0;
  int OptIterX = -1, OptIterY = -1, IterY;
  OptCX = 0.0;
  OptCY = 0.0;

  CX -= 0.40; CY -= 0.40;
  double CX0 = CX, Step = 0.08;
  for (IterY = 0; IterY < 11; IterY++)
  {
    CX = CX0;
    for (int IterX = 0; IterX < 11; IterX++)
```

```
{
  for (int i = 0; i < 4; i++)
  {
    A = (F / (v[i].X - width / 2) + CX);
    B = CY;
    C = width / 2 * F / (v[i].X - width / 2) + CX * width / 2 + CY *
        height / 2 + F;
    D = CX;
    E = (F / (v[i].Y - height / 2) + CY);
    G = height / 2 * F / (v[i].Y - height / 2) + CX * width / 2 + CY *
        height / 2 + F;
    Det = A * E - B * D;
    xc[i] = (C * E - B * G) / Det;
    yc[i] = (A * G - C * D) / Det;
    zc[i] = F - CX * (xc[i] - width / 2) - CY * (yc[i] - height / 2);
  }
  dev1 = dev2 = dev3 = 0.0;

  dev1 = ((xc[0] - xc[1]) * (xc[2] - xc[1]) + (yc[0] - yc[1]) * (yc[2] -
  yc[1]) + (zc[0] - zc[1]) * (zc[2] - zc[1])) /
    Math.Sqrt(Math.Pow((xc[0] - xc[1]), 2.0) + Math.Pow((yc[0] -
    yc[1]), 2.0) + Math.Pow((zc[0] - zc[1]), 2.0));

  dev2 =
    Math.Sqrt(Math.Pow((xc[3] - xc[2]), 2.0) + Math.Pow((yc[3] -
    yc[2]), 2.0) + Math.Pow((zc[3] - zc[2]), 2.0)) -
    Math.Sqrt(Math.Pow((xc[0] - xc[1]), 2.0) + Math.Pow((yc[0] -
    yc[1]), 2.0) + Math.Pow((zc[0] - zc[1]), 2.0));

  dev3 =
  Math.Sqrt(Math.Pow((xc[2] - xc[1]), 2.0) + Math.Pow((yc[2] - yc[1]), 2.0) +
                                  Math.Pow((zc[2] - zc[1]), 2.0)) -
  Math.Sqrt(Math.Pow((xc[3] - xc[0]), 2.0) + Math.Pow((yc[3] - yc[0]),
  2.0) + Math.Pow((zc[3] - zc[0]), 2.0));

  Crit=Math.Sqrt(Math.Pow(dev1, 2.0)+Math.Pow(dev2, 2.0)+Math.Pow(dev3,
  2.0));
```

```
    if (Crit < MinCrit)
    {
      MinCrit = Crit;
      OptIterX = IterX;
      OptIterY = IterY;
      OptCX = CX;
      OptCY = CY;
      for (int i = 0; i < 4; i++)
      {
        xopt[i] = xc[i];
        yopt[i] = yc[i];
        zopt[i] = zc[i];
      }
    }
    CX += Step;
  } //============= end for (int IterX... ========================
  CY += Step;
} //============= end for (int IterY... ========================
CX = OptCX; CY = OptCY;
CX -= 0.05; CY -= 0.05;
CX0 = CX;
double step=0.01;
for (IterY = 0; IterY < 11; IterY++)
{
  CX = CX0;
  for (int IterX = 0; IterX < 11; IterX++)
  {
    for (int i = 0; i < 4; i++)
    {
      A = (F / (v[i].X - width / 2) + CX);
      B = CY;
```

```
        C = width / 2 * F / (v[i].X - width / 2) + CX * width / 2 + CY *
            height / 2 + F;
        D = CX;
        E = (F / (v[i].Y - height / 2) + CY);
        G = height / 2 * F / (v[i].Y - height / 2) + CX * width / 2 + CY *
            height / 2 + F;
      Det = A * E - B * D;
      xc[i] = (C * E - B * G) / Det;
      yc[i] = (A * G - C * D) / Det;
      zc[i] = F - CX * (xc[i] - width / 2) - CY * (yc[i] - height / 2);
    }
    dev1 = dev2 = dev3 = 0.0;

    // deviation from a 90° angle:
    dev1 = ((xc[0] - xc[1]) * (xc[2] - xc[1]) + (yc[0] - yc[1]) *
    (yc[2] - yc[1]) + (zc[0] - zc[1]) * (zc[2] - zc[1])) /
      Math.Sqrt(Math.Pow((xc[0] - xc[1]), 2.0) + Math.Pow((yc[0] -
      yc[1]), 2.0) + Math.Pow((zc[0] - zc[1]), 2.0));

    dev2 =  // difference |pc[3] - pc[2]| - |pc[0] - pc[1]|:
      Math.Sqrt(Math.Pow((xc[3] - xc[2]), 2.0) + Math.Pow((yc[3] -
      yc[2]), 2.0) + Math.Pow((zc[3] - zc[2]), 2.0)) -

      Math.Sqrt(Math.Pow((xc[0] - xc[1]), 2.0) + Math.Pow((yc[0] -
      yc[1]), 2.0) + Math.Pow((zc[0] - zc[1]), 2.0));

    dev3 =  // difference |pc[2] - pc[1]| - |pc[3] - pc[0]|:
    Math.Sqrt(Math.Pow((xc[2] - xc[1]), 2.0) + Math.Pow((yc[2] - yc[1]),
    2.0) + Math.Pow((zc[2] - zc[1]), 2.0)) -

    Math.Sqrt(Math.Pow((xc[3] - xc[0]), 2.0) + Math.Pow((yc[3] - yc[0]),
    2.0) + Math.Pow((zc[3] - zc[0]), 2.0));

    Crit =Math.Sqrt(Math.Pow(dev1,2.0)+Math.Pow(dev2,2.0)+Math.
    Pow(dev3,2.0));
```

```
        if (Crit < MinCrit)
        {
          MinCrit = Crit;
          OptIterX = IterX;
          OptIterY = IterY;
          OptCX = CX;
         OptCY = CY;
          for (int i = 0; i < 4; i++)
          {
            xopt[i] = xc[i];
            yopt[i] = yc[i];
            zopt[i] = zc[i];
          }
        }
      CX += step;
    } //============== end for (int IterX... ========================
    CY += step;
  } //============== end for (int IterY... ========================
} //**************** end Optimization ****************************
```

Conclusion

This project brings good results and is easy to use: It provides graphical support for the
user and notes when the user makes a mistake.

CHAPTER 11

Polygonal Approximation of Region Boundaries and Edges

This chapter describes a method of representing curves in two-dimensional digital images as polygons. This kind of curve representation is useful for image analysis because the shape of a polygon can be easily investigated by simple geometrical means such as measuring lengths and angles. Polygonal approximation also suggests a new method of estimating curvature of digital curves. For this purpose a polygon can be replaced by a smooth sequence of circular arcs and straight line segments. *Smooth* means that each straight segment is the tangent to the previous and the subsequent arc.

This chapter contains a short review of related publications, a short description of the known methods of polygonal approximation, the definition of a new measure of the similarity of digital curves suggested by Schlesinger (2000), and a new approximation method using this measure. It also contains the theory of the new method of estimating the curvature and some experimental results.

The Problem of Polygonal Approximation

Given is a digital curve C in a two-dimensional image. We want to approximate C by a polygon that has as few edges as possible and is "similar" to C. One of the possible criteria of the similarity is the Hausdorff distance: Let S_1 and S_2 be two sets of points.

© Vladimir Kovalevsky 2019
V. Kovalevsky, *Modern Algorithms for Image Processing*, https://doi.org/10.1007/978-1-4842-4237-7_11

Denote the distance between the points p and q by $d(p, q)$. Then the following definitions hold:

> $D(p, S) = \min d(p, q)\ \forall q \in S$ is the distance from point p to set S.
>
> $D(S_1, S_2) = \max D(p, S_2)\ \forall p \in S_1$ is the distance from set S_1 to set S_2.
>
> $D(S_2, S_1) = \max D(q, S_1)\ \forall q \in S_2$ is the distance from set S_2 to set S_1.
>
> $H(S_1, S_2) = \max (D(S_1, S_2), D(S_2, S_1))$ is the Hausdorff distance between S_1 and S_2.

However, the Hausdorff distance is not always a suitable measure of the similarity of two curves. The Hausdorff distance between the red and the black polygons shown in Figure 11-1 is less than 2 pixels; however, the true deviation is much greater: The polygons are not similar. Schlesinger (2000) suggested a more adequate measure of the similarity of curves.

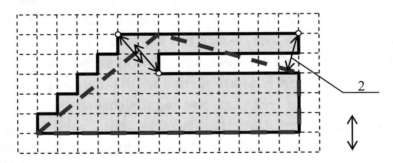

Figure 11-1. *Example of two polygons with the Hausdorff distance less than 2; all arrows have the length 2*

Schlesinger's Measure of Similarity of Curves

Given are two digital curves C_1 and C_2. Take m equally spaced points along C_1 and n points along C_2. Thus one gets two *ordered* sets M_1 and M_2 of points. The smaller the distance between subsequent points along the curve, the more precise the estimate of the similarity. Let us denote the distance between two points p and q as $d(p, q)$.

Find the monotonic map $F\colon M_1 \rightarrow M_2$ with the smallest value of the maximum distance between the corresponding points. The map of an ordered set M_1 onto another ordered set M_2 is called *monotonic*, if for any two points $P_1 < P_2$ of M_1 the condition $F(P_1) < F(P_2)$ holds.

The smallest value of the maximum distance between the corresponding points is the *Schlesinger's distance DS* between the curves C_1 and C_2.

$$DS(M_1, M_2) = \min \max \left(d(p, F(p)) \right)$$

Schlesinger (2000) also suggested an efficient algorithm for computing the distance *DS* for any two digital curves. The value of *DS* for our example can be computed as follows. Let the black curve be *B* and the red one be *R*. The curves are subdivided into corresponding segments (a, b), (b, d), (d, f), and (f, a). (The points a, b, d, and f are lying on both polygons.) Map each point of a segment of *B* onto the nearest point of the corresponding segment of *R* as shown in Figure 11-2.

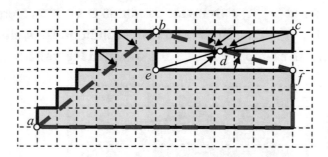

Figure 11-2. *Definition of Schlesinger's similarity*

The value of *DS* for the example of Figure 11-2 is defined by the length of (c, d) (or (e, d)) and is equal to 3.6. It is essentially greater than the Hausdorff distance equal to 2 and is more exact.

Statement of the Approximation Problem

Given a digital curve *C* and a tolerance value ε find the polygonal line *P* with the minimum number of edges such that the Schlesinger's distance $DS(C, P)$ is not greater than ε.

In the next section we consider various methods for solving this problem.

Algorithms for Polygonal Approximation

We present here some algorithms known from the literature and some new algorithms.

The Split-and-Merge Method

The advantage of this method is that it is very simple to understand and to program. Given are a closed curve C and the maximum allowed distance ε from the points of C to the polygon. Take an arbitrary point V_1 on C. Find the point V_2 with the greatest distance from V_1. Now the curve is subdivided into two segments: (V_1, V_2) and (V_2, V_1). Each segment (V_i, V_k) has its chord (at the start of the algorithm two segments have the same chord). For each segment find the point V_m with the greatest distance D from the corresponding chord. If $D > \varepsilon$, split the segment (V_i, V_k) into two segments (V_i, V_m) and (V_m, V_k). Repeat this until $D \le \varepsilon$ for all segments. The split phase is finished.

Now check each pair of adjacent segments (V_i, V_m) and (V_m, V_k) for whether the distance D of V_m to the chord (V_i, V_k) satisfies the condition $D \le \varepsilon$. If so, merge the segments (V_i, V_m) and (V_m, V_k). When all pairs fulfill the condition $D > \varepsilon$, stop the merge phase and the algorithm. An example with $\varepsilon = 1.5$ is shown in Figure 11-3.

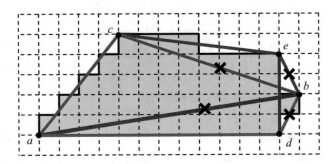

Figure 11-3. *An illustration of the split-and-merge method*

The sequence of new points is a, b, c, d, e. The segments (e, b) and (b, d) have been merged. The given curve is shown by the black step-wise line surrounding the pink region. The starting point is a. The point farthest from a is b. The point of the upper segment with the greatest distance from the chord (a, b) is c, which becomes connected with a and b. The point of the lower segment with the greatest distance from the chord (a, b) is d. It also becomes connected with a and b. The point with the greatest distance from the chord (c, b) is e. It becomes connected with c and b. After this step the condition $D \le \varepsilon$ with $\varepsilon = 1.5$ is fulfilled for all segments. The split phase is finished. For the pair of adjacent segments (e, b) and (b, d) the distance of their common vertex b to the chord (e, d) is less than $\varepsilon = 1.5$. Thus, these segments should be merged. The final approximating polygon has the vertices a, c, e, d.

The Sector Method

The split-and-merge method is rather slow because each point must be tested many times, depending on the number of splits of the segment to which it belongs. This method minimizes the Hausdorff distance, not the Schlesinger distance.

An efficient method called the sector method was suggested by Williams (1978). Start with some point V_1 of the curve C (Figure 11-4). Test all subsequent points. For each point V_i with $i > 1$ and $D(V_1, V_i) > \varepsilon$, draw a circle with the radius equal to the tolerance ε and draw two tangents from V_1 to the circle.

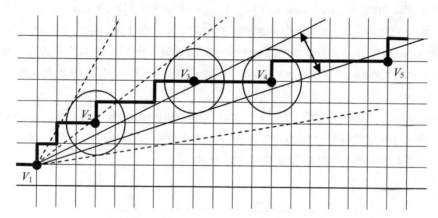

Figure 11-4. *The sector method*

The space between the tangents is a sector, and for each straight line L through V_1 lying in the sector, the distance from the center of the circle to L is less than the tolerance ε. If the next point V_i (V_3 or V_4 in Figure 11-4) lies in the sector, then a new circle with its center at V_i and a sector S of this circle are constructed. The new sector is the intersection of S with the old one. If the next point V_i (e.g., V_5 in Figure 11-4) lies outside of the new sector, then there is no straight line L through V_1 and V_i such that all points between V_1 and V_i have a distance to L less than ε. Therefore, the segment (V_1, V_i) cannot serve as a polygon edge. The point V_{i-1} before V_i is then the last point of the current segment; $[V_1, V_{i-1}]$ is the edge of the polygon. The construction of the next polygon edge starts at the point V_{i-1}.

The Improvement of the Sector Method

The sector method is fast because it tests each point of the given curve only once. However, it guarantees only that the Hausdorff distance between the curve and the polygon is less than the prescribed tolerance ε. The following additional condition has been introduced for interrupting the current segment of the curve that should be approximated by the current edge of the polygon. The point V_{max} of the current segment, which has the greatest distance from the starting point of the segment, must be defined during the processing of the segment. If the distance of the projection of the actual point V_i onto the straight line segment $[V_1, V_{max}]$ is less than $|V_1, V_{max}| - \varepsilon$, then the point V_{max} is the last point of the current segment and the starting point of the next one. This test guarantees that the sequence of the projections of the points of the curve onto the polygon is monotone and therefore the conditions for defining the Schlesinger's distance are fulfilled.

In the example shown in Figure 11-5, the approximating polygon has the vertices a, b, c, d, and e. Red points are those at which the algorithm comes to the decision to interrupt the current segment. The tolerance $\varepsilon = 1.5$.

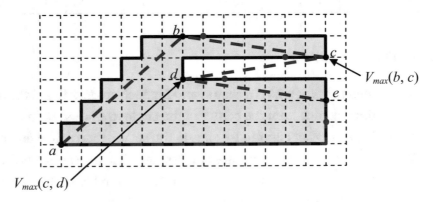

Figure 11-5. *Improvement of the sector method*

The project WFpolyArc presented later in this chapter uses the improved sector method.

Replacing Polygons by Sequences of Arcs and Straight Lines

Definitions and the Problem Statement

Definition 11.1: A sequence of circular arcs and straight line segments is called *smooth* if the following conditions are fulfilled:

1. Each straight line segment L follows an arc A_p and is followed by another arc A_f.

2. The segment L is tangent both to A_p and to A_f at their common end points.

3. If an arc is followed by another arc, then they have a common tangent at their common end point.

Definition 11.2: The *ε-tolerance tube* of a closed polygonal line P is the area between two other polygonal lines P_1 and P_2 such that each edge of P_1, $i = 1, 2$, is parallel to a corresponding edge of P and the shortest distance between P and P_i is exactly equal to the tolerance ε of the approximation. The closed polygonal line P_1 contains P in its interior and P contains P_2 in its interior.

We consider the following problem: Given a polygon P that is known to approximate a digital curve C with the tolerance ε, find a smooth sequence S of circular arcs and straight line segments such that its polygonal approximation with the tolerance ε is equal to P, and the sum of the absolute values of the curvatures of the arcs is minimal.

We suppose that the curvature of the arcs of the sequence S is a good estimate of the curvature of the curve C because the distance between S and C is less than ε. The sum of the absolute values of the curvatures of the arcs must be minimal because otherwise another smooth sequence S^* of small arcs with higher curvature values could be found for which the distance to C is less than the distance between S and C, whereas the curvature values of the arcs of S^* can be arbitrarily high and have nothing to do with curvature of C.

The exact solution of the problem is unknown. We suggest the following approximate solution.

The Approximate Solution

Definition 11.3: A vertex W of the boundary of the tolerance tube T is called *concave* if the obtuse angle between the edges of T incident to W lies outside of T.

In what follows we describe the procedure calculating the curvature values. The procedure calculates for each vertex V (Figure 11-6) of the approximating polygon two candidate values of the curvature C_1 and C_2 of two circular arcs being tangent to the polygon edges incident to V.

Consider first the arc A going through the vertex W and being tangent to the polygon edges. If the distances D_1 and D_2 of the points T_1 and T_2 of tangency of the arc A (both distances are obviously equal to each other) to V are less than or equal to the half length $S_{min}/2$ of the shorter edge of the polygon incident to V, then the radius of the arc should be calculated from the triangle OP_1W (Figure 11-6) as follows:

$$(P_1O) = R_1 - \varepsilon = R_1 \cdot \cos\beta$$

or

$$R_1 - R_1 \cdot \cos\beta = \varepsilon$$

or

$$R_1 = \varepsilon/(1 - \cos\beta) \tag{11.1}$$

where β is the half of the angle γ between the edges of the polygon.

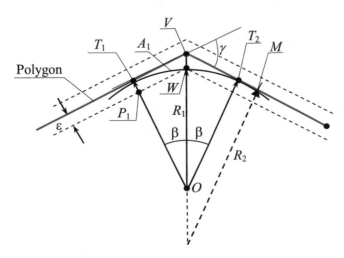

Figure 11-6. *Calculation of the curvature value*

212

If, however, the distances D_1 and D_2 are greater than the distance from V to the middle point M of the shorter of the two polygon edges incident to V, then it is impossible to use this arc because it can overlap with the arc at the next polygon vertex. In this case it is necessary to construct another arc not going through the point W and tangencing the shorter edge at its middle point M and the other edge at a point symmetric to M on the other edge (Figure 11-7).

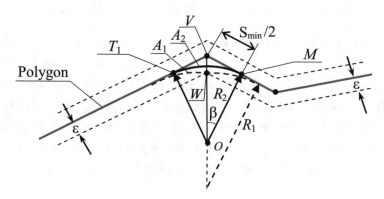

Figure 11-7. *Calculation of the curvature value*

The radius R_2 of this arc should be calculated from the triangle OMV (Figure 11-7):

$$R_2 = \text{ctg}\beta \cdot S_{min}/2; \tag{11.2}$$

The described calculations are performed by the method Curvature desribed next. The method does not calculate the radii but rather the values of the curvature values that are the inverses of the radii:

$$C_1 = 1/R_1; \text{ and } C_2 = 1/R_2. \tag{11.3}$$

The method calculates both C_1 and C_2. It is easily seen that if the distances D_1 and D_2 are shorter than the half-length of the shorter edge (as in Figure 11-6), then $R_1 < R_2$, $C_1 > C_2$, and $C_1 \neq 0$. In this case the resulting value C of the curvature is set to C_1 and the distance D of both points of tangency of the sought for arc to the vertex V is set to $D = R_1 \cdot \tan\beta$.

In the case shown in Figure 11-7, the radius $R_2 < R_1$. the resulting value C of the curvature is set to C_2 and the distance D of both points of tangency of the sought for arc to the vertex V is set to $D = S_{min}/2$.

After calculating the curvature, the method calculates the end points of the arc, which are equal to the points of tangency. For this purpose the length S_1 of the polygon edge preceding V is subdivided in the ratio $a_1:(1 - a_1)$ with $a_1 = D/S_1$. The length S_2 of the edge following V is subdivided in the ratio $a_2:(1 - a_2)$ with $a_2 = D/S_2$.

Finally the method tests whether the length of the arc is zero. This can happen if a small closed polygon contains only three vertices. In this case the procedure returns an error message and the arc is not saved. Here is the code of the method Curvature.

```
public int Curvature(int x1, int y1, int x2, int y2, int x3, int y3,
                                               double eps, ref CArc arc)
/* Calculates the curvature 'k' of an arc lying in the tolerance tube
around the given two polygon edges [(x1,y1), (x2,y2)] and  [(x2,y2),
(x3,y3)] and having the outer boundary of the tube as its tangent. The
tangency point should not be farther than the half-length of the shorter
edge from (x2,y2). The radius of the arc should be as large as possible. */
{
  double a1, a2, lp,  // Variables for calculating the projections
  dx1, dy1, dx2, dy2, len1, len2,    // Increments, lengths of edges
  cosgam, // cosine of the angle between the edges
  sinbet, cosbet,    // cosine and sine of the half-angle between the edges
  strip = 0.6,       // correcture of the deviation
  k, cru1, cru2;     // curvature for long and short edges

  dx1 = (double)(x2 - x1); dy1 = (double)(y2 - y1);  // first edge
  len1 = Math.Sqrt(dx1 * dx1 + dy1 * dy1);
  dx2 = (double)(x3 - x2); dy2 = (double)(y3 - y2);  // second edge
  len2 = Math.Sqrt(dx2 * dx2 + dy2 * dy2);
  if ((len1 == 0.0) || (len2 == 0.0)) return (-1);

  cosgam = (dx1 * dx2 + dy1 * dy2) / len1 / len2;     // cosine of angle
                                                      // between the edges

  if (Math.Abs(cosgam) <= 1.0)
    sinbet = Math.Sqrt((1.0 - cosgam) * 0.5);          // sine of half-angle
  else sinbet = 0.0;
  cosbet = Math.Sqrt((1.0 + cosgam) * 0.5);

  cru1 = (1.0 - cosbet) / (eps - strip);     // long edges, it is important
  // that the arc goes throught the vertex
```

```
double min_len = len1;
if (len2 < min_len) min_len = len2;
if (min_len != 0.0 && cosbet != 0.0)
  cru2 = 2.0 * sinbet / cosbet / min_len;     // short edges, it is
                                                  important
else cru2 = 0.0;                            // that the tangency is in the
                                               middle of the shortest edge

if ((Math.Abs(cru1) > Math.Abs(cru2)) && cru1 != 0.0)
{
  if (cosbet != 0.0 && cru1 != 0.0)
    lp = sinbet / cosbet / cru1;        // distance of the point of
                                           tangency from (x2, y2)
  else lp = 100.0;
  k = cru1;     // first curvature
}
else
{
  lp = min_len / 2.0;
  k = cru2 * 0.95;     // second curvature
}
if (dx1 * dy2 - dy1 * dx2 > 0.0) k = -k;      // the sign

// the first edge is divided in relation a1 : a2
a1 = lp / len1;
a2 = 1.0 - a1;

if (k != 0.0) arc.rad = 1.0F / (float)k;
else arc.rad = 0.0F;

arc.xb = (float)(x1 * a1 + x2 * a2);  // first tangency (begin of the arc)
arc.yb = (float)(y1 * a1 + y2 * a2);

a1 = lp / len2; a2 = 1.0 - a1;
arc.xe = (float)(x3 * a1 + x2 * a2);  // second tangency (end of the arc)
arc.ye = (float)(y3 * a1 + y2 * a2);
```

```
  double AbsR, R, chord_X, chord_Y, Length, Lot_x, Lot_y;
  R = arc.rad;
  AbsR = R;
  if (R < 0.0) AbsR = -R;

  chord_X = arc.xe - arc.xb; chord_Y = arc.ye - arc.yb; // the chord
  Length = Math.Sqrt(chord_X * chord_X + chord_Y * chord_Y); // length of
  chord

  if (R < 0.0)          // 'Lot' is orthogonal to chord
  {
    Lot_x = chord_Y; Lot_y = -chord_X;
  }
  else
  {
    Lot_x = -chord_Y; Lot_y = chord_X;
  }

  if (2 * AbsR < Length) return -1;
  if (Length < 0.1) return -2;

  double Lot = Math.Sqrt(4 * R * R - Length * Length);
  arc.xm = (float)((arc.xb + arc.xe) / 2 - Lot_x * Lot / 2 / Length);
  arc.ym = (float)((arc.yb + arc.ye) / 2 - Lot_y * Lot / 2 / Length);

  if ((arc.xe == arc.xb) && (arc.ye == arc.yb))
  { // can be a closed line of three points ??
      return -2;
  }
  return 0;
} // ****************** end Curvature ********************************
```

The Project WFpolyArc

The form of this project is shown in Figure 11-8.

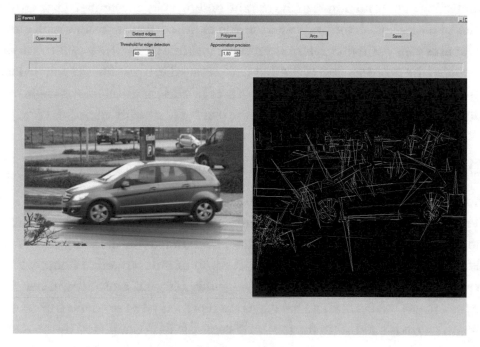

Figure 11-8. *The form of the project WFpolyArc*

Just as our other projects, the form contains an Open image button enabling the user to open an image.

The next button is Detect edges. Clicking this button starts the procedure of edge detection described in Chapter 7. Clicking Polygons starts the procedure of the polygonal approximation of the edges. The precision of the approximation is defined by the value shown in the Approximation precision setting. The displayed value presets the maximum approximation error in pixels. The polygons are shown in the right-hand picture box. Each polygon is tested to determine whether it is smooth or not. This is important for the definition of arcs: It is expedient to determine the arcs only for smooth polygons. The smoothness is defined in the following way. A subroutine defines for each vertex of the polygon whether the sign of the angle between the two edges at this vertex is different from the sign of the angle between the first and the second edges of the polygon. The value of the angle is compared with the maximum angle allowed for smooth polygons.

If the percentage of nodes where the angle is either too large or has the wrong sign, exceeds a predetermined threshold, then the polygon is considered not smooth.

Clicking Arcs starts the method defining the arcs of smooth polygons. The radius vectors starting at the end points of the arc and ending at its curvature center are drawn. The color of the radius vectors indicates the sign of the curvature: Yellow radii are drawn for arcs with positive curvature and violet indicates arcs with negative curvature. Parameters of the polygons and of the arcs can be saved in a text file as explained later. The user can save the lists of polygons and of arcs by clicking Save. It is possible to see the values of the parameters when reading the text file (e.g., with Microsoft Word).

Methods Used in the Project `WFpolyArc`

Methods used for edge detection were introduced in Chapters 6 and 7.

Methods realizing the polygonal approximation of the edges can be made simpler and more understandable when using the representation of the detected edges in a cell complex (Kovalevsky, 2008). The idea of a cell complex is described in Chapter 7.

To make the processing of the detected edges simpler and more comprehensible we use the image `CombIm` in which the edges are represented as sequences of cracks. The image `CombIm` is filled, as in the project `WFcompressPal` (Chapter 8) by the method `LabelCellsNew`. The method reads the image `EdgeIm` produced by the method `ExtremVarColor` or a similar method for grayscale images. It looks for pairs of adjacent pixels with colors that differ by more than the predefined threshold. For each such pair of pixels the crack lying between them is labeled by 1. Also the points (0-cells) at the ends of such a crack are labeled, and the label is equal to the number of cracks belonging to the edge and incident to the point.

Here is the code of the method `LabelCellsNew`.

```
public void LabelCellsNew(int th, CImage Image3)
/* Looks in "Image3" for all pairs of adjacent pixels with color
differences greater than "th" and labels the corresponding cracks in "this"
with "1". The points incident with the crack are also provided with labels
indicating the number and locations of incident cracks.  This method works
both for color and gray value images. ---*/
{ int difH, difV, nComp, NXB=Image3.width, x, y;
   byte Lab = 1;
   if (Image3.N_Bits==24) nComp=3;
```

```
else nComp=1;
for (x=0; x<width*height; x++) Grid[x]=0;

byte[] Colorh = new byte[3];
byte[] Colorp = new byte[3];
byte[] Colorv = new byte[3];
for (y = 0; y < height; y += 2)
  for (x = 0; x < width; x += 2) // through the points
    Grid[x + width * y] = 0;
for (y=1; y<height; y+=2)
  for (x=1; x<width; x+=2) // through the right and upper pixels
  { if (x>=3) //-------------- vertical cracks: abs.dif{(x/2, y/2)-
  ((x-2)/2, y/2)} ----------
    { for (int c=0; c<nComp; c++)
      { Colorv[c]=Image3.Grid[c+nComp*((x-2)/2)+nComp*NXB*(y/2)];
        Colorp[c]=Image3.Grid[c+nComp*(x/2)+nComp*NXB*(y/2)];
      }
      if (nComp==3) difV=ColorDif(Colorp,Colorv);
      else difV=(Colorp[0]-Colorv[0]);
      if (difV < 0) difV = -difV;
      if (difV>th)
    {
      Grid[x - 1 + width * y] = Lab;   // vertical crack
      Grid[x - 1 + width * (y - 1)]++; // point above the crack;
      Grid[x - 1 + width * (y + 1)]++; // point below the crack
    }
  } //-------------------- end if (x>=3) -----------------------------

    if (y>=3) //------------ horizontal cracks: abs.dif{(x/2, y/2)-(x/2,
    (y-2)/2)} ---------
    { for (int c=0; c<nComp; c++)
      { Colorh[c]=Image3.Grid[c+nComp*(x/2)+nComp*NXB*((y-2)/2)];
        Colorp[c]=Image3.Grid[c+nComp*(x/2)+nComp*NXB*(y/2)];
      }
```

```
        if (nComp==3) difH=ColorDif(Colorp,Colorh);
        else difH=Math.Abs(Colorp[0]-Colorh[0]);
        if (difH>th)
      {
        Grid[x + width * (y - 1)] = Lab; // horizontal crack
        Grid[x - 1 + width * (y - 1)]++;  // point left of crack
        Grid[x + 1 + width * (y - 1)]++; // point right of crack
        }
      } //-------------------------- end if (y>=3) ---------------------
    } //================= end for (x=1;... ============================
} //********************* end LabelCellsNew ***************************
```

Polygonal approximation of the edges starts with the method SearchPoly. The method scans the points in the image CombIm. When it finds a point with the label equal to 1, 3, or 4, it calls the method ComponPoly. The method encodes in the object of the class CListLines the polygons of the edge component containing the starting point (X, Y) found by SearchPoly. The method uses a queue that is first-in-first-out. The method puts the starting point Pinp into the queue and starts a while loop. It tests each labeled crack incident to the point P fetched from the queue. If the next point of the crack is a branch or an end point, then the crack is being ignored. Otherwise the function TraceApp is called. TraceApp traces the edge until the next end or branch point and calculates the vertices of the approximating polygon. The tracing ends at a point called Pterm. If the point Pterm is a branch point, it is put into the queue. ComponPoly returns when the queue is empty.

Here is the code for ComponPoly.

```
public int ComponPoly(CImage Comb, int X, int Y, double eps)
{ int dir, dirT;
  int LabNext, rv;
  iVect2 Crack, P, Pinp, Pnext, Pterm;
  Crack = new iVect2();
  P = new iVect2();
  Pinp = new iVect2();
  Pnext = new iVect2();
  Pinp.X = X;
  Pinp.Y = Y; // comb. coord.
```

```
int CNX = Comb.width;
int CNY = Comb.height;
pQ.Put(Pinp);
while(!pQ.Empty()) //=========================================
{
  P = pQ.Get();
  if ((Comb.Grid[P.X + CNX * P.Y] & 128) != 0) continue;
  for (dir=0; dir<4; dir++) //====================================
  {
    Crack.X = P.X + Step[dir].X;
    Crack.Y = P.Y + Step[dir].Y;
    if (Crack.X < 0 || Crack.X > CNX - 1 || Crack.Y < 0 ||
                                       Crack.Y > CNY - 1) continue;
    if (Comb.Grid[Crack.X+CNX*Crack.Y]==1) //---- ------------ --------
    {
     Pnext.X = Crack.X + Step[dir].X;
     Pnext.Y = Crack.Y + Step[dir].Y;
     LabNext = Comb.Grid[Pnext.X + CNX * Pnext.Y] & 7;
     if (LabNext==3) pQ.Put(Pnext);
     if (LabNext==2) //--------------------------------------------------
     {
       Polygon[nPolygon].firstVert = nVert;
       dirT = dir;
       Pterm = new iVect2();
       rv=TraceApp(Comb, P.X, P.Y, eps, ref Pterm, ref dirT);
       if (rv<0)
       { MessageBox.Show("ComponPoly, Alarm! TraceApp returned " + rv);
         return -1;
       }
       if (nPolygon>MaxPoly-1)
       { MessageBox.Show("ComponPoly: Overflow in Polygon; nPolygon=" +
                                   nPolygon + " MaxPoly=" + MaxPoly);
          return -1;
       }
```

```
             else      nPolygon++;
             if ((Comb.Grid[Pterm.X+CNX*Pterm.Y] & 128)==0 && rv>=3)
                                                        pQ.Put(Pterm);
      } // ------------- end if (LabNest==2) ----------------------------
      if ((Comb.Grid[P.X+CNX*P.Y] & 7)==1) break;
      } //-------------- end if (Comb.Grid[Crack.X ...==1) --------------
    } //========= end for (dir ... ====================================
    Comb.Grid[P.X+CNX*P.Y] |=128;
  } //========== end while    ====================================
    return 1;
} //************ end ComponPoly    *************************************
```

When the approximating polygons are calculated, the user can start the calculation of the arcs. The method FindArcs reads the list of the polygons, investigates three subsequent vertices of each polygon, and computes the curvature and the end points of an arc corresponding to the middle vertex of the triple by means of the method Curvature already described. The principles of these calculations were described earlier in this chapter. The method FindArcs produces the list of arcs. Each entry in the list contains the coordinates of the end points, those of the curvature center, and the value of the curvature radius of the arc, all in pixels. Here is the code of FindArcs.

```
public int FindArcs(PictureBox pictureBox, CImage EdgeIm, double eps, Form1 fm1)
/* The method calculates the parameters of the arcs contained in the
polygons. Fills the array 'Arc []' of structures "CArc". Shows the contents
of this array graphically. */
{
  bool deb = false, disp = true;
  int j, ip, first, last, Len, rv,
    x1, y1, x2, y2, x3, y3,        // three polygon vertices composing an arc
    xb, yb, xe, ye, old_xe = 0, old_ye = 0;      // "int" boundaries of arcs
  nArc = 0;
  Pen linePen = new System.Drawing.Pen(Color.LightBlue);
  int marginX = fm1.marginX;
  int marginY = fm1.marginY;
  double Scale1 = fm1.Scale1;
```

```
for (ip = 0; ip < nPolygon; ip++) // ==============================
{
  int cntArc = 0;
  Polygon[ip].firstArc = -1;
  Polygon[ip].lastArc = -2;
  if (!Polygon[ip].smooth) continue;
  first = Polygon[ip].firstVert;
  last = Polygon[ip].lastVert;
  old_xe = -1;
  old_ye = -1;

  if (last > first + 1) // ------- are there sufficient vertices?--------
  {
    if (disp) // here are three points of a polygon calculated but not
    drawn
    {
      x1 = (int)(Scale1 * Vert[first].X + 0.5);  // starting point
      y1 = (int)(Scale1 * Vert[first].Y + 0.5);
    }
    x2 = Vert[first].X;          // will become the first point of the arc
    y2 = Vert[first].Y;
    x3 = Vert[first + 1].X;        // second point
    y3 = Vert[first + 1].Y;

    Polygon[ip].firstArc = nArc;


    // Points from the second one until the one before the last
    Len = last - first + 1;
    for (j = 2; j <= Len; j++) // ==============================
    {
      x1 = x2; y1 = y2;
      x2 = x3; y2 = y3;
      x3 = Vert[first + j % Len].X;
      y3 = Vert[first + j % Len].Y;
```

```
CArc arc = new CArc();
// 'Curvature' calculates and saves parameters of an arc in 'arc'.
rv = Curvature(x1, y1, x2, y2, x3, y3, eps, ref arc);
if (rv < 0) continue;
if (Math.Abs(arc.xb - arc.xe) < 1.0 &&
        Math.Abs(arc.yb - arc.ye) < 1.0 || Math.Abs(arc.rad) < 2.0)
        continue;

// The arc is saved in the list of arcs:
Arc[nArc] = arc;
if (cntArc == 0) Polygon[ip].firstArc = nArc;

cntArc++;
nArc++;
if (disp) //----------------------------------------------------------
{
  xb = marginX + (int)(Scale1 * arc.xb + 0.5);
  yb = marginY + (int)(Scale1 * arc.yb + 0.5);
  if (j == Len)
  {
    xb = marginX + (int)(Scale1 * Vert[last].X + 0.5);
    yb = marginY + (int)(Scale1 * Vert[last].Y + 0.5);
  }
  xe = marginX + (int)(Scale1 * arc.xe + 0.5);
  ye = marginY + (int)(Scale1 * arc.ye + 0.5);
  rv = DrawArc(arc, true, fm1);
  if (rv < 0) return -1;

  Pen bluePen = new System.Drawing.Pen(Color.LightBlue);
  if (j > 2 && j < Len && last - first > 2 && old_xe > 0)
                                fm1.g2Bmp.DrawLine(bluePen, old_xe,
                                old_ye, xb, yb);
  old_xe = xe; old_ye = ye;
} //--------------------- end if (disp) -------------------------
```

```
      if (j == Len - 1) Polygon[ip].lastArc = nArc - 1;
    } // ============== end for (j... ================================
   } // ----------------------- end if (last > first+1 ) ---------------
  } // =============== end for (ip... ================================
  return 0;
} // ****************** end FindArcs ***********************************
```

The lists of the polygons and of the arcs can be saved on the hard disk by clicking Save, resulting in a text file with the extension .txt that contains the list of polygons and the list of arcs. It contains for each polygon its parameters like firstVertex, lastVertex, firstArc, and lastArc. After the list of polygons comes the list of arcs. For each arc it contains the coordinates (xb, yb) of the starting point, the coordinates of the end point, the coordinates of the curvature center, and the radius. The file can be read by means of any text processing program (e.g., Microsoft Word). The directory TEXT and the name of the text file are calculated automatically from the name of the opened image. The TEXT directory should be located near the directory containing the opened image. A version of the Save enabling the user to chose the directory and the name of the text file can be seen in the project WFcircleReco described in Chapter 12. Save circles is also decribed in Chapter 12.

Precision of the Calculation of the Radii

We have investigated the precision of the described method using an artificial image with an ideal ellipse with half axes of 328 and 95 pixels (Figure 11-9).

Figure 11-9. *Artificial image of an ellipse used in the experiment*

It was possible to calculate the curvature radius at each point of the boundary because we know the parameters of the ellipse. The comparison of the calculated values with the values produced by FindArcs has shown that at points of the boundary with the true curvature radius under 174 pixels the errors of the produced values are less than 15 percent. At greater radii, the errors are less than 20 percent. This precision is sufficient for some applications.

To test the value of the errors in the case of small radii we have used another artificial image with radii of 100 and 200 pixels (Figure 11-10). In the tests of both artificial images the errors in estimation of the curvature radius were under 20 percent. This is in agreement with the theoretical investigation (Kovalevsky, 2001) showing that errors of the estimation of derivatives of curves in digital images are specified by the intensity of digitization noise making the coordinates of pixels rather imprecise.

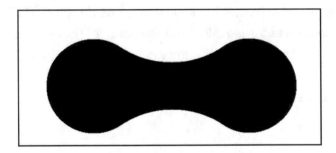

Figure 11-10. *Digital photograph of a link of a bicycle chain used in the experiment (the holes are artificially filled with black color to make the image simpler)*

The boundary of this image contains a point of inflation where the curvature changes its sign. The average curvature in the neighborhood of this point is near zero, which corresponds to rather large values of the radius. At other points the error of estimating the curvature radius was under 20 percent.

Conclusion

The results reported here show that the precision of the method is satisfactory.

CHAPTER 12

Recognition and Measurement of Circular Objects

This chapter describes a method of recognizing and measuring the parameters of objects that have a boundary shape similar to a circle. We use a modified method of least squares I developed some years ago for checking the quality of solder bumps in wafers. Here we describe a development of this method that can be applied to any color or grayscale images to recognize objects with a boundary that approximates a circle. The method calculates the estimates of the radius and the center coordinates. Figure 12-1 shows an example using the method for sorting apples according to their sizes.

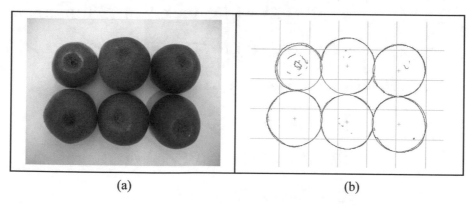

(a)   (b)

Figure 12-1. *Example of (a) an image and (b) the results*

V. Kovalevsky, *Modern Algorithms for Image Processing*, https://doi.org/10.1007/978-1-4842-4237-7_12

Mathematical Foundation of the Method

This method is similar to the classical method of least squares with the essential difference that we minimize not the sum of the squares of the deviations of the given points from the sought for circle, but rather the sum of the squares of the difference of the areas of the circle with unknown radius R and the circle with the unknown center (x_c, y_c) through the given point (x_i, y_i):

$$\text{Deviat} = \sum (R^2 - (x_i - x_c)^2 - (y_i - y_c)^2)^2. \tag{12.1}$$

The sum is calculated according to the index i of the points, where i gets N values from 0 to $N - 1$. This criterion differs from the classical one

$$\text{Crit} = \sum (R - \sqrt{(x_i - x_c)^2 - (y_i - y_c)^2})^2 \tag{12.2}$$

in that instead of the difference (distance of a point from the middle point) - radius, we use the difference radius² - distance². This makes the solution much easier and faster, and the difference between the resulting circle and the classical one is very small.

Let us derive the necessary equations. We take the partial derivatives of Equation 12.1 after x_c, y_c, and R.

$$\star\text{Deviat}/\star x_c = 4^* \sum (R^2 - (x_i - x_c)^2 - (y_i - y_c)^2)^* (x_i - x_c) \tag{12.3}$$

$$\star\text{Deviat}/\star y_c = 4^* \sum (R^2 - (x_i - x_c)^2 - (y_i - y_c)^2)^* (y_i - y_c) \tag{12.4}$$

$$\star\text{Deviat}/\star R = 4^* \sum (R^2 - (x_i - x_c)^2 - (y_i - y_c)^2)^* R \tag{12.5}$$

and set them equal to 0. We obtain three equations:

$$\sum (R^2 - (x_i - x_c)^2 - (y_i - y_c)^2)^* (x_i - x_c) = 0 \tag{12.6}$$

$$\sum (R^2 - (x_i - x_c)^2 - (y_i - y_c)^2)^* (y_i - y_c) = 0 \tag{12.7}$$

$$\sum (R^2 - (x_i - x_c)^2 - (y_i - y_c)^2) = 0 \tag{12.8}$$

The left parts are polynoms containing the variables x_c, y_c, and R with powers 1, 2, and 3. We demonstrate in what follows how to transform Equations 12.6 and 12.7 to linear ones.

We open the round brackets in Equation 12.8 and obtain

$$\sum (R^2 - x_i^2 + 2^* x_i {}^* x_c - x_c^2 - y_i^2 + 2^* y_i {}^* y_c - y_c^2) = 0$$

or

$$\sum (R^2 - x_c^2 - y_c^2) = \sum(x_i^2 - 2^* x_c ^* x_i + y_i^2 - 2 ^* y_c ^* y_i)$$

or

$$N^*(R^2 - x_c^2 - y_c^2) = \sum(x_i^2 - 2^* x_c ^* x_i + y_i^2 - 2 ^* y_c ^* y_i). \qquad (12.9)$$

The sum is calculated for N values of i from 0 to N-1. The sum $\sum(R^2 - x_c^2 - y_c^2)$ can be replaced by $N^*(R^2 - x_c^2 - y_c^2)$ since $(R^2 - x_c^2 - y_c^2)$ does not depend on i.

Let us now transform Equation 12.6 to separate the expression $R^2 - x_c^2 - y_c^2$.

$$\sum (R^2 - (x_i - x_c)^2 - (y_i - y_c)^2)^* (x_i - x_c) =$$

$$\sum (R^2 - (x_i - x_c)^2 - (y_i - y_c)^2)^* x_i - \sum (R^2 - (x_i - x_c)^2 - (y_i - y_c)^2)^* x_c =$$

$$\sum(R^2 - (x_i - x_c)^2 - (y_i - y_c)^2)^* x_i - x_c^* \sum(R^2 - (x_i - x_c)^2 - (y_i - y_c)^2) = 0.$$

The second term $x_c^* \sum(\ldots)$ is according to Equation 12.8 equal to 0. Thus:

$$\sum(R^2 - (x_i - x_c)^2 - (y_i - y_c)^2)^* x_i = 0.$$

After opening the round brackets we obtain:

$$(R^2 - x_c^2 - y_c^2)^* \sum x_i - \sum(x_i^2 - 2^* x_i^* x_c + y_i^2 - 2^* y_i^* y_c)^* x_i = 0.$$

According to Equation 12.9, we replace $(R^2 - x_c^2 - y_c^2)$ with $\sum(x_i^2 - 2^* x_c ^* x_i + y_i^2 - 2 ^* y_c ^* y_i) / N$ in the first term and perform the multiplication with x_i in the second one:

$$\sum x_i^* \sum(x_i^2 - 2^* x_c^* x_i + y_i^2 - 2 ^* y_c ^* y_i) / N - \sum(x_i^3 - 2^* x_i^2 {}^* x_c + x_i^* y_i^2 - 2^* y_i^* y_c^* x_i) = 0.$$

Let us denote each sum $\sum x_i^{m*} y_i^n$ with S_{mn}. Then:

$$S_{10}^*(S_{20} - 2^* x_c^* S_{10} + S_{02}^* S_{01} - 2^* y_c^* S_{01}) - (S_{30} + 2^* x_c^* S_{20} + S_{12} + 2^* y_c^* S_{11})^* N = 0.$$

or

$$2^* x_c^*(N^* S_{20} - S_{10}^2) + 2^* y_c^*(N^* S_{11} - S_{10}^* S_{01}) = (S_{30} + S_{12})^* N - S_{10}^* S_{20} - S_{02}^* S_{01}. \quad (12.6a)$$

This is a linear equation in x_c and y_c. After similar transformations, Equation 12.7 also becomes a linear equation:

$$2*x_c*(N*S_{11} - S_{10}*S_{01}) + 2*y_c*(N*S_{02} - S_{02}{}^2) = (S_{03} + S_{21})*N - S_{01}*S_{20} - S_{02}*S_{01}. \qquad (12.7a)$$

Equations 12.6a and 12.7a can be easily solved. The solutions can be set in Equation 12.9 rewritten in the S_{mn} notation:

$$R^2 - x_c{}^2 - y_c{}^2 = (S_{20} - 2*x_c*S_{10} + S_{02} - 2*y_c*S_{01})/N. \qquad (12.9a)$$

to obtain the value of R.

We present here the source code of the method MinAreaN2 performing these solutions. Two other similar slightly simpler methods, MinArea2 and MinAreaN, are also used in the project. MinAreaN2 is a combination of these two methods.

```
public double MinAreaN2(int ia, iVect2[] P, int Start, int np, ref double
radius, ref double x0, ref double y0)
/* Calculates the estimates "x0" and "y0" of the coordinates of the center
and the estimate "radius" of the radius of the optimal circle with the
minimum deviation from the given set "P[np]" of points. The found values
and the 13 sums used for the calculation are assigned to the arc with the
index "ia". -- */
{
  double SumX, SumY, SumX2, SumY2, SumXY, SumX3, SumY3,
  SumX2Y, SumXY2, SumX4, SumX2Y2, SumY4;
  double a1, a2, b1, b2, c1, c2, Crit, det, fx, fy, mx, my, N, R2;
  int ip;
  N = (double)np;
  SumX = SumY = SumX2 = SumY2 = SumXY = SumX3 = SumY3 = 0.0;
  SumX2Y = SumXY2 = SumX4 = SumX2Y2 = SumY4 = 0.0;

  for (ip = Start; ip < Start + np; ip++) //==== over the set of points ====
  {
    fx = (double)P[ip].X;
    fy = (double)P[ip].Y;
    SumX += fx;
    SumY += fy;
```

```
    SumX2 += fx * fx;
    SumY2 += fy * fy;
    SumXY += fx * fy;
    SumX3 += fx * fx * fx;
    SumY3 += fy * fy * fy;
    SumX2Y += fx * fx * fy;
    SumXY2 += fx * fy * fy;
    SumX4 += fx * fx * fx * fx;
    SumX2Y2 += fx * fx * fy * fy;
    SumY4 += fy * fy * fy * fy;
} //============ end for (ip...) =============================

a1 = 2 * (SumX * SumX - N * SumX2);
b1 = 2 * (SumX * SumY - N * SumXY);
a2 = 2 * (SumX * SumY - N * SumXY);
b2 = 2 * (SumY * SumY - N * SumY2);
c1 = SumX2 * SumX - N * SumX3 + SumX * SumY2 - N * SumXY2;
c2 = SumX2 * SumY - N * SumY3 + SumY * SumY2 - N * SumX2Y;
det = a1 * b2 - a2 * b1;
if (Math.Abs(det) < 0.00001) return -1.0;

mx = (c1 * b2 - c2 * b1) / det;
my = (a1 * c2 - a2 * c1) / det;
R2 = (SumX2 - 2 * SumX * mx - 2 * SumY *my + SumY2) / N + mx*mx + my*my;
if (R2 <= 0.0) return -1.0;
x0 = mx;
y0 = my;
radius = Math.Sqrt(R2);
elArc[ia].Mx = mx;
elArc[ia].My = my;
elArc[ia].R = radius;
elArc[ia].nPoints = np;
Crit = 0.0;
for (ip = Start; ip < Start + np; ip++) //======== point array =========
{
  fx = (double)P[ip].X; fy = (double)P[ip].Y;
```

```
    Crit += (radius - Math.Sqrt((fx - mx) * (fx - mx) + (fy - my)*
    (fy - my))) *
        (radius - Math.Sqrt((fx - mx) * (fx - mx) + (fy - my) *
        (fy - my)));
} //============== end for (ip...) ===========================
elArc[ia].SUM[0] = N;
elArc[ia].SUM[1] = SumX;
elArc[ia].SUM[2] = SumY;
elArc[ia].SUM[3] = SumX2;
elArc[ia].SUM[4] = SumY2;
elArc[ia].SUM[5] = SumXY;
elArc[ia].SUM[6] = SumX3;
elArc[ia].SUM[7] = SumY3;
elArc[ia].SUM[8] = SumX2Y;
elArc[ia].SUM[9] = SumXY2;
elArc[ia].SUM[10] = SumX4;
elArc[ia].SUM[11] = SumX2Y2;
elArc[ia].SUM[12] = SumY4;

return Math.Sqrt(Crit / (double)np);
} //************** end MinAreaN2 *********************************/
```

The Project **WFcircleReco**

The corresponding project WFcircleReco contains the following:

1. The class Form1 containing the necessary data structures and calls of the processing methods.

2. Methods for the edge detection described in Chapter 7.

3. Methods for approximating the edges by polygon lines described in Chapter 11.

4. A method MakeArcs3 for dissolving polygon lines in subsets called arcs with approximately constant curvature.

5. A method MakeCirclesEl for finding the best matching circle for each group of passing arcs.

6.   A method GetAngle calculating for each arc the angle between the radius vectors from the center of the matching circle to the end points of the arc.

7.   The method MakeCircles calculating for each group of arcs with close centers of curvature the optimal circle according to the minimum deviation of the points of the arcs from the circle.

8.   Service methods displaying the polygons, the arcs, and the optimal circles.

We start here with the description of the project WFcircleReco.

The Form of the Project WFcircleReco

The form of the project WFcircleReco is shown in Figure 12-2.

The code of the form consists of five parts, each of which starts when the user clicks the corresponding button.

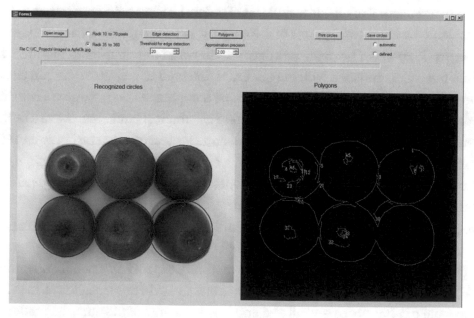

Figure 12-2. *The form of the project WFcircleReco*

The Open image part allows the user to choose a directory and select an image. The user can open a .bmp or a .jpg image. The image will be opened and shown in the left-hand picture box. This part of the code defines five work images and displays the original image.

After clicking Edge detection, the user can define the threshold of edge detection. He or she can see the edges in the right-hand picture box and change the threshold if necessary (standard is 20).

Edge detection calls the methods SigmaSimpleUni and ExtremLightUni necessary for the edge detection according to the binarized gradient method described in Chapter 7. The edges are defined in the image ExtremIm as sequences of pairs of adjacent pixels having the color difference or gray value difference greater than the Threshold setting. The color difference is the sum of absolute differences of the intensities of the color channels provided with the sign of the difference in the lightness.

To make the processing of the edges simpler and more convenient, the image CombIm is created with combinatorial coordinates (see Chapter 7) and doubled values of width and height.

In this project we slightly changed the labeling of points: We now use only the bits 0, 1, and 2 for specifying the number of edge cracks incident to the points; the bits 3, 4, 5, and 6 are not used. The bit 7 is used to label points already being put into the queue. For specifying the cracks and points of the edges, we use the method LabelCellsSign described in Chapter 7. The detected edges are shown in the right-hand picture box.

When the user is satisfied with the quality of detected edges, he or she can click Polygons. Because the variety of the circles to be recognized is very large we consider eight variants of intervals for the allowed radii: The smallest circles can have a radius between 10 and 20 pixels, whereas the radius of the largest one can be between 180 and 360 pixels. For each of these intervals the value of the parameter epsilon defining the precision of the polygonal approximation is specified: It changes from 1.05 pixel for the smallest circles to 2.00 pixel for the largest ones.

The part Polygons contains a for loop running through all eight variants. For each variant the method SearchPoly is started again. This method tests the image CombIm containing the detected edges and starts the method ComponPoly at each end or branch point. These two methods are members of the class CListLines (file CListLines.cs). When ComponPoly has processed all end and branch points of the edge, it is called again to start at points that are not end or branch points. Then ComponPoly makes the approximation of all closed edge curves.

The method ComponPoly is almost the same as in the project WFcompressPal (Chapter 8) with the following small difference: The short lines containing a single crack that were detected and saved by the method ComponLin are now ignored. They were important for image compression; however, they are of no importance for circle recognition. The method TraceLin called by ComponLin in the project WFcompressPal is replaced here by the method TraceAppNew, which also traces a line of the edge; however, it makes the polygonal approximation of the line. The method is designed in such a way that it never produces sequences of collinear points: If three subsequent approximating points appear to be collinear, then the middle point is not saved. For this purpose a small method ParArea (see the source code that follows) is used. It calculates the area of the parallelogram spanned on three subsequent vertices Vert of the polygon.

Here is the source code of TraceAppNew. Instructions necessary for debugging are omitted.

```
public int TraceAppNew(CImage Comb, int X, int Y, double eps, ref iVect2
Pterm, ref int dir)
/* This method traces a line in the image "Comb" with combinatorial
coordinates, where the cracks and points of the edges are labeled: bits
0, 1, and 2 of a point contain the label 1 to 4 of the point. The label
indicates the number of incident edge cracks. Bits 3 to 6 are not used.
Labeled bit 7 indicates that the point should not be used any more. The
crack has only one label 1 in bit 0. This function traces the edge from
one end or branch point to another one while changing the parameter "dir".
It makes polygonal approximation with precision "eps" and saves STANDARD
coordinates in "Vert".  ----------*/
{
  int br, Lab, rv = 0;
  bool BP = false, END = false, deb = false;
  bool atSt_P = false;
  iVect2 Crack, P, P1, Pold, Pstand, StartEdge, StartLine, Vect;
  Crack = new iVect2();
  P = new iVect2();
  P1 = new iVect2();
  Pold = new iVect2();
  Pstand = new iVect2();
  StartEdge = new iVect2();
  StartLine = new iVect2();
  Vect = new iVect2();
```

```
int iCrack = 0;
P.X = X; P.Y = Y;
Pstand.X = X / 2;
Pstand.Y = Y / 2;
P1.X = Pold.X = P.X;
P1.Y = Pold.Y = P.Y;
StartEdge.X = X / 2;
StartEdge.Y = Y / 2;
StartLine.X = X / 2;
StartLine.Y = Y / 2;

int[] Shift = { 0, 2, 4, 6 };
int StartVert = nVert;
Vert[nVert].X = Pstand.X;
Vert[nVert].Y = Pstand.Y;
nVert++;
Vect = new iVect2();
int CNX = Comb.width;
int CNY = Comb.height;
CheckComb(StartEdge, Pstand, eps, ref Vect);

while (true) //=================================================
{
  Crack.X = P.X + Step[dir].X;
  Crack.Y = P.Y + Step[dir].Y;
  if (Comb.Grid[Crack.X + CNX * Crack.Y] == 0)
  {
    MessageBox.Show("TraceAppNew, error: dir=" + dir + " the Crack=(" +
    Crack.X
                            + "," + Crack.Y +        ") has label 0; ");
  }
  P.X = P1.X = Crack.X + Step[dir].X;
  P.Y = P1.Y = Crack.Y + Step[dir].Y;
  Pstand.X = P.X / 2;
  Pstand.Y = P.Y / 2;
  br = CheckComb(StartEdge, Pstand, eps, ref Vect);
```

```
Lab = Comb.Grid[P.X + CNX * P.Y] & 7; // changed on Nov. 1
switch (Lab)
{
  case 1: END = true; BP = false; rv = 1; break;
  case 2: BP = END = false; break;
  case 3: BP = true; END = false; rv = 3; break;
  case 4: BP = true; END = false; rv = 4; break;
}
if (Lab == 2) Comb.Grid[P.X + CNX * P.Y] = 0; // deleting all labels of P
iCrack++;
if (br > 0) //-------------------------------------------------------------
{
  if (nVert >= MaxVert - 1)
  {
    MessageBox.Show("Overflow in 'Vert'; X="+X+" Y="+Y + " nVert=" +
    nVert);
    return -1;
  }

  if (br == 1)
  {
    if (nVert > (StartVert + 1) && ParArea(nVert, Pold) == 0.0)
    {
      Vert[nVert - 1].X = Pold.X / 2;
      Vert[nVert - 1].Y = Pold.Y / 2;
    }
    else
    {
      Vert[nVert].X = Pold.X / 2;
      Vert[nVert].Y = Pold.Y / 2;
    }
  }
  else
  {
    if (nVert>(StartVert + 1) && ParArea(nVert, Pold)==0.0)
    Vert[nVert-1] = Vect;
```

```
      else Vert[nVert] = Vect;
   } //------------------ end if (br == 1) ----------------------------
   if (nVert > (StartVert + 1) && ParArea(nVert, Pold) == 0.0)
   {
      StartEdge = Vert[nVert - 1];
   }
   else
   {
      StartEdge = Vert[nVert];
      if (StartEdge.X > 0 || StartEdge.Y > 0) nVert++; // very important!
   }
   br = 0;
} //---------------- end if (br > 0) -----------------------------------
atSt_P = (Pstand == StartLine);
if (atSt_P)
{
   Pterm.X = P.X; // Pterm is a parameter of TraceAppNew
   Pterm.Y = P.Y;
   Polygon[nPolygon].lastVert = nVert - 1;
   Polygon[nPolygon].closed = true;
   rv = 2;
   break;
}

if (!atSt_P && (BP || END))
{
   Pterm.X = P.X;
   Pterm.Y = P.Y;
   Vert[nVert].X = Pstand.X;
   Vert[nVert].Y = Pstand.Y;

   Polygon[nPolygon].lastVert = nVert;
   Polygon[nPolygon].closed = false;
   nVert++;
   if (BP) rv = 3;
   else rv = 1;
```

```
      break;
    }
    if (!BP && !END) //-----------------------------
    {
      Crack.X = P.X + Step[(dir + 1) % 4].X;
      Crack.Y = P.Y + Step[(dir + 1) % 4].Y;
      if (Comb.Grid[Crack.X + CNX * Crack.Y] == 1)
      {
        dir = (dir + 1) % 4;
      }
      else
      {
        Crack.X = P.X + Step[(dir + 3) % 4].X;
        Crack.Y = P.Y + Step[(dir + 3) % 4].Y;
        if (Comb.Grid[Crack.X + CNX * Crack.Y] == 1) dir = (dir + 3) % 4;
      }
    }
    else break;
    Pold.X = P.X;
    Pold.Y = P.Y;
  } //================== end while ===============================
  Polygon[nPolygon].nCrack = iCrack;
  return rv;
} //********************* end TraceAppNew **************************
```

Now Form1 calls the method CheckSmooth, checking all polygons to determine whether they are smooth. A polygon is smooth if the relative number of large angles between its edges is less than a predefined proportion.

Then the method MakeArcs3 is started, which subdivides the polygon lines into subsets called arcs with approximately constant curvature. The method ThreePoints calculates for each three subsequent vertices of a polygon line the curvature of the circle going through the three points. It is a value of one divided by the radius of this circle. The method calculates the coordinates of the curvature center and returns the value of the curvature. In this project an arc can contain any number of vertices different from the project WFpolyArc where an arc had always exactly three vertices.

The method MakeArcs3 implements the following definition of an arc:

1. All values of the local curvature at all vertices of an arc have the same sign. Curvature equal to zero cannot appear because of the property of TraceAppNew mentioned earlier.

2. Absolute values of the angles between subsequent polygons' edges have an approximate value less than a threshold depending on the local curvature of the arc and of the precision of the approximation.

3. The lengths of the polygons' edges must be less than a threshold.

The method MakeArcs3 calculates for each location in the polygon line four logical variables—bAngle, bCurve, bEdge, and bSign—specifying whether the conditions just indicated are fulfilled. The bSign variable is true if the sign of the curvature changes.

If all four logical variables are okay, certain values are assigned to the variables Start[iSign] and End[iSign] specifying the start and the end location of an arc. The variable bSign specifies the sign of the local curvature. Parameters of the arcs are saved in the array elArc, which is a member of the class CListLines).

The method MakeCirclesEl then calculates the optimal circle for groups of arcs having similar parameters. It tests all pairs of arcs and checks whether their center points are closer to each other than a predefined distance MD and whether their curvature radii are approximately equal: The relation must be between 0.5 and 2.0. Indexes of arcs satisfying these conditions are saved in an array and are used for the calculation of the optimal circle containing all these arcs.

For the calculation of the optimal circle the project uses a modified procedure of least squares that is realized by the method MinAreaN2. The procedure and the method were described earlier in this chapter. The procedure is very fast and robust.

The project WFcircleReco has the important property of using numerous arcs having similar centers and similar radii for the calculation of a circle. They are put together in a group and the optimal circle is calculated for the group. To find all arcs having similar centers and similar radii, all pairs of arcs are tested.

The project was tested on many various images, some of which were the old images from the original project designed for checking solder bumps in wafers and some new images containing apples, mushrooms, nuts, and other circular-shaped objects. Figure 12-3 and Figure 12-4 are examples of images in which all circular objects have been recognized and their parameters correctly estimated.

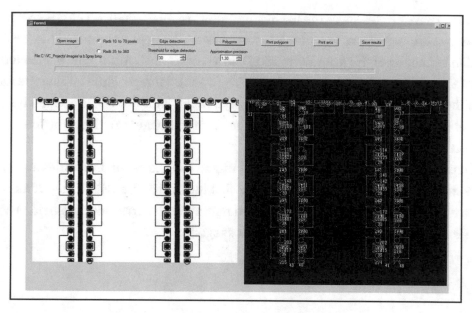

Figure 12-3. *Form with 93 recognized circles of wafer bumps*

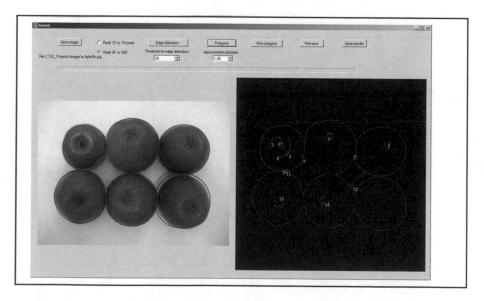

Figure 12-4. *Form of the project with recognized apples*

Recognized circles are drawn in red over the original image in `pictureBox1` on the left-hand side. On the right side in `pictureBox2`, the detected polygons are drawn in green.

Clicking Save circles saves the list of parameters of all recognized circles in a text file. The user can choose one of two possible ways of specifying the name and the location of this file by means of the Automatic and Defined options. If Automatic is selected, the name of the text file is based on the name of the opened image while adding the name TEXT of the directory located near the directory images containing the opened image. The extension .bmp or .jpg of the name of the opened image is replaced by the extension .txt.

If Defined is selected, the user has the ability to see the list of directories and choose the directory and the name of the text file by clicking one of the visible files. If there is no suitable name, the user can enter the desired name in the corresponding field. After the text file is saved, its contents are shown by MessageBox.

CHAPTER 13

Recognition of Bicycles in Traffic

Due to the good properties of the presented method for circle recognition, I had the idea to use this method to recognize bicycle wheels, which are ideal circles. However, if the bike is positioned so that the plane of its frame makes an acute angle with the viewing direction, then the wheels look like ellipses rather than circles. We thus also need a method of recognizing ellipses. Unfortunatelly we have not succeded with generalizing our method of circle recognition (see Chapter 12) for ellipses. We have tried to use the well-known method of conjugate gradients, but our experiments have shown that this method is not robust: Sometimes it fails when the points to which the ellipse is to be fitted do not lie near an ellipse.

Because an ellipse is defined by only a small number of parameters, namely five, it is possible to use the classical procedure of least squares as described in the next section.

Mathematical Foundation of Ellipse Recognition

An ellipse with axes parallel to the coordinate axes of a Cartesian coordinate system and with the center lying in the origin has the well-known equation

$$x^2 / a^2 + y^2 / b^2 = 1.$$

However, we need to consider the general case of a shifted and inclined ellipse. We use the general equation of a conic section:

$$Ax^2 + Bxy + Cy^2 + Dx + Ey + F = 0.$$

© Vladimir Kovalevsky 2019
V. Kovalevsky, *Modern Algorithms for Image Processing*, https://doi.org/10.1007/978-1-4842-4237-7_13

Our aim is to find parameters of an ellipse for which the sum of the squared distances of a set of given points from the ellipse is minimal. Thus our objective function is

$$f = \sum_i \left(Ax_i^2 + Bx_i y_i + Cy_i^2 + Dx_i + Ey_i + F \right)^2 . \tag{13.1}$$

The expression in the parentheses is approximately proportional to the distance of the point (x_i, y_i) from the ellipse. It contains six unknown coefficients A, B, C, D, E, and F. However, it is well known that an ellipse is uniquely defined by five parameters. Therefore we divide all terms of Equation 13.1 by A and denote the new coefficients as follows:

$B / A = 2k_1$

$C / A = k_2$

$D / A = 2k_3$

$E / A = 2k_4$

$F / A = k_5$

The transformed objective function is

$$f = \sum_i \left(x_i^2 + 2k_1 x_i y_i + k_2 y_i^2 + 2k_3 x_i + 2k_4 y_i + k_5 \right)^2 . \tag{13.1a}$$

The partial derivative of f to k_1 is

$$\frac{\partial f}{\partial k_1} = 4\sum_i \left(x_i^2 + 2k_1 x_i y_i + k_2 y_i^2 + 2k_3 x_i + 2k_4 y_i + k_5 \right) * x_i y_i .$$

After multiplying all terms in the parentheses by $x_i * y_i$ we obtain

$$\frac{\partial f}{\partial k_1} = 4\sum_i \left(x_i^3 y_i + 2k_1 x_i^2 y_i^2 + k_2 x_i y_i^3 + 2k_3 x_i^2 y_i + 2k_4 x_i y_i^2 + k_5 x_i y_i \right).$$

We divide it by four and denote each $\sum_i x_i^m y_i^n$ by $S(m, n)$ and obtain

$$\frac{\partial f}{\partial k_1} = S(3,1) + 2k_1 S(2,2) + k_2 S(1,3) + 2k_3 S(2,1) + 2k_4 S(1,2) + k_5 S(1,1).$$

By setting it equal to zero we obtain the first of the five equations for the unknowns k_1, k_2, k_3, k_4, and k_5.

$$2k_1 S(2,2) + k_2 S(1,3) + 2k_3 S(2,1) + 2k_4 S(1,2) + k_5 S(1,1) = -S(3,1)$$

In a similar way we obtain the other four equations:

$$2k_1 S(1,3) + k_2 S(0,4) + 2k_3 S(1,2) + 2k_4 S(0,3) + k_5 S(0,2) = -S(2,2)$$

$$2k_1 S(2,1) + k_2 S(1,2) + 2k_3 S(2,0) + 2k_4 S(1,1) + k_5 S(1,0) = -S(3,0)$$

$$2k_1 S(1,2) + k_2 S(0,3) + 2k_3 S(1,1) + 2k_4 S(0,2) + k_5 S(0,1) = -S(2,1)$$

$$2k_1 S(1,1) + k_2 S(0,2) + 2k_3 S(1,0) + 2k_4 S(0,1) + k_5 S(0,0) = -S(2,0)$$

This system of equations is solved by the well-known Gauss method implemented in the method GetEllipseNew using the method Gauss_K. The sums $S(x^m, y^n)$ are calculated by the method MakeSums2.

The following is the source code of GetEllipseNew.

```
public int GetEllipseNew(Point[] Vert, int iv1, int nPoints1, int iv2, int
nPoints2,
ref double Delta, ref double f, ref double a, ref double b, ref double c,
ref double d)
{
  bool deb = false;
  double[,] A = new double[5, 5];
  double[,] B = new double[5, 1];
  int nSum = 15;
  double[] Sum = new double[nSum];
  MakeSums2(Vert, iv1, nPoints1, iv2, nPoints2, Sum);
  A[0, 0] = 2.0 * Sum[12];
  A[0, 1] = Sum[11];
  A[0, 2] = 2.0 * Sum[8];
  A[0, 3] = 2.0 * Sum[7];
  A[0, 4] = Sum[4];
  A[1, 0] = 2.0 * Sum[11];
  A[1, 1] = Sum[10];
```

```
A[1, 2] = 2.0 * Sum[7];
A[1, 3] = 2.0 * Sum[6];
A[1, 4] = Sum[3];
A[2, 0] = 2.0 * Sum[8];
A[2, 1] = Sum[7];
A[2, 2] = 2.0 * Sum[5];
A[2, 3] = 2.0 * Sum[4];
A[2, 4] = Sum[2];
A[3, 0] = 2.0 * Sum[7];
A[3, 1] = Sum[6];
A[3, 2] = 2.0 * Sum[4];
A[3, 3] = 2.0 * Sum[3];
A[3, 4] = Sum[1];
A[4, 0] = 2.0 * Sum[4];
A[4, 1] = Sum[3];
A[4, 2] = 2.0 * Sum[2];
A[4, 3] = 2.0 * Sum[1];
A[4, 4] = Sum[0];

B[0, 0] = -Sum[13];
B[1, 0] = -Sum[12];
B[2, 0] = -Sum[9];
B[3, 0] = -Sum[8];
B[4, 0] = -Sum[5];

Gauss_K(A, 5, B, 1);

f = -0.5 * Math.Atan2(2.0 * B[0, 0], 1.0 - B[1, 0]);
c = (B[0, 0] * B[3, 0] - B[1, 0] * B[2, 0]) / (B[1, 0] - B[0, 0] * B[0, 0]);
d = (B[0, 0] * B[2, 0] - B[3, 0]) / (B[1, 0] - B[0, 0] * B[0, 0]);
Delta = B[1, 0] - B[0, 0] * B[0, 0];
double BigDelta = B[1, 0] * B[4, 0] + B[0, 0] * B[3, 0] * B[2, 0] +
    B[0, 0] * B[3, 0] * B[2, 0] - B[2, 0] * B[1, 0] * B[2, 0] - B[3, 0]
    * B[3, 0] - B[4, 0] * B[0, 0] * B[0, 0];
double S = 1.0 + B[1, 0];
double a2, b2;
```

```
double aprim = (1.0 + B[1, 0] + Math.Sqrt((1.0 - B[1, 0]) *
(1.0 - B[1, 0]) + 4.0 * B[0, 0] * B[0, 0])) * 0.5;
double cprim = (1.0 + B[1, 0] - Math.Sqrt((1.0 - B[1, 0]) *
(1.0 - B[1, 0]) + 4.0 * B[0, 0] * B[0, 0])) * 0.5;
a2 = -BigDelta / aprim / Delta;
b2 = -BigDelta / cprim / Delta;
a = Math.Sqrt(a2);
b = Math.Sqrt(b2);
if (Delta > 0.0)  return 1;
return -1;
} //*************** end GetEllipseNew *******************************
```

The Project WFellipseBike

The form of this project is shown in Figure 13-1.

Figure 13-1. *The form of the project WFellipseBike*

The user clicks Open image, then selects the folder and the image. The image appears in the left picture box. Then the user clicks Detect edges. There is a numeric up and down tool for the selection of the threshold for edge detection. However, the preselected value of 20 is good for all images and should not be changed. The program runs automatically. It uses the methods described in Chapter 12 for edge detection and polygonal approximation of the edges. Then it uses the method MakeArcsTwo for subdividing the polygons into arcs. This method is slightly different from the MakeArcs3 method described in Chapter 12.

The method FindEllipsesMode is then called to find the ellipses of the wheels of a bike. The method uses arcs sorted according to the number of points. The sorting is performed by the method SortingArcs writing the indexes of the sorted arcs into the array SortArcs. The arc with the greatest number of points stays in SortArcs[0]. Thus the arcs can be taken in the order of decreasing number of points.

The recognition of ellipses is not as simple as that of circles: If the arc transferred to the method GetEllipseNew to find the ellipse containing the arc contains fewer than ten points, sometimes false parameters of the ellipse can be calculated. Therefore we have developed additional means to fix this problem. The method QualityOfEllipseNew calculates the number of points in arcs lying near the ellipse as displayed in Figure 13-2.

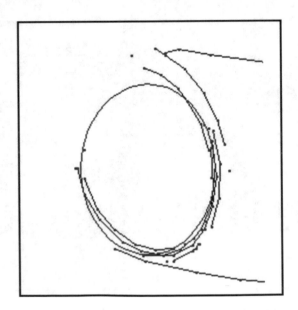

Figure 13-2. *Fragment of a bike image with a recognized ellipse*

In Figure 13-2, black lines are the arcs, blue points are the polygon vertices contained in the arcs, and the red line is the recognized ellipse. The quality of the ellipse is estimated as the number Sum of blue points in the tube around the ellipse. This number is compared with the value maxPoints, which is the number of points in the arc ia passed as a parameter to the method GetEllipseNew multiplied with 2π and divided by the angle of the arc. Thus maxPoint is the maximum possible number of points in a closed curve. The ellipse is regarded as good if the value Sum is greater than 0.5*maxNumber. Here is the code for QualityOfEllipseNew.

```
public int QualityOfEllipseNew(int ia, Ellipse Ellipse, int[] SortArcs,
Form1 fm1)
// Returns the sum of the numbers of points of arcs near the ellipse.
{
  bool deb = false, Disp = false; //true; //
  int Dif, goodDartIa, locDart, i, iv, ivm, ive, ja, Sum = 0, x, y, xm, ym,
  xe, ye;
  double angleDart, a = Ellipse.a, b = Ellipse.b, c = Ellipse.c,
  d = Ellipse.d;
  double maxPoints = elArc[ia].nPoints * 6.28 / elArc[ia].Angle;
  int ivStart, ivMid, ivEnd, xMain, yMain;
  ivStart = elArc[ia].Start;
  ivMid = ivStart + elArc[ia].nPoints / 2;
  ivEnd = ivStart + elArc[ia].nPoints - 1;
  x = Vert[ivStart].X;
  y = Vert[ivStart].Y;
  double AngleStart = Math.Atan2(y - d, x - c);
  xe = Vert[ivEnd].X;
  ye = Vert[ivEnd].Y;
  double AngleEnd = Math.Atan2(ye - d, xe - c);
  xMain = Vert[ivMid].X;
  yMain = Vert[ivMid].Y;
  double AngleMid = Math.Atan2(yMain - d, xMain - c);
  double minAngle = Math.Min(AngleStart, AngleEnd);
  double maxAngle = Math.Max(AngleStart, AngleEnd), help;
  bool Plus2PI = false;
```

```
if (minAngle < 0.0 && maxAngle > 0.0 && !(AngleMid >= minAngle &&
                                           AngleMid < maxAngle))
{
  Plus2PI = true;
  help = maxAngle;
  maxAngle = minAngle + 2 * Math.PI;
  minAngle = help;
}
angleDart = 57.3 * Math.Atan2(yMain - elArc[ia].My, xMain - elArc[ia].Mx)
+ 15.0;
if (angleDart < 0.0) angleDart += 360.0;
goodDartIa = 6 + (int)angleDart / 30;
if (goodDartIa > 11) goodDartIa -= 12;
double AngleJa, Fx, Fxe;
for (i = 0; i < nArcs; i++) //===============================
{
  ja = SortArcs[i];
  if (ja == ia || elArc[ja].nPoints < 5) continue;
  iv = elArc[ja].Start;
  ivm = iv + elArc[ja].nPoints / 2;
  ive = iv + elArc[ja].nPoints - 1;
  x = Vert[iv].X;
  y = Vert[iv].Y;
  xm = Vert[ivm].X;
  ym = Vert[ivm].Y;
  xe = Vert[ive].X;
  ye = Vert[ive].Y;
  Fx = (x - c) * (x - c) / a / a + (y - d) * (y - d) / b / b;
  Fxe = (xe - c) * (xe - c) / a / a + (ye - d) * (ye - d) / b / b;
  if (Fx < 0.6 || Fx > 1.67 || Fxe < 0.6 || Fxe > 1.67) continue;

  angleDart = 57.3 * Math.Atan2((ym - d) * a * a, (xm - c) * b * b);
  if (angleDart < 0.0) angleDart += 360.0;
  locDart = (int)angleDart / 30;
  if (locDart > 11) locDart -= 12;
  Dif = Math.Abs(elArc[ja].Dart - locDart);
```

```
    if (Dif > 6) Dif = 12 - Dif;
    if (Disp) DrawOneLongArc(ja, fm1);
    if (Dif < 2)
    {
      if (Disp) DrawOneLongArc(ja, fm1);
      for (iv = elArc[ja].Start; iv < elArc[ja].Start + elArc[ja].nPoints;
      iv++)
      {
        x = Vert[iv].X;
        y = Vert[iv].Y;
        AngleJa = Math.Atan2(y - d, x - c);
        if (AngleJa < 0.0 && Plus2PI) AngleJa += 6.28;
        if (!(AngleJa > minAngle && AngleJa < maxAngle)) Sum += elArc[ja].
        nPoints;
      }
    }
  } //================= end for (i = 0; ... =============================
  return Sum;
} //******************* end QualityOfEllipseNew *************************
```

If the ellipse is not good, the method HelpArcNew is called. This method obtains the arc ia as an argument and finds different arcs ja lying inside the curvature circle of the arc ia. If the arc ja has a proper orientation and is not too close to the arc ia, it forms a pair with the arc ia. For each pair of arcs (ia, ja) an ellipse is calculated and its quality is estimated. The ellipse with the best quality is returned as the result. Here is the code for HelpArcNew.

```
public int HelpArcNew(int ia, int[] SortArcs, ref Ellipse Ellipse, int
SumStart, Form1 fm1)
{
  bool disp = false;
  int Dif, i, ivMid, ivm, ja, xMain, yMain, xm, ym;
  ivMid = elArc[ia].Start + elArc[ia].nPoints / 2;
  xMain = Vert[ivMid].X;
  yMain = Vert[ivMid].Y;
```

```
double angleDart, a = Ellipse.a, b = Ellipse.b, c = Ellipse.c,
d = Ellipse.d;
int goodDartIa;
angleDart = 57.3 * Math.Atan2(yMain - elArc[ia].My, xMain - elArc[ia].Mx)
+ 15.0;
if (angleDart < 0.0) angleDart += 360.0;
goodDartIa = 6 + (int)angleDart / 30;
if (goodDartIa > 11) goodDartIa -= 12;

double R = elArc[ia].R, Mx = elArc[ia].Mx, My = elArc[ia].My;
CBox Box = new CBox();
Box.minX = (int)(Mx - R) - 10;
if (c - a < Box.minX) Box.minX -= 20;

Box.maxX = (int)(Mx + R) + 10;
if (c + a > Box.maxX) Box.maxX += 20;

Box.minY = (int)(My - R) - 10;
if (d - b < Box.minY) Box.minY -= 20;

Box.maxY = (int)(My + R) + 10;
if (d + b > Box.maxY) Box.maxY += 20;

DrawRectangleSmart(Box, fm1);
int Dist2 = 0, minDist2 = (int)(1.5 * elArc[ia].R * elArc[ia].R);
int[] jBest = new int[100];
int nBest = 0;
for (i = 0; i < nArcs; i++) //=====================================
{
  ja = SortArcs[i];
  if (!ArcInBox(ja, Box)) continue;
  if (elArc[ja].nPoints < 4) continue;
  if (disp) DrawOneLongArc(ja, fm1);
  Dif = Math.Abs(elArc[ja].Dart - goodDartIa);
  if (Dif > 6) Dif = 12 - Dif;
  if (Dif > 3) continue;
  ivm = elArc[ja].Start + elArc[ja].nPoints / 2;
  xm = Vert[ivm].X;
  ym = Vert[ivm].Y;
```

```
    Dist2 = (xm - xMain) * (xm - xMain) + (ym - yMain) * (ym - yMain);
    if (Dist2 > minDist2)
    {
       jBest[nBest] = ja;
       nBest++;
    }
    if (nBest >= 5) break;
 } //================= end for (i = 0;  ==============================

double Delta = 0.0, F = 0.0;
Ellipse Ellipse1 = new Ellipse();
int jbestOpt = -1, maxSum = SumStart, Sum = 0;
for (i = 0; i < nBest; i++) //==========================================
{
   if (disp) DrawRedArc(jBest[i], fm1);
   GetEllipseNew(Vert, elArc[ia].Start, elArc[ia].nPoints,
   elArc[jBest[i]].Start,
          elArc[jBest[i]].nPoints, ref Delta, ref Ellipse1.f,
                                     ref Ellipse1.a, ref Ellipse1.b,
                                     ref Ellipse1.c, ref Ellipse1.d);
   Sum = QualityOfEllipseNew(ia, Ellipse1, SortArcs, fm1);
   if (disp) DrawEllipse(Ellipse1, fm1);
   if (!(Ellipse1.a > 5.0 && Ellipse1.b > 5.0) ||
                                     Ellipse1.d - Ellipse1.b < fm1.
                                     height * 2 / 5) Sum = 0;
   else
   {
     if (Sum > maxSum)
     {
       if (disp) DrawEllipse(Ellipse1, fm1);
       if (disp) DrawRedArc(jBest[i], fm1);
       maxSum = Sum;
       jbestOpt = jBest[i];
       Ellipse = Ellipse1;
     }
   }
}
```

```
  } //================== end for (i ... i < nBest; ======================
  DrawRedArc(jbestOpt, fm1);
  Pen pen = new Pen(Color.Red);
  DrawEllipsePen(Ellipse, pen, fm1);
  return jbestOpt;
} //****************** end HelpArcNew ******************************
```

The rear wheel of the bicycle is sometimes obscured by the cyclist's legs so that the ellipse cannot be detected. If a high-quality ellipse of the front wheel is already recognized, a copy of this ellipse is assigned to the rear wheel. So that this assignment can be done right, the tangent at the midpoint MP of an arc ia1 of the rear wheel must be calculated. A point P is found on the ellipse of the front wheel, which has the same tangent and the same orientation as the orientation of the arc ia1. The copy of the ellipse of the front wheel is placed so that the point P lies on the point MP. Then, the parameters of the copy of the ellipse are specified with the method HelpArcNew. The relative position of both ellipses, especially their distance to each other, is checked with the method CminusCel before and after the call of HelpArcNew. All these procedures are performed in the method FindEllipsesMode. Here is the code for this method.

```
public int FindEllipsesMode(CImage SigmaIm, Ellipse[] ListEllipse, ref int
nEllipse, Form1 fm1)
{
    int[] SortArcs = new int[nArcs];
  int maxNP = 0, k = SortingArcs(SortArcs, ref maxNP);

  int i, ia, ia1, i0, i1;
  nEllipse = 0;
  double a = 0.0, b = 0.0, c = 0.0, d = 0.0; //, fret = 0.0;
  int[,] List = new int[20, 1200];
  int[] nArcList = new int[20];
  SCircle[] Circle = new SCircle[20];
  for (i = 0; i < 20; i++)
  {
    Circle[i] = new SCircle();
    Circle[i].goodCirc = true;
  }
  Ellipse[] smalList = new Ellipse[20];
```

```
for (i = 0; i < 20; i++) smalList[i] = new Ellipse();
int Sum1 = 0;
double AnglePerPoint = 0.0, maxPoints = 0.0;
fm1.progressBar1.Visible = true;
fm1.progressBar1.Step = 1;
int jump, Len = nArcs, nStep = 20;
if (Len > 2 * nStep) jump = Len / nStep;
else
  jump = 2;
double Delta = 0.0, f = 0.0, F = 0.0;
Ellipse Ellipse1 = new Ellipse();
Ellipse Ellipse2 = new Ellipse();
int[] Pattern = new int[100000];
double aa = 0.0, bb = 0.0, cc = 0.0, dd = 0.0;
for (i0 = 0; i0 < nArcs; i0++)   //=====================================
{
  if ((i0 % jump) == jump - 1) fm1.progressBar1.PerformStep();
  ia = SortArcs[i0];
  DrawRedArc(ia, fm1);
  if (elArc[ia].nPoints <= 5) break;

  GetEllipseNew(Vert, elArc[ia].Start, elArc[ia].nPoints, 0, 0, ref
  Delta, ref f,

                                        ref a, ref b, ref c, ref d);
  DrawEllipse(f, a, b, c, d, fm1);
  if (b < 20.0 || a < 6.0 || d + b > fm1.height || d - 4 * b < 0.0)
  continue;
  int jbestOpt = -1;
  Ellipse1.a = a;
  Ellipse1.b = b;
  Ellipse1.c = c;
  Ellipse1.d = d;
  Point P1 = new Point(0, 0);
  Point P2 = new Point(0, 0);
  if (a > 5.0 && b > 5.0)
  {
```

```
    Sum1 = QualityOfEllipseNew(ia, Ellipse1, SortArcs, fm1);
    AnglePerPoint = elArc[ia].Angle / elArc[ia].nPoints;
    maxPoints = 2 * Math.PI / AnglePerPoint;
    if (b > fm1.height / 4 || elArc[ia].nPoints < 10) Sum1 = 0;
    Pen pen = new Pen(Color.Red);
    if (elArc[ia].nPoints < 10 || d + b > fm1.height * 2 / 5)
    {
      jbestOpt = HelpArcNew(ia, SortArcs, ref Ellipse1, Sum1, fm1);
      DrawEllipse(Ellipse1, fm1);
    }
  }

  for (i1 = i0 + 1; i1 < nArcs; i1++) //===================================
  {
    ia1 = SortArcs[i1];
    if (!Position(ia1, Ellipse1, fm1)) continue;
    if (elArc[ia1].nPoints <= 5)
    {
      MessageBox.Show("Finishing the search for ia1");
      break;
    }
    CBox BoxP1 = new CBox();
    CBox BoxP2 = new CBox();
    int iv = elArc[ia].Start, x = Vert[iv].X, y = Vert[iv].Y;
    int iv1 = elArc[ia1].Start, x1 = Vert[iv1].X, y1 = Vert[iv1].Y;
    GetEllipseNew(Vert, elArc[ia1].Start, elArc[ia1].nPoints, 0, 0, ref
    Delta, ref f,
                                                ref a, ref b, ref c, ref d);
    DrawEllipse(f, a, b, c, d, fm1);
    if (!(a > 5.0 && b > 5.0)) continue;
    DrawRedArc(ia1, fm1);
    double K2 = DrawTangent(ia1, ref P2, fm1);
    P1 = PointWithTangent(Ellipse1, K2, elArc[ia1].Dart, fm1);
    if (P1.X == 0 && P1.Y == 0) continue;
    Ellipse2 = Ellipse1;
    Ellipse2.c = P2.X + Ellipse1.c - P1.X;
```

256

```
    Ellipse2.d = P2.Y + Ellipse1.d - P1.Y;
    DrawEllipse(Ellipse2, fm1);
    if (d + b > fm1.height || d - b < fm1.height * 2 / 5) continue;
    jbestOpt = -1;
    if (Ellipse2.a > 5.0 && Ellipse2.b > 5.0)
    {
      Sum1 = QualityOfEllipseNew(ia1, Ellipse2, SortArcs, fm1);
      AnglePerPoint = elArc[ia1].Angle / elArc[ia1].nPoints;
      maxPoints = 2 * Math.PI / AnglePerPoint;
      Pen pen = new Pen(Color.Red);
      if ((elArc[ia1].nPoints < 10 || d + b > fm1.height * 2 / 5) &&
                                    CminusCel(Ellipse1, Ellipse2, fm1))
      {
        jbestOpt = HelpArcNew(ia1, SortArcs, ref Ellipse2, Sum1, fm1);
        DrawEllipse(Ellipse2, fm1);
      }
    }

    bool CMINC = CminusCel(Ellipse1, Ellipse2, fm1);
    if (!CMINC) continue;
    ListEllipse[nEllipse] = Ellipse1;
    nEllipse++;
    ListEllipse[nEllipse] = Ellipse2;
    nEllipse++;
    if (nEllipse >= 2)
    {
      fm1.progressBar1.Step = fm1.progressBar1.Maximum - Len / (100 / 6) -
                                            fm1.progressBar1.Value;
      fm1.progressBar1.PerformStep();
      return 1;
    }
  } //============= end for (i1 = 0; ... ============================
  } //============= end for (i0 = 0; ... ============================
  MessageBox.Show("FindEllipsesMode: no bike recognized");
  return -1;
} //***************** end FindEllipseMode ****************************
```

The recognition of the wheels is the most important part of the bicycle recognition. When both ellipses of the wheels are recognized, the method RecoFrame is called. It recognizes the direction of travel of the bicycle. This method contains several simple models of different types of the frame. Each type of the frame is presented two times: one with the fork of the front wheel of the bicycle to the left and one with the fork to the right. These models are tested one after the other. Each model is transformed so that the positions of the wheel axles match the centers of the ellipses. A narrow rectangle is formed around each straight segment of the frame. Then all polygons in the processed image are passed through and the lengths of the polygon edges that fit into the rectangles are summed. The model with the greatest sum prevails. In this way the direction of the movement of the bicycle is recognized. An example of the model of the frame is shown in Figure 13-3.

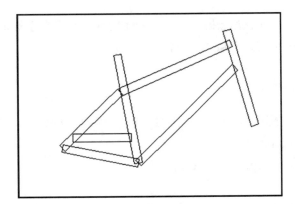

Figure 13-3. *Example of a model of the frame*

Another Method of Recognizing the Direction

The method just described works when the plane of the frame is at an acute angle to the viewing direction as, for example, in Figure 13-1. In addition, parts of the frame are often obscured by the cyclist's legs. Therefore we have developed another method DarkSpots which returns the direction of the bike movement: 0 for right and 2 for left. The method makes a box inside of each wheel, calculates histograms of the lightness and sums SumLengths of lengths of almost horizontal polygon edges in these boxes and decides about the drawing direction of the bike. The decision is made by comparing the sum of histogram values below a threshold, i.e. the number of dark pixels in the box, plus 6*SumLenths in both boxes. The greater value indicates the rear wheel and with it also the direction of drawing: if the rear wheel is on the right hand side then the bike moves to left.

When the ellipses of the wheels and the direction of movement are recognized, the ellipses of the wheels and the model of the frame are shown in the right picture box. The message box in the middle of the display shows the message "Bicycle going to left is recognized." If the user clicks Save result, a text file will be saved on the disk with context corresponding to the following example:

"A bicycle going to left has elliptical wheels.

First: a = 113; b = 173; c = 864; d = 796.

Second: a = 114; b = 173; c = 469; d = 790."

The notations are as follows: a is the horizontal half-axis of the ellipse, b is its vertical half-axis, c is the x coordinate of the center of the wheel, and d is its y coordinate.

We have tested about 100 photographs showing bicycles on streets in a city. The bicycles were recognized in all photograps except large images of about 2000 × 1500 pixels with small bicycles of about 150 pixels in length (Figure 13-4).

Figure 13-4. *Example of an image with a nonrecognized bicycle*

Figure 13-5 provides some examples of images with recognized bicycles.

Figure 13-5. *Examples of images with recognized bicycles*

CHAPTER 14

A Computer Model of Cell Differentiation

This chapter does not belong to the area of image processing. The reason for including it in this book is the broad and versatile interest circle of the author. The topic of this chapter is related to biology.

One can ask how is it possible that cells of different types are developed during the growth of an organism in spite of the fact that they all have exactly the same deoxyribonucleic acid (DNA). It can be supposed that each cell must obtain some information indicating its position in the growing organism, perhaps some kind of coordinates. The DNA must then contain different instructions for the development of cells having different coordinates. The coordinates can be produced during the division of cells: A new cell adjacent to an old cell with coordinate set (X, Y, Z) must get the coordinate set in which one of the coordinates of the old cell has been increased or reduced by 1. Which of the three coordinates is changed depends on the direction of the vector from the old cell to the new one. Thus the two main ideas of this chapter are that cells must get some kind of coordinates and that DNA instructions specifying the properties of a cell must depend on its coordinates.

We have developed a project WFcellDivision in which a multicellular organism is modeled by an array Org (organism) of 63×63 cells (an odd number is better to exactly define the middle cell).

The process of producing a new cell is simulated by specifying and saving its features. Each cell can possess the coordinates X and Y as its features, a variable Property (which is a color index), and the array DNA[63×63] as its genetic information. A cell is an object of the class CCelln.

© Vladimir Kovalevsky 2019
V. Kovalevsky, *Modern Algorithms for Image Processing*, https://doi.org/10.1007/978-1-4842-4237-7_14

```
int const Cwidth=63, Cheight=63;

class CCelln
{ public:
    int X, Y, Property;
    unsigned char DNA[Cwidth*Cheight];
}
```

The aim of the project is to simulate the generation of one cell after another and the assignment of a value to the variable Property of each cell. The value depends on the coordinates of this cell and on the contents of DNA saved in this cell. Directly copying the values of DNA to Properties of all cells of Org is supposed to be impossible. It is only possible to copy the DNA from one cell to the neighboring new originating cell and to copy inside the originating cell one certain value from the DNA of the cell to the Property of this cell. The aim of the project is to demonstrate that in spite of these limitations, it is possible to assign correct values of Property to all cells of Org.

Let us describe the functioning of the project. The method Form1 begins by defining and initializing the array Org possessing memory for 63 × 63 cells. Initializing Org consists of setting the Property and the elements of the array DNA[63×63] of each cell of Org to -1, which means that the cell does not exist.

Then one of the cells in the middle of the array Org, namely that with the coordinates (31, 31), becomes "filled": It obtains the coordinates $X = 31$ and $Y = 31$. Its array DNA is filled with the color indexes of a small digital Image of 63 × 63 pixels. The image has been chosen arbitrarily to demonstrate that concrete content can be assigned to the properties of the cells. The content of DNA becomes a copy of a digital image where each element is a color index, a number between 0 and 255 that can be transformed to a color by means of a color table Palette. In Palette a color (RED, GREEN, BLUE) is saved for each color index. All other cells of the array Org initially have at the coordinates equal to -1 and the array DNA is empty (i.e., it is filled with -1).

The method Grow is called next. It simulates the growth of the organism while generating coordinates of cells starting with a cell adjacent to the central cell (31, 31). The coordinates are generated in such a way that all originating cells lie in a spiral turning around the central cell. During the growth process, more and more cells obtain a copy of the array DNA from one of the neighboring cells. They also obtain their coordinates and certain values of Property depending on the content of DNA and of the coordinates of a cell.

The Property of the cell with the coordinates (31, 31) obtains the value of a single element of the array DNA (see Figure 14-1), DNA[31, 31], i.e. the color index of the pixel (31, 31).

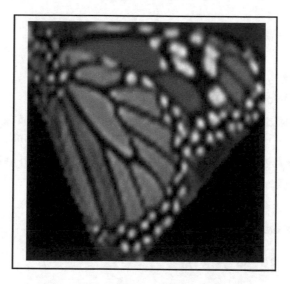

Figure 14-1. *The image copied to* Org[31, 31].DNA

The shape of the growing organism is specified by the boundary of the area with the black color assigned to some elements of DNA around the color area representing the growing organism. This array contains a color index different from (0, 0, 0) in each element corresponding to a cell that should be present in the organism and an index pointing to (0, 0, 0) (black color) for each element corresponding to a cell that should not be present in the organism.

A cell of the array Org is filled if it has nonzero coordinates, a value of Property pointing to a color different from (0, 0, 0), and contents of DNA different from -1.

When the growth process is started, each cell in the array Org that is adjacent to a filled cell obtains an exact copy of the array DNA that is the same for all cells. The coordinates of this cell obtain values differing by 1 from the coordinates of the filled neighbor cell. For example, if the new cell lies to the right of a filled cell with coordinates (X, Y) then its X coordinate obtains the value $X1 = X + 1$ and its Y coordinate $Y1$ the value Y. The new cell obtains the standard copy of the DNA and its Property becomes equal to DNA[X1, Y1] where $X1$ and $Y1$ are the coordinates of the new cell.

Here is the code for Grow.

```
int Grow(CCelln[] Org, int width, int height)
{ int cnt=0, i, k, x=(width-1)/2, y=(height-1)/2, nCount=1, X, Y;
  do
  { for (i=0; i<nCount && x<width-1; i++)
    { x++;
      X=Org[x+width*y].X=Org[x-1+width*y].X+1;
      Y=Org[x+width*y].Y=Org[x-1+width*y].Y;
      for (k=0; k<width*height; k++) Org[x+width*y].DNA[k] =
                                          Org[x-1+width*y].DNA[k];
      Org[x+width*y].Property=Org[x+width*y].DNA[X+width*Y];
    }
    cnt+=nCount;
    if (cnt==width*height) break;

    for (i=0; i<nCount && y<height-1; i++)
    {   y++;
      X=Org[x+width*y].X=Org[x+width*(y-1)].X;
      Y=Org[x+width*y].Y=Org[x+width*(y-1)].Y+1;
      for (k=0; k<width*height; k++) Org[x+width*y].DNA[k] =
                                          Org[x+width*(y-1)].DNA[k];
      Org[x+width*y].Property=Org[x+width*y].DNA[X+width*Y];
    }
    cnt+=nCount;
    if (cnt==width*height) break;

    nCount++;
    for (i=0; i<nCount && x>0; i++)
    {   x--;
      X=Org[x+width*y].X=Org[x+1+width*y].X-1;
      Y=Org[x+width*y].Y=Org[x+1+width*y].Y;
      for (k=0; k<width*height; k++)
                          Org[x+width*y].DNA[k]=Org[x+1+width*y].DNA[k];
      Org[x+width*y].Property=Org[x+width*y].DNA[X+width*Y];
    }
```

```
  cnt+=nCount;
  if (cnt==width*height) break;

  for (i=0; i<nCount && y>0; i++)
  { y--;
    X=Org[x+width*y].X=Org[x+width*(y+1)].X;
    Y=Org[x+width*y].Y=Org[x+width*(y+1)].Y-1;
    for (k=0; k<width*height; k++)
                    Org[x+width*y].DNA[k]=Org[x+width*(y+1)].DNA[k];
    Org[x+width*y].Property=Org[x+width*y].DNA[X+width*Y];
  }
  cnt+=nCount;
  if (cnt==width*height) break;
  nCount++;
} while(1);
return 1;
}
```

The process finishes when all cells of the array Org are filled. Then the values of Property of all cells are copied into a new array (image) of 63 × 63 pixels with the aim of making the results visible. This image is displayed with the color table Palette, and the user can see that the image is identical to the original Image copied to DNA[31, 31] except the pixels where the array DNA has indexes pointing to the black color. These pixels are shown as black (see Figure 14-2).

Figure 14-2. *The resulting image copied from* Org[*].Property

Thus all cells of the array Org are different: They contain different values of Property despite all of them having exactly the same copy of the array DNA.

Conclusion

We have demonstrated that it is possible to generate an organism with different cells in spite of the fact that all cells of the organism have exactly the same copy of genetic information and in spite of the fact that directly copying the array DNA to the array Org[x, y].Property was prohibited.

References

Aksak, I., C. Feist, V. Kijko, R. Knoefel, V. Matsello, V. Oganovskij, M. Schlesinger, D. Schlesinger, and G. Stanke. 1997. Detection of the objects with given shape on the grey-valued pictures. In *Computer analysis of images and patterns, CAIP 97,* 551–58. Berlin: Springer.

Canny, J. 1986. A computational approach to edge detection. *IEEE Transactions on Pattern Analysis and Machine Intelligence 8*(6):679–98.

Chochia, P. A. 1988. Image enhancement using sliding histograms. *Computer Vision, Graphics, and Image Processing 44*(2):211–29.

Dempster, A. P., N. M. Laird, and D. B. Rubin. 1977. Maximum likelihood from incomplete data via the EM algorithm. *Journal of the Royal Statistical Society, Series B 39*: 1-38.

Gallert, B. A., and M.J. Fisher. 1964. An improved equivalence algorithm. *Communications of the ACM 7*(5):301–03.

Hazewinkel, M., ed. (2001) [1994], Graph theory, Encyclopedia of Mathematics, Springer Science+Business Media B.V. / Kluwer Academic Publishers, ISBN 978-1-55608-010-4.

Hlaváč, V., T. Pajdla, and M. Sommer. 1994. Improvement of the curvature computation. In *Proceedings of the 12th international conference on pattern recognition,* Vol. 1, 536–38. Piscataway, NJ: IEEE Press.

Kimmel, R., and A. M. Bruckstein. 2003. On regularized Laplacian zero crossings and other optimal edge integrators. *International Journal of Computer Vision 53*(3):225–43.

Kovalevsky, V. 1990. *Lecture notes in image processing.* Berlin: University of Applied Sciences Berlin, Department of Computer Science.

Kovalevsky, V. 2001. Curvature in digital 2D images. *International Journal of Pattern Recognition and Artificial Intelligence 15*(7):1183–1200.

Kovalevsky, V. 2004. Algorithms in digital geometry based on cellular topology. *Lecture Notes in Computer Science 3322*:366–93.

© Vladimir Kovalevsky 2019
V. Kovalevsky, *Modern Algorithms for Image Processing,* https://doi.org/10.1007/978-1-4842-4237-7

REFERENCES

Kovalevsky, V. 2008. *Geometry of locally finite spaces.* Berlin: Editing House Baerbel Kovalevski ISBN 978-3-9812252-0-4.

Lee, J.-S. 1983. Digital image smoothing and the sigma filter. *Computer Vision, Graphics, and Information Processing 24*(2):255–69.

Lowe, D. G. 1989. Organization of smooth image curves at multiple scales. *International Journal of Computer Vision 3*:119–30.

Rosenfeld, A. 1970. Connectivity in digital pictures. *Journal of the ACM 17*:146–60.

Rosenfeld, A., and J. L. Pfalz. 1966. Sequential operations in digital picture processing. *Journal of the ACM 13*:471–94.

Press, W.H., Flannery, B.P., Teukolsky, S.A. and Vetterling, W.T. 1990, Numerical Recipes in C (Cambridge University Press, Cambrige).

Schlesinger, M. I. 2000. *Investigation of metrical properties of images and development of efficient algorithms for image pattern recognition under non-linear deformations.* Technical report, Institute of Information Technologies, Kiev, Ukraine.

Tomasi, C., and R. Manduchi. 1998. Bilateral filtering for gray and color images. In *Proceedings of the 1998 IEEE International Conference on Computer Vision*, 839-846. Piscataway, NJ:IEEE Press.

Vialard, A. 1996. *Geometric parameter extraction from digital paths.* In *Discrete geometry for computer imagery*, ed. S. Miguet, A. Montanvert, and S. Ubéda, 24–35. Berlin: Springer.

Williams, C. 1978. An efficient algorithm for the piecewise linear approximation of planar curves. *Computer Graphics and Image Processing 8*:286–93.

Worring, M. 1993. *Shape analysis of digital curves.* Doctoral thesis, University of Amsterdam.

Worring, M., and A. W. M. Smeulders. 1993. Digital curvature estimation. *Computer Vision, Graphics, and Image Processing: Image Understanding, 58*(3):366–82.

Index

A

Abstract cell complex (ACC)
    advantages, 103
    Cartesian two-dimensional, 104
    combinatorial coordinates, 105
    cracks, 103
    edges, 105
    pixels, 104
    points, 103
Array DNA, 261–263, 265–266
Array Org, 261–263, 265–266
Averaging filters, 6

B

Bilateral filter, 18
Bilinear transformation, 189–190
Binarization of the gradient, 101
BitmapToGrid method, 26–27
BitmapToGridOld method, 28
BitmapToImage method, 131
Boundary crack, 104
Boundary curve, 104
Breadth-first algorithm, 141
BreadthFirst_D( )
    method, 35–37, 39
BreadthFirst_L method, 40
Breadth-first search
    method, 121, 171, 181–183

C

Canny algorithm, 122
Canny edge detector, 119
Cell differentiation
    DNA, 261–262
    growth process, 262–263
Cell list, 128
Central projection, 190
Central transformation, 190
CImage, 3
Circular object, recognizing and
    measuring, 227
    mathematical foundation, 228–230, 232
    MinAreaN2 code, 230–232
    WFcircleReco (*see* WFcircleReco project)
Classical topology, 168
CleanCombNew method
    cell complex, 121
    CombIm, 120–121
    DrawComb, 120
    example, 121–122
    trace, 121
Color differences method,
    improvement
    binarized gradients, 107
    CleanCombNew method, 120
    gradient direction, 108
    LabelCellsSign (*see* LabelCellsSign
    method)

Printed in the United States
By Bookmasters